Evangelism for "Normal" People

Good News for Those Looking for a Fresh Approach

John P. Bowen

Augsburg Fortress

Minneapolis

For Deborah—

friend, lover, companion, catalyst, fellow-learner

EVANGELISM FOR "NORMAL" PEOPLE
Good News for Those Looking for a Fresh Approach

Editors: Scott Tunseth and James Satter
Cover design: David Meyer
Text design: James Satter
Cover art: copyright © 2002, Eyewire

ISBN 0-8066-4191-6

The paper used in this publication meets the minimum requirements of American National Standard for Information Sciences—Permanence of Paper for Printed Library Materials, ANSI Z329.48-1984.

Manufactured in the U.S.A.

10   09   08   07   06   05   04   5   6   7   8   9   10

Contents

Foreword

NORTH AMERICAN CULTURE—and Canadian society in particular—has limited space for faith flavored with fundamentalism. We prefer the disarray of diversity to the conviction that any one way is the right way. It is no wonder that the very idea of evangelism triggers emotional trauma for many committed followers of Jesus Christ. Whether one's background is mainline Protestant, Catholic, or conservative evangelical, the "E" word often is a dreaded one.

John P. Bowen's *Evangelism for "Normal" People* is tuned in to today's world. As a self-described introvert, John has given us a treatment of evangelism that is both sensitive and sensible. He is very aware of the anxiety that "normal" people can feel when it comes to telling others about their personal faith. His book is experientially illustrated, methodologically balanced, and biblically rooted. The biblical journey takes us through Babylon, focuses on Jesus, and rejoices in Paul's enthusiasm for the gospel. There is a chapter addressing the difficult evangelistic issue of Christians' attitudes toward other religions, and another dealing with the often ignored subject of hell.

The author's commitment to the biblical text and balanced methodology does not result in a treatise of theoretical lessons about evangelism. On the contrary, the brightly colored threads of practical illustration run through all the chapters. Without being over-stated or self-serving, John's personal commitment to Christ is evident throughout, as it translates into intentional witness and willed obedience. Readers cannot help but admire his perseverance.

John's view of evangelism is integrated. For John, the gospel is not a program. Evangelism is not a project. Sharing one's faith is simply part of wholesome Christian commitment. Planned methods of evangelistic outreach are affirmed, but not without a proper place for prayer. Both words and deeds are given their due. Communicating with others about life in Christ is assumed to be part of the Christian life, whether one is a member of the clergy, a student worker, or a lay believer.

This book is a lot like John himself. Without being simplistic, it gives clear direction. It challenges routine with calls to risk. The specifics are realistic and reachable. Rather than being triumphal, the tone is confessional and empathetic. The absence of rhetoric and the presence of insight and understanding are integral to "being Bowen."

Early in the book, Bowen asks the question, "Can evangelism be redeemed?" Throughout the book, readers are invited to take "yes" steps toward God and encourage others to do the same. John's contribution to the evangelistic cause moves us forward and beckons all of us in the right direction.

DON POSTERSKI
Vice President, National Programs
World Vision Canada

Acknowledgments

THIS BOOK HAS BEEN GROWING for many years, and the number of people who have influenced my living and my thinking has also grown as the years have gone by, till I am hardly able to list them all. I am grateful to God for all of them.

First and most relevantly, I am thankful to the many student and church groups that have listened to different parts of this material, interacted with it, and sharpened my thinking about it. Some of their stories are told in these pages.

Geraint Morgan was a teacher of religious education in my high school in Wales. When I was sixteen, he explained to me what I had never understood before, that Christianity was primarily being a disciple of Jesus, not a matter of outward religious observance, however conscientious. In the Christian fellowship group Geraint started in the school, I first learned (among other things) that I could read the Bible for myself and have it make sense, and that it was important to share my faith. He still prays for me, nearly forty years later.

I realize now (though I did not at the time) that I had many fine models of evangelistic speaking during my formative years as a student in England, notably David Watson, David McInnes, Michael Green, John Stott, and Roger Forster. They were clear, witty, widely read, biblical, academically responsible but not arid, respectful, relevant, and challenging. At the time, I assumed this was normal for evangelists.

I have known Andrew Cornes since our student days. He has taught and modeled faithfulness in evangelism (to God, to the gospel, and to people) for many. He also helped my wife become a Christian at university and so is, I suppose, my spiritual father-in-law. His is the sermon I retell in chapter 9.

Phyllis Clutterbuck was a dear friend in Bristol, England. She never married but became a mother to the innumerable employees under her supervision in the department store where she worked, and the kind of Christian whom people simply want to be with.

Four years in the church in York, England, where David Watson was the pastor, provided a wonderful model of how evangelism can be integrated into the regular flow of parish life, and be the more powerful because of it. There I also met John Freeth, then Anglican chaplain at York University, who taught me more about evangelism (and many other things) than I realized at the time.

In Canada, Don Posterski not only breathed new life into Inter-Varsity Christian Fellowship's evangelistic vision, but he was a marvelous friend and mentor to me personally, not least helping me to worry less and enjoy the Christian life more. I have also learned from him something of the generosity and creativity of God, which are crucial in evangelism.

Jim Berney, who until the end of 2001 was the President of IVCF Canada, believed in me and encouraged me along the way. In the story I tell in chapter 9, it was he who refused my resignation in 1988 and helped open new doors for me in ministry. Michael Pountney affirmed my new calling, generously funded my change of direction, and was more patient with me than I was with myself.

Gene Thomas's love of Jesus has helped shape the way many people in North America, including myself, read the Gospels and has thus shaped our approach to evangelism.

Cynthia Taylor encouraged me to believe I could take the risk of pursuing a calling to a ministry in evangelism. Brian Walsh, Harold Percy, Brian McLaren, and John Irwin have also helped me in indispensable ways. I am grateful, too, to Michael Knowles, Margaret Norman, George Piggford, T. V. Thomas, and Nicky Laxton Ward for reading the manuscript, for being the kind of friends who will "speak the truth in love," and for their insightful suggestions.

I have greatly appreciated Scott Tunseth at Augsburg Fortress, who has been a patient and painstaking editor as we have tried to "squeeze a quart into a pint pot."

Special thanks to my family for their unfailing love and support, and not least for putting up with many absences over the years when I went to speak in universities across the country. My daughter Anna also did a lot of the initial work of seeking permissions for this book: thanks, sweetheart.

To all these people, my thanks. You have been good news to me in a thousand ways.

Introduction:

The Abolition of Evangelism?

There was part of me that secretly felt evangelism was something you shouldn't do to your dog, let alone your friend.

Rebecca Manley Pippert, *Out of the Saltshaker* [1]

I COULDN'T BELIEVE IT. The plane out of Hamilton had been cancelled. Now the three of us flying to Pittsburgh had been bundled into a taxi to take us to the airport in Toronto, an hour away. There, we were assured, we could catch a later flight.

During that hour in the taxi, careening down the highway, we got talking. Julie, the woman in the front seat, told us almost at once that she was a member of the Church of Spiritual Science in California. Dave, sitting with me in the back, was a scientist from the National Research Centre in Ottawa, and an agnostic. And there was me, a teacher of evangelism from an Anglican seminary. (The taxi driver kept very quiet, so I don't know where he was coming from.)

I wish I had a tape recording of the conversation. For Dave, all religion was foolish and irrational. To him, the very idea of "spiritual science" was an oxymoron. For Julie, on the other hand, all religion was good and valid. I found myself pulled in two directions. To the scientist I wanted to say, "Christianity is a rational faith, though probably not in the sense you mean." I wanted to say to Julie, "Yes, I agree, the spiritual is the most important thing in life, but I think Jesus is quite different from anything and anyone you will find in other religions."

I felt as if I was being required to be bilingual, to speak one language to the secular scientist and a different language to someone who follows New Age spirituality. That hour was one of the most stimulating, stretching, confusing, and hilarious I have ever had.

In some ways, that conversation was a reminder for me of where our world is at. People may believe any one of a thousand different things. There is far more diversity of belief than there was fifty years ago. If you use words like "God," "faith," or "reason," there is no longer any guarantee that another person will have the same understanding of those words as you do.

Everything changes. In some cultures, of course, the rate of change is so slow from one generation to the next that you might be deceived into thinking that nothing has changed. Yet even there, little by little, change comes. Rocks wear down. The course of a riverbed changes. Animals migrate. People are born, and people die. In other cultures, however, such as that of the Western world in the twenty-first century, the rate of change is breathtaking.

What does this mean for those of us who try to follow Jesus of Nazareth? Surely nothing can change with "the faith that was once for all entrusted to the saints" (Jude 3). God doesn't change, so why should the faith change that is based on an unchanging God? Perhaps because we see things this way, change often seems slower inside the church than in the world outside. For those in liturgical traditions I know, one new prayer book in fifty years is too fast a rate of change. Others look back to Augustine, Aquinas, or Luther (depending on their theological taste) for inspiration and to strengthen their sense that nothing changes.

Is change then bad for a Christian? A.W. Tozer once said that our salvation rests on two facts: (1) that God does not change, and (2) that we can and do change. He is right. In fact, God seems to have built change, both the slow kind and the fast kind, into our world. This doesn't mean that all change is for the best, of course. But change itself seems to be one of God's ideas. Presumably God likes the world that way.[2]

Learning to like change

Where do we go to learn how the church should handle change? One source of help is cross-cultural missionaries. Those who have done the work of the church overseas understand the importance of change simply because they have had to. They have experienced firsthand the fact that cultures are different, and that what seemed solid and reliable and unchanging in one can crumble to dust in another. They have discovered, often from bitter experience, that knowing how to be church in one culture doesn't mean that you know how to be church in another culture. But they, too, have experienced that God is present in change, through change, and on the other side of change.

Lesslie Newbigin has urged us that if we want to learn to be church in the Western world in the twenty-first century, our theologians must learn from "the experience of missionaries in the cross-cultural transmission of the gospel." [3] We need to listen carefully to what these folks have to tell us. They know some things about change, and how to respond to it wisely.

The primary change taking place in our world involves the shorthand terms "modern" and "postmodern." I'm not going to describe that shift in detail, but I am convinced that, just as overseas missionaries have had to change their approach to faith and church in light of a different culture, so the church in the West needs to change in order to minister in this new postmodern world. Many have written on this subject, too, so I want to concentrate on just one aspect of church life and how it is affected by this new culture: evangelism.

I toyed with calling this book *The Abolition of Evangelism*. That has a nice, dramatic ring to it, don't you think? But in the end it seemed to me rather too negative, and, in any case, who wants to read a book on the abolition of something they didn't care to know about in the first place?

Yet there was something useful in that title. I believe that much of what has gone under the name of "evangelism" for over a hundred years happened in a modernist culture and within a modernist understanding of the faith. Indeed, the word *evangelism* itself was only coined in sixteenth century (it is not in the Bible), and the first reference to it is in the writings, not of a theologian, nor even of an evangelist, but of Francis Bacon, one of the inventors of the scientific method. That alone should be a clue to the fact that maybe "evangelism" is due for an overhaul.

I for one would be happy to stop using the word *evangelism* altogether. Jesus seems to have managed without it. But maybe it can serve as the scaffolding of a building. Scaffolding is very useful while the building is going up (indeed, the building could hardly go up at all without it), but, once the building is up, the scaffolding has served its purpose. Unless the builder removes it then, it will spoil the view! So I will continue to use the word *evangelism*, but maybe in the end we will find we can dispense with it.

Interpreting the Bible today

Some words of explanation about my own background and perspective are in order. There are many tribes within the Christian family. My own could be described as Anglican and evangelical. For me, evangelical simply means those within the broader Christian tradition who stress two things: (1) the Bible as the Christian's primary source of authority, and (2) the gospel as the good news of Christ for the world. Most of this book will be about the gospel, one way or another, but it may be helpful to say something at this point about my attitude to the Bible, since I will be referring to it frequently.

I have been helped in thinking about this by an image of New Testament scholar N. T. Wright, who compares it to a previously unknown Shakespeare play, most of whose fifth act has been lost. Everybody is excited to see this previously unknown play. So what can be done? It would be possible, I suppose, to commission some great Shakespearean scholar to write the missing act. But Wright suggests that it would be:

> better . . . to give the key parts to highly trained, sensitive and experienced Shakespearean actors, who would immerse themselves in the first four acts . . . and who would then be told to work out a fifth act for themselves. . . . They cannot go and look up the right answers. Nor can they simply imitate the kinds of things that their particular character did in the early acts. A good fifth act will show a proper final development, not merely a repetition of what went before. [4]

They will speak and act, says Wright, "with both innovation and consistency." This, he suggests, is an appropriate attitude to the Bible. It is the Christian's authority in the same sense that acts one through four of the play are the actors' authority. Shakespeare's text gives direction but does not dictate. It offers characters and plot lines to which the actors must be faithful. But the actors have freedom as to how they develop those characters and play out those plots.

In these pages I frequently reflect on the text of the Bible. You won't find me considering questions of authorship and historicity, however, important though these are. My job is to consider the text of the story as we have it, to try and understand such things as how and why the plot works the way it does, what the characters are about, and what the

imagery is saying. Then, in the light of the story thus far, I want to speculate as to what this might mean for us as we write our own act of God's
play. As with everything else in the Christian life, I believe our approach
to evangelism will combine "consistency" with the story thus far with
"innovation" as we think about what it means for today.

Who this book is for

Writers always are advised to have a particular reader in mind as they
write. So who was my imaginary reader? The first thing to say is that I had
in mind someone who is already a follower of Jesus, though I would be
happy if the book were also of interest to those who would not call themselves Christians. I also hope that the book may be of use to brothers and
sisters of Christian tribes other than my own. I am painfully aware that my
experience and knowledge are limited to particular parts of the Christian
spectrum.

On the other hand, we all start from the limited world of our own culture. We can't help that. What we can help, however, is whether we behave
as if our little world is the only one and seek to keep the doors closed to
the outside, or whether we acknowledge and respect other worlds, and
keep the doors open to the possibilities of hospitality, conversation, and
friendship with those worlds. I hope this book keeps the doors open.

Among other Christians, I was also writing for those who, like myself,
have been put off by many modern manifestations of "evangelism," but
who still feel we do have something worth sharing. We just need a better
way to do it. My conviction is that there is a better way; in fact, that there
are many better ways.

So who is the reader? I have used the phrase "'normal' people." The
book is for "'normal' people." The problem, of course, is to define normal.
Who has any right to do so? Biologists? Anthropologists? Sociologists?
I hope not. To be honest, I use that phrase "'normal' people" in the title in
a tongue-in-cheek way. (Put it down to the British sense of humor.)
After all, we all like to think we are normal. In fact, we probably measure
other people's "normality" by our own standards or those of our culture.
So the title of this book refers to those people who think to themselves,
"I'm normal, therefore I'm not much interested in evangelism," those
people who think evangelism is somehow abnormal (even for Christians)
and therefore only for weird Christians, "them" as opposed to "us."

My hope is to show that evangelism is, or at least can be, "normal" for all those who consider themselves followers of Jesus. After all, Jesus, the archetypal evangelist, is also the most normal person who ever lived, in the sense that he most fully illustrated the Creator's intentions for human life.

What this book is and is not

This is, in the first place, a book about vision and understanding and attitude. My desire, as someone has expressed it, is to help rescue evangelism from the red light district of the church and put it back on the main street of church life, where it belongs.

At the same time, I need to warn you: this is not a "how-to" book. Certainly there are practical ideas on evangelism, born of my own or others' experience, and I trust you will enjoy using them and improving on them. But, in fact, I suspect that the hunger for "how-to" books (not to mention how-to lectures, seminars, conferences, videos and tapes) is the fruit of a particular modernist culture, one that say things such as these:

You can do it.

You don't need help (apart from this book).

You are competent (once you watch this video).

What matters is to get the job done.

You get more achieved if you think of life as a series of projects.

Get the results you want.

I believe that kind of attitude has hampered the life of the church, and not least the activity we call evangelism. After all, Christian faith is about relationship—above all, relationship with God, but also our relationships with one another, whether inside or outside the church. And, while we can find practical help with all those relationships, an over-emphasis on techniques for "doing relationships" can actually work against the very relationships they were meant to help.

The book falls into two main parts: chapters 1 through 9 trace the story of evangelism from the beginning of the Bible to (almost) the end. Then, chapters 10 through 16 look at some implications of the story and consider what might be our practical responsibilities in God's ongoing story.

Part one follows a broadly chronological sequence, and it probably makes most sense to read those chapters in order. Part two is more fragmented, and you may want to pick and choose those parts of particular interest to you.

The final thing to say is that I have written this book in terms of my own personal journey in thinking about evangelism, and I invite you to come with me on that journey. You may guess that the changes in my thinking weren't quite as neat as the book makes them sound. Neither did the journey take several months, as the text might suggest. It took years, and, indeed, it still continues, and (God willing) will continue till I die.

Now let's make a start. Let me tell you one of my own stories that got me going on this journey in the first place.

1.

Flasher Evangelism

We shall not cease from exploration
And the end of all our exploring
Will be to arrive where we started
And know the place for the first time.

T. S. Eliot, "Little Gidding" [1]

I RECENTLY SHAVED OFF MY BEARD. I had it for seven years, so some of my friends have never seen me without it. I felt particularly flattered when one colleague told me I looked ten years younger. That's how I wanted to see myself. (She didn't tell me how old she thought I had looked before, but I only realized that later.) However, a seven-year-old who lives across the road from me said, "Boy, you look so much older." As far as I was concerned, that was the wrong answer—he was not seeing me as I wanted to be seen.

"Seeing ourselves as others see us." Sounds like a neat idea, doesn't it? Brave and honest and unafraid. Yet in practice, we don't always want to know how others see us. Too often it's painful. But it can also be the kind of pain the dentist produces by probing an aching tooth and telling us he can fix it.

Christians—those who try to follow Jesus in our world—have differing opinions of evangelism. Some churches make evangelism the number one priority. Others—particularly in what are called the mainline denominations—shy away from it as from a skunk that has wandered by mistake into a garden party. [2] But how must evangelism appear and feel to those outside the church community? How do others see that particular side of church life?

My wife, Deborah, is an English professor, and from time to time she reads a book that she then passes on to me for me to enjoy, too. One book was *Bluebeard's Egg,* a collection of Margaret Atwood's short stories.

I always find Atwood stimulating, so recently I settled down to enjoy this latest book. All went well until I read the story "Scarlet Ibis." In the middle was a section that made me blink, stop, read it again, and then think very hard. The character Christine is on a trip to see the scarlet ibises of Florida. On the way, she gets into conversation with a woman who tells her that she used to be a missionary. Atwood writes:

> Christine had been raised Anglican, but the only vestige of this was the kind of Christmas cards she favored: prints of mediaeval or renaissance old masters. Religious people of any serious kind made her nervous: they were like men in raincoats who might or might not be flashers. You would be going along with them in the normal way, and then there could be a swift movement and you would look down to find the coat wide open and nothing on under it but some pant legs held up by rubber bands. This had happened to Christine in a train station once.[3]

Not exactly a pleasant image; it's quite repulsive in fact. Atwood is telling us how it feels to be on the receiving end of a certain kind of evangelism: it is disgusting. For many years I had worked with university students, and much of my work had been in the area of evangelism, both teaching about it and doing it, and I loved my work. But now a writer whom I respect and enjoy, looking at evangelism as an observer, was saying it struck her as being like indecent exposure, a criminal offense.

The next time I was discussing evangelism with a group of Christians, I read them that passage from Atwood and asked them what they thought she was trying to convey by her use of the flasher image. The answers were very revealing. They said things like this:

- The action of a flasher is totally inappropriate to the relationship.
- A private and personal thing is made public, and cheapened.
- Something that should be an expression of intimacy and tenderness—sexual arousal—is used as a form of violence.
- The victim feels violated and dehumanized, and the perpetrator acts in a way that is less than human.

So this is how one of Canada's most articulate and sensitive writers views evangelism: it is dehumanizing, violent, and inappropriate. Strong words. No wonder many Christians back away from the "E" word.

We have no desire to be spiritual flashers. We just don't want to be seen that way.

What then of my work in evangelism? What about the things I was teaching to churches and to students? I began to rethink. Surely evangelism was never meant to be the way Atwood describes it. Christian evangelism, after all, was started by Jesus, who consistently affirmed people's humanity and dealt with them gently and appropriately. Nobody could have described his approach, in evangelism or in life, as dehumanizing, violent, or inappropriate.

Yet much of the language around evangelism has overtones (some of them not too subtle) of violence and objectivization. People speak of such things as:

- Evangelistic "crusades," as though evangelism were warfare, with unbelievers as the "enemy," or, at best, "prisoners of war."
- Evangelistic "tools," as though evangelism were an industrial process with unbelievers as the raw material.
- Evangelistic "strategies," as though evangelism were a marketing campaign with unbelievers as the consumer. [4]
- "Friendship evangelism," which makes friendship appear a means to an end, rather than a God-given end in itself.
- "Lifestyle evangelism," which sounds as if Christian discipleship were a lifestyle adopted not out of obedience to Christ but in order to impress and attract those outside Christian faith.

So what had gone wrong? A second experience pushed me further in the direction of a new understanding of evangelism. Once again it was not from an overtly Christian source.

A Christmas surprise

My wife and I were visiting with a couple of English friends for an afternoon tea, with Christmas cake and mince tarts. While the children watched a video, we talked. Our friend Jane, who would not consider herself a Christian, had developed some strong views on gender issues during the ten years we had known her. Over the third cup of tea, I asked Jane what had made those convictions grow.

Had she, for instance, been reading books about gender issues?

"No," she replied thoughtfully—but certainly books by women.

"Books about women?" I asked.

Again, no—books about anything, including novels by Margaret Laurence and Margaret Atwood, and stories by Alice Munro. Their points of view as women were persuasive. They struck an answering chord in Jane, a chord that male writers had never found.

Jane also had taken a union job a few years back, as a representative on affirmative action. That had put her into a position where she had been forced to face issues of sexism head on, and to become painfully aware of how other women were hurting in ways she herself had never experienced. That job also put her alongside people who had thought through a lot of the issues—equality in the workplace, day care, sexual abuse, gender discrimination—people who were putting their lives on the line to work toward a better day for women.

Anything else, I asked? "Well," replied Jane, "when I began to look back on my life from this new vantage point, I realized how much I had put up with over the years simply because I was a woman." What this new outlook had done for Jane was to give her a framework for critiquing that experience. Her new vision helped her make sense of her experience, and gave her a community of friends who had been through the same sort of thing.

As we left the warmth of the fireside and started the drive back home, my mind couldn't let the conversation go. Jane had had a conversion experience, though not the one I hoped (and still hope) for her. We tried to figure out how it had happened.

First, she had been attracted by the creative work of people who all happened to hold the same philosophy. Not that they were writing about their philosophy. They were simply writing about life, but they did so in a way that was attractive and that made sense.[5]

Then she had worked alongside people who had impressed her by their wholeheartedness, their willingness to sacrifice for their cause, and by the clear-cut truth and justice of much they were saying. These were not people who had studied gender issues in school. They were just thoughtful, passionate people—amateurs, in the literal sense of people who act for the love of their cause.

Finally, Jane had found a new way of making sense of her life, almost a philosophy of life. It explained her past, it gave her purpose for the present, and it offered bright hope for the future.

No crusades. Not a lot of preaching. No door-to-door visitation. Certainly no aggressive confrontations. Just convinced people doing their thing. Personal stories of the non-preachy variety. People who integrated their faith and their work, people who practiced what they believed.

Of course, it's not just Jane who has converted. All of Western society has been touched by discussion of these same issues. Certainly the church has become a different place. Is it just possible that the women's movement has done a better job of communicating its message in the past thirty years than Christians have of communicating theirs?

As we pulled into the driveway, I sighed. This was supposed to have been a relaxing visit. Certainly, I had hoped to say something appropriate about my faith if the opportunity came. But it turned out to be a time for listening more than for talking. I hadn't bargained on God's speaking to me, least of all to say something about evangelism through a friend who's not yet a Christian. But, after all, it was Christmas, God's traditional time for surprises.

Can evangelism be redeemed?

So my rethinking of evangelism began. Margaret Atwood helped me understand how deeply our society resents many traditional forms of evangelism. Could evangelism be redeemed? My conversation with Jane, on the other hand, helped me see that people are still "converted" even in a tolerant society like ours, through (what shall I say?) more humane and holistic methods of "evangelism." But that was not evangelism on behalf of Christian faith or conversion to Christ.

It was another Canadian woman writer who made me think there was a kind of Christian evangelism that was possible in our world. Sandra Tsing Loh is writing about a former boyfriend in her collection of stories *Depth Takes a Holiday*:

> We were half way through a lovely Thai dinner; we had discussed the music of John Coltrane; we had discovered a common love of volleyball. Our faces were flushed. Lanterns swayed hypnotically. Grasping my hand, Jeff impulsively leaned forward. "Sandra?"
>
> "What?" I asked huskily.
>
> "Have you accepted the Lord Jesus Christ as your savior?"

Just like that. No warm-up. No mood music. No idle teasing around the
God issue to loosen the soil. Had Jeff grabbed my breast I would not have
been more shocked.[6]

At first, I was simply disturbed to find another writer who, like
Atwood, instinctively turns to the language of sexual inappropriateness to
describe how she felt at this sudden, clumsy effort at "evangelism." But
then I noticed a hint of something else, more positive. The words, "No
warm-up. No mood music. No idle teasing around the God-issue to
loosen the soil," suggest to me that Tsing Loh is not opposed to talking
about "the God-issue" in principle. She is no closed-minded atheist. (Few
people are.) In fact, quite the opposite. She implies that she would be
happy to talk about God under appropriate circumstances—circumstances
that would include just a little more sensitivity.

So could there be a different kind of evangelism? An evangelism acces-
sible to "'normal' people" inside and outside the church? A kind of
evangelism that would look so different from our stereotypes that we
might even have to find a new word for it?

The other factor that spurred my thinking was the realization that
"good evangelism" happens all the time. After all, everyone who follows
Jesus has been evangelized, in the sense that at some point they heard the
story of Jesus from someone, and believed it. Presumably they didn't feel
they were being flashed at. Presumably there was suitable "warm up" and
"mood music." It may have been in childhood from parents or godparents;
the story may have been told at church or at Sunday school. Or the evangelizing may have happened in adult life through one means or another.
However it took place, every Christian has been successfully evangelized.
Maybe there is something we can learn from the experience of those who
are happy and grateful they were evangelized.

One of these is my friend Nicky Laxton Ward. I met Nicky shortly
after she came from England to Canada as a graduate student at Carleton
University in Ottawa. At the time this manuscript was written Nicky was
working for Inter-Varsity Christian Fellowship at the University of
Toronto, helping students figure out issues of faith and spirituality.

But Nicky was not always a Christian. I had heard bits of her story over
the years we have known each other, but in preparing this book I realized
how helpful it would be to have her whole story as an example of what

"good evangelism" can look like, so she wrote out the whole thing for me. I will quote pieces of her story as the book goes on, but here is a summary of Nicky's story, in her own words.

Nicky's story

I became a Christian in my first year at university. When I arrived in residence, I found a big empty room, but there was a friendly face: Sarah, who was to be my roommate. Sarah was very popular and very trendy. She had long curly hair, big green glasses, and shocker lipstick. She had a very attractive personality, too. She was very friendly, fun, and bubbly—basically the life and soul of the party.

We set about unpacking and decorating the room. For me, the first thing to go was the Gideon Bible on my shelf. "Won't be needing that," I said. I then removed the Bible and placed it at the bottom of my bottom drawer, while commenting to Sarah that I had no idea why they wasted all this money putting Bibles in all these rooms when no one ever read them anyway. What a waste of paper! Sarah was strangely silent at this point but didn't say anything.

During Frosh Week, we had a blast. We spent a lot of time getting to know one another and having a good laugh. We went to every Frosh event, danced for hours, then drank coffee in various people's rooms until the early hours of the morning. Basically we had an excellent time.

Then Sunday came. Sarah got up early and told me she was going to church. I could not believe it! Why on earth would she want to go to church? She was so cool, I could not imagine why she could possibly want to do such an uncool thing. However, I went with her. Surprisingly enough, I kept going. In fact, I went to lots of Christian events with Sarah, including her Christian fellowship group on the campus every week, simply because I respected her and was interested to find out what she believed. Besides, she kept inviting me.

As I spent more and more time with these Christians, and as I learned more and more about what they believed, I became more and more intrigued. Conversations about God would come up frequently and naturally, probably because I was spending so much time thinking about it all.

Before long, people began to assume that I was a Christian. I went to the weekly fellowship meeting and listened (and even sang) with the others. Then I would go to a study group where four or five of us would meet together to study the Bible. During these meetings I would say absolutely nothing. I would simply listen. Sometimes I would be intrigued or confused, and at other times I was amused.

Before long I realized what was missing in my life, that I had a yearning inside me, an emptiness that needed feeding, a hole that no amount of good marks or achievements would fill. I later heard this described as a God-shaped vacuum, a yearning that only the love of God could satisfy.

A significant moment for me was standing up in a church service on my birthday at the end of my first year in university. It happened at a confirmation service, when the rector asked if there was anyone who had already been confirmed but who, at the time of their confirmation, didn't really mean it. (At least, that's how I interpreted it.) Well, I had been confirmed at the age of fifteen, at a time when I doubted the existence of God but thought it would be cool to be able to take the bread and wine at communion! I hesitantly stood up. For me, this was a public declaration of my new faith before my friends, and I appreciated the "congratulations" that I received from many of them afterward.

Several things struck me in this story. First, the kind of evangelism Nicky experienced was very relational. Sarah was a good friend to her. They had fun together as well as having serious discussions. What's more, Sarah would have been her friend even if Nicky had not gone to church with her.

Then I noticed that Nicky's conversion took place gradually over the course of a year. She had time and space to figure things out, time to watch how the Christians lived, space to figure out what they meant when they said "prayer" or "the Holy Spirit" or "discipleship." I can't say that nobody pressured Nicky to "become a Christian" because they did (I will describe that incident later), but, fortunately, she was not put off by it. Nicky also experimented with prayer, and she tentatively engaged in worship. And in the Holy Spirit's time, Nicky came to the point where she could (though "hesitantly" at first) identify herself as a follower of Jesus.

For Nicky, that year was one of turmoil and confusion. Yet that is not necessarily a bad thing. Confusion can give us a chance to sort out our feelings and to grow as people. So it was for Nicky. Confusion gave way to clarity; atheism melted away, and faith grew green.

Evangelism, it seems, can be dehumanizing, as Margaret Atwood suggests. But it can also be a wonderful thing, as Nicky discovered. If Atwood's view is the only one, then the sooner the church gives up on evangelism, the better. But if Nicky's experience is the way evangelism should be, there are probably many people who would love to be evangelized. Some of them may currently be agnostics or atheists, as Nicky was. Others are exploring their spirituality, though they might well qualify that by saying they are "spiritual, not religious." To date, no one has given them any reason to connect their interest in spirituality with the rich resources of the Christian church.

How could I figure this out? Where should I begin? Philosopher Alasdair MacIntyre once wrote: "I can only answer the question, 'What am I to do?' if I can answer the prior question, 'Of what story or stories do I find myself a part?'" [7]

All of us have stories that give direction to our lives, stories that tell us what kind of world this is, what is worth living for, and where we are going. For Christians, that is the story of God making the world, sustaining the world, and redeeming the world through Christ. What should we think and do in terms of evangelism? If MacIntyre is right, we consult our story. I decided some serious Bible study was in order. And presumably I should begin at the beginning.

2.

Evangelism B.C.:
An Old Testament Vision

There is nothing actively missionary yet, but there is a sense of the infinite worth of the treasure entrusted to Israel in her faith, and the profound conviction that her God embraces all . . . in His love, and wills that they shall share her treasure.

H. H. Rowley, *The Missionary Message of the Old Testament* [1]

I HAVE TO CONFESS that the Old Testament did not seem a promising place to begin thinking about evangelism. Apart from anything else, evangelism has to do with good news. But what good news is there in the Old Testament? So much of it seems violent, sexist, and downright boring to a contemporary reader. Once again, there were surprises in store for me.

Good news, bad news, better news

The beginning of the Bible describes an idyllic scene: people live in harmony with God, they love one another and serve a creation that is fresh and totally unspoiled. Good news indeed. Then, however, comes the bad news. Human beings decide to restructure the management of the universe with themselves at the center. They try to lock God out.

As humans, however, we function best when we are in relationships. We function best of all in the greatest relationship of all—our relationship with God. As a result, when we tried to walk away from God like this, all sorts of dysfunction followed. We became fragmented inside, we drew back from intimacy with one another, and our symbiotic relationship with the world around became strained and destructive. We experienced a kind of death.

If you have experienced the end of a close relationship, either through physical death or through alienation of one kind or another, you will know that, although you learn to exist without the one you love, it is never the same again. There is part of us that dies when we are separated from someone we love. It is like that with God: living at a distance from God causes death in our relationship with God. We may learn to exist without God, but we are never the same again. Part of us has died.

Now the stage is set to understand the distinctive good news of the Bible. The night sky has been spread against which the stars can shine. We don't have long to wait for evangelism to begin.

Imagine the scene. The sun is setting. The world still looks perfect, but at the heart of it is now a cancer that will quickly spread and take over every corner of creation. Into this world steps the Creator for an evening stroll with Adam and Eve. God clearly knows what has happened, though the story veils the fact. And what does God say to those who have spit in his face? God asks, "Where are you?" These are such simple, poignant words. Like a mother searching for a child, like a teenager with a lost puppy. Words of deep affection but also urgent concern.

Under the circumstances, God might have said other things. I'm afraid I might have said, "You jerks! How dare you do this to me?" Indeed, God might have said nothing, merely acted once and for all to scour those specks of moral pollution off the planet there and then. But no. God's first words are words that reach out, essentially saying, "Come out. Don't hide. Let's talk. Let's figure this thing out." It is amazingly gracious of God. God's attitude right there is good news for scared wrongdoers.

What God has to say to Adam and Eve is not all good news, however. All actions have their consequences, however compassionate the judge. So the pair is expelled from their idyllic home, and they begin to suffer in a way previously unknown.

What is so good here is that God does not give them up forever. Even outside the garden of perfection, God cares and provides for them. And God promises that one day someone will come who can destroy the evil they have let into the world.

Well, I reflected, isn't that evangelism? Doesn't God feel toward all of us, in a sense, as God felt toward Adam and Eve? Evangelism at its core is God coming after us, even at our very worst, to invite us to come home.

Evangelism is God coming with outstretched hands to seek reconciliation with those who have set themselves up as his enemies. And those outstretched hands are the driving force of the Bible story until humankind cannot stand them any more, and they are nailed down to stop them coming any closer. But that is to leap ahead.

Evangelism, then, begins early in the story. In fact, it could hardly have begun any earlier. As soon as there is bad news, God's posture is to step in with good news. In other words, there seems to be something pretty close to the heart of God that compels God to evangelize. Maybe love is the right word for it. Evangelism is one form the love of God takes in the face of sin.

Good news for Abraham

So where does the story of evangelism go next? I flipped the pages of my Bible from Genesis chapter 3 to chapter 12, where the story of Abraham and Sarah begins. A new phase in the Bible's story, the beginning of the Jewish nation. Any evangelizing there? These were God's first words to Abraham:

> Go from your country and your kindred and your father's house to the land that I will show you. I will make of you a great nation, and I will bless you . . . so that you will be a blessing . . . and in you all the families of the earth shall be blessed. (Genesis 12:1-3)

I had read this many times before, but now, as I read it with the question of evangelism in mind, I realized how often I had noticed only the first half of God's promise— "I will make of you a great nation . . . I will bless you"—and been puzzled, even irritated. After all, why just one nation? How come other nations are not chosen? What about the rest of us? God, it doesn't seem fair.

The objection, however, assumes that God was not interested in any other nation. I noticed that in fact the story says precisely the opposite. God's intention in calling Abraham is not to shower blessings on one favorite child and turn away from the rest. God's desire is to bless the whole world. God is not the parent who says to one child, "You're the only one I'm going to give an allowance to because I like you best."

Rather, God is the parent who says, "Here, you take this week's allowance and share it with your sisters and brothers." The blessing is for all. Abraham's family is merely the channel.

There is a link between God's words to Abraham and God's words to Adam. The blessing to Adam and Eve was the joy of living as God's people in God's world in God's way. Now the people of Abraham and Sarah are going to be responsible for putting people back in touch with their Creator and inviting the whole world to live as God's people in God's world in God's way. Abraham's descendants are invited to become God's hands reaching out with God's blessing. They are to be God's evangelists.

Of course, it takes a long time for this to come about. God does not appear to be in a hurry. Abraham has only one son, Isaac, by his wife, Sarah. Isaac has only two sons, Esau and Jacob. Then Jacob, making up for lost time, has twelve sons. Then, through four hundred years in Egypt, the people grow until by the time they set out to return to the land God has promised them, they are a significant number—enough to make Pharaoh worry about losing the majority of his labor force.

Their leader, Moses, is commissioned by God to lead these people to the place where they will establish their identity as a new nation. Before they get very far, however, God delivers to them a new constitution to go along with their new independence. Unlike many constitutions, there is little in it about rights (they are children of God, after all—what other right can compare with that?) and a great deal about responsibilities.

Then, for what amounts to about two hundred pages in most versions of the Bible, God—through Moses—lays down the law about everything from farming to worship, from childbirth to clothing, from immigration to hygiene. Why is this necessary? If God's plan is to bless the world, why not get together a group of zealous missionaries to go and evangelize the world? Surely that would be much quicker and less frustrating?

A working model

Then I realized that there is a clue in Leviticus 19. Now I have to be honest. I do not spend a lot of time reading Leviticus. But, as I pondered this question, something came to mind that my Old Testament professor had said many years ago about this (apparently) obscure chapter among the laws of Moses. One of the strange things about the chapter is how diverse the laws are. They include care for the poor, fair payment for laborers, care for people who are disabled, harvesting of fruit orchards, not allowing one's daughters to become prostitutes, respect for the elderly, and concern for refugees.

Yet in spite of the wild variety, there is a refrain that binds the contents of the chapter together. After many of the laws, the words "I am the LORD" occur. (The word LORD rendered in capital letters indicates the personal name of God, often written as Yahweh or YHWH.) Is this then a threat? Keep this law, or else you will have me to answer to? No, argued Alec Motyer, my professor. The chapter says, "You shall be holy, for I the LORD your God am holy" (Leviticus 19:2). Thus, each of the commands indicates a particular way that Israel's God is holy—Yahweh cares for people who are poor, or disabled, or elderly, or refugee, and so on—and so a people being remade in the image of their Creator will imitate God's concerns.

Through Moses and the people of Israel, God is creating a community that once more bears the image of the Creator just as human beings were intended to do at the beginning. The image has not been destroyed, but it has been distorted by sin. Now God takes steps to restore that original perfection.

What does this have to do with evangelism, or, at least, with God's intention to reach out to the whole world? Everything. Listen to the words of Moses as he summarizes the whole giving of the law:

> So just as the LORD my God has charged me, I now teach you statutes and ordinances for you to observe in the land that you are about to enter and occupy. You must observe them diligently, for this will show your wisdom and discernment to the people, who, when they hear all these statutes, will say, "Surely this great nation is a wise and discerning people!" (Deuteronomy 4:5-8)

God's intention is that others will look at Abraham's people and say in effect, "Boy, those people really know how to live. Look at how they care for one another. See how they take care of people with disabilities? And they have some neat farming techniques. What makes them that way? They say it's something to do with their religion. Maybe we'd better check it out."

Richard Middleton and Brian Walsh put it this way: "Israel's distinctive practice of justice was meant to shine as a beacon in the ancient Near East, attracting other nations to the distinctive God who wills such justice." [2]

God, it seems, is not interested in announcing a verbal ultimatum to the world. God's rescue mission has never happened through words alone. God's reaching out to the world begins through the lived-out message of a God-centered life. Eventually there will be a place for words, words that can explain the life. But it is the life that needs to come first.

God is concerned in the first place to create a community committed to twin foci: love of God and love of neighbor—a community that will be intriguing and attractive to outsiders. As God's people live in God's world in God's way, their life will be a powerful magnet for everyone searching for truth and compassion, for justice and dignity, for meaning and hope. The outstretched hands cannot achieve much unless they are attached to a healthy body.

Maybe there is a reason that evangelism is not front and center in the Old Testament. C. S. Lewis argues that there is little in the Old Testament about heaven and hell because God wished to teach people to value their relationship with him for its own sake, "quite apart from anything he can bestow or deny." Lewis thinks it would have been almost impossible for people to learn to value their relationship with God as "their true goal and the satisfaction of their needs" because "personal hopes and fears" would get in the way. [3]

Perhaps, in the same way, if God had introduced the idea of evangelism earlier, the desire to follow God and live as God's people for God's own sake would never have had the opportunity to grow. And the way the people represented God would have been distorted, their words outstripping their lives.

The scarlet thread

Time after time, kings and prophets remind the people of this vision of worldwide influence. I began to follow this scarlet thread through the highlights of the Old Testament story.

Here is David, for instance, boasting of how he will defeat Goliath, and promising that through this victory "all the earth may know that there is a God in Israel" (1 Samuel 17:46). His vision reaches far beyond making Israel safe from its Philistine enemies. He wants the world to know about Israel's God.

Then there is David's son, Solomon, dedicating his great temple. As he prays, he betrays the fact that he shares his father's heart by asking that "foreigners, who are not of your people Israel, [may] come from a distant land because of your great name and your mighty hand and your outstretched arm" (2 Chronicles 6:32). He asks God to hear their prayers, too. Why? "In order that all the peoples of the earth may know your name and fear you, as do your people Israel" (2 Chronicles 6:33).

Not only kings but prophets also yearn for that day to come when the world will love and follow God. Here, for example, is Micah in the time before the exile in Babylon:

> Many nations shall come and say: "Come, let us go up to the mountain of the LORD, to the house of the God of Jacob; that he may teach us his ways and that we may walk in his paths. For out of Zion shall come instruction, and the word of the LORD from Jerusalem." (Micah 4:2)

Micah foresees that "many nations" (the Hebrew word is *goyim*, still used today to indicate non-Jews) will want to come to the place where God is to be found. Why? Because this God is a teacher who gives instruction, and because they want to learn, not just in our limited academic sense, but so that they may "walk in his paths." The nations, too, want to live as God's people in God's world in God's way.

The experience of seventy years in exile does not quench this vision. If anything, it gets stronger. Certainly what is perhaps the most vivid picture of this future turning to God from all over the world comes once the exiles have returned home to Jerusalem. The prophet Zechariah foresees a day when:

> Many peoples and strong nations shall come to seek the LORD of hosts in Jerusalem, and to entreat the favor of the LORD. Thus says the LORD of hosts: In those days, ten men from the nations of every language shall take hold of a Jew, grasping his garment and saying, "Let us go with you, for we have heard that God is with you." (Zechariah 8:22-23)

Where is all this coming from? The passion of these kings and prophets that the world should know God stretches all the way back to the day when God shared his heart for a hurting world with Abraham.

A limited response

Does the passion find fulfillment? Do "the nations" turn to Israel's God? I tried making a list. There are not a lot of examples, but there are some. For example:

- Moses tells his father-in-law Jethro all that God has done for the Israelites in rescuing them from Egypt. Jethro is deeply impressed, confessing, "Now I know that the LORD is greater than all other gods" (Exodus 18:11).

- Then, when the people of Israel first cross into the land of Palestine, there is one woman, Rahab the prostitute, who discerns the reality of what is going on. She recognizes that Yahweh is not just another petty tribal deity. She says:

  I know that the LORD has given you the land . . . for we have heard how the LORD dried up the water of the Red Sea before you . . . the LORD your God is indeed God in heaven above and in earth below. (Joshua 2:8-11)

Because of Rahab's commitment to the God of Israel, she is protected when Jericho is destroyed, and indeed, the author notes that "her family has lived in Israel ever since" (Joshua 6:25). In fact, her son Boaz plays a part in the life of another woman who came to trust Israel's God, Ruth.

- The widow Ruth, like Rahab, though for different reasons, finds herself drawn to the God of the Israelite religion. She says to her Israelite mother-in-law, Naomi, as they set out to return from Moab to Israel:

  > Where you go, I will go;
  > Where you lodge, I will lodge;
  > your people shall be my people,
  > and your God my God.
  > (Ruth 1:16f)

Ruth's attachment is not only to Naomi but also to Naomi's God and Naomi's faith. As the story unfolds, God honors this new faith of Ruth's. She not only finds a home among the Israelites, but she also marries Boaz, and they become the parents of Obed, who in turn becomes a grandfather of King David. Hundreds of years later, both Ruth and her mother-in-law are given places of honor as ancestors in the family tree of Jesus Christ (Matthew 1:5).

- When the Queen of Sheba visits King Solomon in Jerusalem, she has already heard of his God-given wisdom, so she comes "to test him with hard questions" (2 Chronicles 9:1). When she hears his answers and sees the impressive way Solomon's kingdom is organized, the Chronicler says (literally), "there was no more breath in her" (9:4). [4] She understands that Solomon's wisdom and strength come from the God he worships, and so she responds, "Blessed be the LORD your God, who has delighted in you" (9:8).

- Naaman is a general in the army of the King of Aram, in the time of the prophet Elisha. With Elisha's guidance, he is miraculously cured of leprosy, and his response is eloquent: "Now I know that there is no God in all the earth except in Israel" (2 Kings 5, especially verses 15-19).

There are two interesting notes concerning this story. First, he asks for two mule-loads of earth to take home with him, so that he can erect an altar for the worship of Israel's God, perhaps believing that Israel's God can only be worshiped on his own soil. Second, he asks Elisha's forgiveness because he will have to continue to worship with the king in the temple of Rimmon, the god of Syria. Elisha responds, "Go in peace"— not just a casual farewell, but an affirmation of Naaman's new faith.

- Another foreign ruler touched by the reality of Israel's God is Nebuchadnezzar, during the time the people of Judah are in exile in Babylon. One of the exiles, a young man named Daniel, makes a deep impression on the king, and finds a prominent place at court. While there, he is able to interpret a dream of the king's, warning him that unless he repents of his pride, he will experience God's judgment. The king is indeed punished, but once he has recovered his response is:

Now I, Nebuchadnezzar, praise and extol and honor the King of heaven, for all his works are truth, and his ways are justice; and he is able to bring low those who walk in pride. (Daniel 4:37)

- One Old Testament event that we might almost recognize as an "evangelistic crusade" is the preaching of Jonah at Nineveh. Jonah's message is a classic "turn or burn" message: "Forty days more," he thunders, "and Nineveh shall be overthrown" (Jonah 3:4).

And then, to Jonah's dismay, "the people of Nineveh believed God, including the king, who ordered his people to dress in sackcloth and to turn from their evil ways" on the grounds that, "Who knows? God may relent and change his mind; he may turn from his fierce anger, so that we do not perish" (Jonah 3:9). The king's uncertainty makes it sounds as though Jonah had not thought to mention this possibility: he was more interested in judgment. God does indeed turn from his fierce anger,[5] and the city is spared. Jonah is not exactly pleased at the results of his preaching, but that's another story.

Well, this was not exactly a long list. Not the sort of mass turning to the God of Israel that Abraham might have hoped for, or that Micah and Zechariah dreamed of. Still, sometimes outsiders to Israel really do catch a glimpse of the reality of God among God's people, whether on the macro level—Rahab believing in the God who parted the Red Sea—or on the micro level—Ruth being drawn by the humble faith of an elderly woman. And at least some of them are drawn to join the community of faith, to play their part in the unfolding of God's story for the world. Sadly, however, such cases are the exception rather than the rule.

The problem seems to be not so much lack of interest on the part of outsiders as that God's people fail to live up to God's norms, and there is little about them that might attract an outsider. Indeed, at one point, they beg God to give them a king so that they can be like the nations round about them (1 Samuel 8:5). How can they ask such a thing? Don't they get it? The whole point is that they should be different and distinctive from the other nations. Yet here, as on other occasions, they are seeking to minimize the differences and be like everyone else.

Pulled in opposite directions

What next? I thought on to the end of the Old Testament story. Seventy years after going into exile in Babylon, the people return to their own city of Jerusalem to make a fresh start. The books of Ezra and Nehemiah pick up the story. It would be nice to think that they finally learned something about God's hopes for them. Now perhaps they will create a community faithful to God's norms for human life, and attract the neighbors like wasps to honey.

Well, you might think so, but no. The pendulum has certainly moved but, as so often happens, it has gone too far in the opposite direction. If they had wanted at one time to be "like the other nations," now they have grasped the importance of being different, with a vengeance. They become almost paranoid in their determination to be separate and pure. They cut themselves off from normal interchange with their neighbors.

At first there is some excuse, I suppose. After all, their sole chance of survival as a tiny, fragile, new nation surrounded by hostile powers is to have as little to do with them as possible. When the returning exiles first arrive in Jerusalem and begin to rebuild their city, the surrounding states are initially nervous, then mocking, and finally antagonistic. Crown prince Zerubbabel, and later Nehemiah, play safe and will have nothing to do with them (Ezra 4:1-3; and Nehemiah 4:1-23; 6:1-19).

Mixed marriages also pose a threat to Jewish identity. Within a short time of the return, both Ezra and Nehemiah find that the returnees have begun marrying wives from the surrounding nations. Since the time of Solomon, with his hundreds of foreign wives and concubines, inter-marriage had been a recipe for disaster. Time after time, the people had learned the hard way that if you marry outside the faith, the faith becomes diluted and useless as a remedy for the world's ills. No wonder, then, when the nation is in such a fragile state of rebuilding, that Ezra and Nehemiah are appalled and make them deal drastically with the problem. It seems impossibly harsh and unfeeling to us, but one can understand the motivation (Ezra 9:1—10:44; Nehemiah 13:23-27).

Between Old and New Testaments, the same two opposite strands emerged in Jewish attitudes to the outside world. On the one hand, there were those who were attracted to non-Jewish culture. In the second century before Christ, some even went so far as to hide or even reverse their circumcision, in order to participate in Greek athletic competitions. On the other end of the spectrum were the Pharisees, convinced that Judaism had to be kept pure by careful observation of the law. A good number of them refused to take the oath of loyalty to Caesar, and were punished.

Neither extreme—strict separation nor enthusiastic assimilation—seems likely to bring the blessing of Abraham to the whole world. There must be another way. There is at least one hint of something better yet to come. When Herod began in 19 B.C. to build the Temple that Jesus would know, it was decorated with rich gifts from foreign rulers, and the temple itself contained a large court of the Gentiles. Here, then, was openness to the nations. But by the time of Jesus, that same court of the Gentiles, instead of being a house of prayer for all the nations, had become "a den of robbers," at least in Jesus' estimation (Mark 11:17).

Where next?

Well, this certainly was a new way of thinking about the Old Testament, and some of it hit home at once. For one thing, it was a relief to realize that evangelism is God's project. It was not invented by TV evangelists or indeed by human beings at all. The desire to reconcile us to God comes in the first place from God's side. That was both a relief and a challenge. A relief because it is no longer something we have to worry about primarily, but something we can look to God for leadership about. A challenge because God may just give that leadership if we ask for it.

I realized, too, that the tension that emerged by the end of the Old Testament still haunts us in our own day. Even now, there are churches and individual Christians who hold passionately to one or the other extreme. Some stress the importance of Christians being distinctive from the world around, but then build themselves walls against the outside world so that their light cannot be seen. Others emphasize the importance of openness to the culture, but gradually lose all distinctiveness so that they have nothing of value to offer. Neither attitude is very productive of healthy evangelism.

How revolutionary it would be if churches, instead of asking themselves, "How can we evangelize?" would ask, "What is the quality of our community life? Is it such that outsiders to the faith might be attracted by it?" But this, it seemed to me, was a whole topic by itself.

3.

Evangelism and Community

I am because we are.
We are because he is.

Kenyan Eucharistic Liturgy

AT THIS POINT, I became aware of a discrepancy. The image of evangelism so detested by Margaret Atwood was that of the "lone ranger" evangelist, the individual who approaches a stranger and asks them whether they are saved. Certainly there are models of what we might call conversational evangelism in the New Testament: Jesus offers some models (one of which we will look at in the next chapter), and Philip in the book of Acts offers another (we'll look at that one in chapter 9). These are by no means flasher-type evangelists, but they might be the origin of the tradition of individual-to-individual evangelism.

The picture I got from the Old Testament, however, had nothing to do with one individual verbalizing their faith to another individual. The normal expectation of the Old Testament, rather, had to do with (1) a community trying to live out its faith, and (2) the world hearing about what God had done for Israel. (There were exceptions, such as Naomi with Ruth, or Daniel with King Nebuchadnezzar, though I somehow suspect they were not spiritual flashers anyway.)

So where does this leave us? Is evangelism an individual responsibility or the effect of the life of a faith community?

My friend Don Posterski recalls speaking to a Christian conference on one occasion and asking the 300 delegates how many of them had prayed to God that morning to give them opportunities to talk about their faith that day. Half a dozen people put up their hands. Don mused over this statistic. These were committed church folk, who had probably heard sermons about the importance of evangelism. They might even have read books or gone to seminars on the subject. In spite of that, only a handful felt it to be their personal responsibility. Were the other 294 people spiritual failures?

Don's conclusion was that the vast majority of Christians will never become lone ranger evangelists and probably will feel a lingering sense of guilt over that for years. Yet they probably were not meant to be that kind of evangelist anyway. That sort of gift is certainly given to some people (the six who raised their hands were presumably perfectly serious). I have been around such people, and they are amazing.

Roger's story

Take my friend Roger, for example. I remember how Roger was once a witness to a crime. A police officer came to see him and, in noting his "particulars," asked him what he did for a living. "I'm an evangelist!" said Roger with an infectious grin. "Do you know what an evangelist is?" One hour later, the officer said, "Well, I guess I'd better start taking down your evidence, hadn't I?" For an hour they had talked about Jesus. Did the officer feel trapped or abused or flashed at? Not in the slightest. He loved it and went away thoughtful, wondering why he'd never thought of religion that way before.

Now the church could definitely benefit from more Rogers. But Rogers, I suspect, are born, not made. I struggled for years, thinking I should be that kind of evangelist, and I have finally come to the conclusion that I'm not and I never will be. (I know it's dangerous to make that kind of dogmatic statement when God might be eavesdropping, but I think I'll risk it.)

If you are not like Roger either, does that mean we simply have to wait for the Rogers of this world to bring people to faith in Christ? Is there nothing we are supposed to do? Part of the answer, I have come to believe, is that we are responsible to make the church an evangelizing community—a safe and inviting place where outsiders to faith can come to figure out their spirituality in a Christian context.[1]

As I turned the pages of the Gospels, it struck me more and more that this is what Jesus was doing. Certainly, he had heart to heart conversations about faith with individuals, certainly he preached to the crowds, but those things were not the heart of what he was about. One clue is in the way Mark, at the beginning of his Gospel, summarizes Jesus' message: "The time is fulfilled and the kingdom of God has come near: repent and believe in the good news" (Mark 1:15).

The kingdom of God is basically the realm where God is king. In the Old Testament, God's kingship found expression among the people of

Israel. After all, when Israel had asked for a (human) king so that they would be "like the other nations," God's response was telling: "They have rejected me from being king over them" (1 Samuel 8:7). In as far as Israel lived as God's people in God's world in God's way, they represented the kingdom of God, the realm where God was loved and followed.

Now Jesus comes along and he has the audacity to proclaim, "the kingdom has come." Everyone knew what he meant. His words were an implied criticism of the Judeans [2] for their failure to live out the kingdom, but it was also a promise, a promise that something new was knocking at the door. And that something was not just the chance for individuals to relate to God in a new way, but the birth of a new community, a new or renewed Israel, where God would once again be acknowledged as king, not just in words or even in the life of godly individuals, but in the life of a community.

There is another clue to what Jesus is about in the simple fact that he called twelve disciples. In a culture that understood symbolism, the choosing of twelve men could signify only one thing: these represented the twelve tribes of Israel. N.T. Wright observes that "Israel had not had twelve visible tribes since the Assyrian invasion in 734 B.C. . . . [yet Jesus] indicated pretty clearly that he was thinking in terms of the eschatological restoration of Israel" [3] In other words, Jesus believed himself to be reconstituting the historic people of Israel, calling the nation to become who God had always intended them to be. And how were they to fulfill this calling? By following Jesus. It was breathtaking and audacious and outrageous. No wonder people either loved him or hated him.

If Jesus' calling of the twelve disciples is the first step in his establishment of a new community, it is not the last. There is much more to come. Jesus calls other people to be members of this new family, he invites them to family celebrations, and he instructs them in the ways of the new community.

A new family

I found an indication of Jesus' new family, for instance, on one occasion, when his mother and his brothers come to look for him, and he responds by saying: "Who are my mother and my brothers?" And looking at those who sat around he said, "Here are my mother and my brothers! Whoever does the will of God is my brother and sister and mother" (Mark 3:34–35).

For Jesus, this new family of people who are committed to following God takes precedence over any biological family loyalties. Gerhard Lohfink underscores the fact that Jesus "did not call [the disciples] into solitude or isolation. That is not the point of discipleship. He called them into a new family of brothers and sisters, itself a sign of the arriving kingdom." [4]

It shouldn't surprise us, then, that while Jesus goes about preaching the kingdom and doing the works of the kingdom, he lives and travels with a group of disciples, both men and women. Luke records that:

> The twelve were with him, as well as some women who had been cured of evil spirits and infirmities: Mary, called Magdalene, from whom seven demons had gone out, and Joanna, the wife of Herod's steward Chuza, and Susanna, and many others, who provided for them out of their resources. (Luke 8:1-3)

These were not just folk curious to see what Jesus would do next. By leaving home to follow him, they had broken or at least strained ties with those back home. Instead, they had become members of the new family. As such, they shared life with Jesus, learned from him, supported him financially, and helped him in his ministry. Thus Jesus doesn't need to say that the kingdom of God is a new kind of community: he demonstrates what it means to be a new kind of community. [5]

It is probably no coincidence that he includes among the twelve at least two social and political opposites—Levi, a collaborator with the Roman army of occupation, and Simon the Zealot, quite possibly a guerrilla fighter against the Romans—and he expects them to break bread together at his table. They have to be reconciled, to learn to live and love as family.

More than this, as the team traveled around, their goal was not to persuade individuals to join the kingdom one by one, and to believe in Jesus in their hearts. That would be inconsistent and (to them at least) meaningless. No. N.T. Wright believes that Jesus' priority was "to establish . . . what we might call cells of followers, mostly continuing to live in their towns and villages, who by their adoption of his praxis, his way of being Israel, would be distinctive within their local communities." [6]

Some who were impressed with his message may have physically left home and followed him. But the majority who stayed at home would begin to live differently, to relate to one another differently—in a word, to become another new family group.[7]

What has all this to do with evangelism? In the Gospels, the message of evangelism is not just about how we relate to God, it's also about a whole new way of being family. There is good news of forgiveness and hope, certainly, but it is not just a message preached by an individual to an individual. The gospel message is communicated by the lives of the community as well as by preaching. And, naturally, the effect of that kind of evangelism is not just that individuals begin to relate to God in a new way, but that they get involved in the new community of God's people. This is a very long way from the solitary flasher and his solitary victim.

If we are to reproduce that pattern in our churches, it means that they need to grow as families centered on God and (as Jesus put it) doing the will of God, whatever they discern that to be. They speak the message of Jesus, certainly, but they also live it out in community.

The problem is often that those communities become closed communities. They do not necessarily make a deliberate decision to shut themselves off from outsiders (though that can happen), but the fact is that as they spend time together both formally and informally they weave a relational web that is difficult for an outsider to penetrate. If the community is meant to be the agent of evangelism, however, it has to be an open community, where outsiders can come in and explore the reality of faith. Consider the power of an open community.

Belonging before believing

I am a member of a group of faculty who teach evangelism in seminaries across North America. At our annual conference a few years back, the then president, George Hunter, told the story of his own coming to faith in Jesus. As I was pondering this issue of evangelism and community, George's story struck me as a wonderful example of how the two are meant to work together.[8]

As a teenager, George first became interested in Jesus through seeing an actor delivering the Sermon on the Mount. His curiosity prompted him to start attending a church youth group. The pastor was "friendly, approachable and interested in me, and . . . the prettiest girls in town attended Fulford Church." But what struck him about the community was that "the people pulled for each other, and interceded for each other.

I observed macho guys become real, and even vulnerable, with each other. I observed people seriously and adventurously living their lives as credible Christians." Three months later, he committed himself to be a follower of the Jesus he had heard about and whose influence had been so real around him.

The next part of his story is less inspiring. He received "training in evangelism," which he summarizes as: (1) explaining to a person his or her need of a savior; (2) encouraging the person to make a personal declaration of trust in Christ and his atoning work on the cross; and (3) bringing the new Christian into a fellowship of believers where spiritual growth may occur.

He conscientiously learned "the method" and tried to put it into practice. His experience, however, was that, more often than not, it just did not work. People did not respond as they were meant to, yet George assumed that the problem was with him rather than "the method."

In retrospect, he reflects, "I now know that this very logical evangelical sequence contrasts with the actual conversion process of many people, not just my own." Whereas the expectation of his training was that people would believe the gospel, and then come to belong to the church, what happened to him was the opposite: for him, belonging came before believing. Indeed, it was only through the experience of belonging to an open Christian community that he was able to believe. As he belonged, he found himself involved in conversations about faith, and, just as important, was able to watch the words lived out in the community, and to encounter Jesus Christ.

Not long after this, I went to speak to a student group at Trent University in Ontario, Canada. Under the leadership of some student friends of mine, Jeremy, Joy, and Hugh, they had worked hard for a couple of years to become the kind of community I have been describing. They had tried to become a family that not only talked about the good news of Jesus but who modeled it in terms of their openness, friendliness, and generosity.

That evening, I met a student named Jennifer. In the course of conversation, it seemed appropriate to ask her if she would call herself a follower of Jesus, or whether she was just checking out Christian faith. "No, I'm not a Christian," she said without embarrassment, "but, you know, this is a great place to ask my questions." I was impressed. I was even more impressed when I visited the group again eighteen months later. Jen was still there, and we got chatting. I told her how I had been struck by our conversation on the previous occasion. "Ah, but I'm not in that space any more," she said brightly, "I'm a follower of Jesus now. I read my Bible and pray every day and try to do what Jesus wants."

What had happened? Like George Hunter, Jen had heard words about Jesus, but she had also been welcomed into a community that was trying to be the kind of family Jesus taught about. There, over a period of time, the words had begun to make sense as she had seen them lived out. One of the problems with other kinds of evangelism is often how to connect "converts" to the church. Frequently it just doesn't happen. With someone like Jen, however, as with George, nobody needed to persuade her of the importance of Christian community. She was already there, and she loved it! That's where she had learned about Jesus and got in touch with Jesus. She didn't have to be persuaded to join: she just had to stay. And why would she not stay there? It had become her family.

The model of evangelism in which George Hunter had been "trained" makes a number of assumptions. One is that individual faith in Christ and life in the Christian community are somehow separate realities. Another is that mental assent to the message of Christ is a separate thing from living by the message of Christ. There is also the assumption that a split-second decision is more significant than a lengthy process.

But there is another conviction underlying this model. It is most simply expressed by saying that you are either in or you are out. Either you are a Christian or you are a "non-Christian" (not a term I like particularly). And the purpose of evangelism is then to persuade outsiders to become insiders, to cross the line from darkness into light.[9] In fact, so deeply has this understanding become embedded in people's understanding (whether or not they approve of evangelism) that they are not aware there is another way of thinking about it.

Bounded sets and centered sets

Jesus demonstrates another way in the Gospels. This model actually opens doors for Christian communities to become evangelizing communities. One of the first people to write about this was missiologist Paul Hiebert, who uses the language of "bounded sets" and "centered sets."[10]

In this way of thinking, a bounded set is a group of things or people that has a clear boundary. "Apples" would be such a grouping: if someone says, "Apple," we have a mental picture of what that means. We are not going to picture a banana or a TV or an alligator. We are clear what kinds of objects are "in" the group called "apples" and which are "out." Now, says Hiebert, for many, "Christian" is just such a term. Depending on the particular Christian tradition, if you are (a) baptized and/or (b) believe certain doctrines and/or (c) behave in a certain way, then you are "in." If not, then you are "out."

A centered set, on the other hand, is a group of things or people defined not by whether they are inside a particular boundary but by how they relate to a particular center. There is a boundary, but it is not the most important thing. What is important is whether people (or things) are moving toward the center or away from the center. According to Hiebert, some things may be far from the center, but they are moving toward the center, therefore they are part of the centered set. On the other hand, some objects may be near the center but are moving away from it, so they are not a part of the set.[11]

Imagine a poll of people's political preferences. Some would say, "I am definitely a supporter of Party X," or "I am definitely not a member of any party." These respondents have identified themselves as members or non-members of those bounded sets we call political parties. But there are some subtleties of political loyalties that this way of measuring misses.

For example, most voters are not card-carrying members of any party, and yet they are much more significant in deciding the results of elections than the minority who are party members. So how can we measure their allegiance (or lack of it) if they do not actually join a party? Pollsters will ask them questions such as: "If there were an election tomorrow, which of the present political parties would you vote for?" This kind of question is not asking about present loyalties but about the direction in which people are heading. Those who express a preference for one party over another are moving toward the center of a political grouping, but they are not there yet, in that they have not taken out party membership nor have they voted. Their inclination may be strong or weak, and for the weaker ones, it may change altogether by election day. But the direction in which they are moving is often what changes the outcome of an election.

Equally, there may some card-carrying members of particular parties who are secretly thinking of jumping ship and changing their allegiance, despite their public stand. By the standard of bounded sets, they are solid insiders. But by the standard of centered sets, they are actually moving in the opposite direction from the undecided voters, away from the center of the grouping. Wise party leaders will be more interested in people's direction than in their official status.

Here is the question for evangelism: Is Christian faith a form of bounded set—either you're in or you're out? Or could we think of it as a centered set—where what is significant is not whether you are in or out, but in what direction you are moving? The answer to that question will determine what we mean by evangelism.

The group at Trent University had worked at becoming a centered set. They made no secret of the fact that this was a Christian group. Yet they stressed the center—their desire to learn from Jesus—more than they emphasized the boundary—"Have you accepted Jesus as your Savior? Yes or no?" As a result, Jen was made welcome, and over time was free to move toward the center, as the Holy Spirit nurtured her interest in Jesus.

Nicky's story, which appears in chapter 1, offers the same lesson. There had been a week of evangelistic talks on her university campus, she recalls:

Some of my Christian friends, I think, wondered whether I had "become a Christian" because every evening of the mission there was an "altar call," and I went up every time. The reason I went up, however, was to find out more about what this Christian thing was about. . . . [My roommate] Sarah was less worried about seeing me "cross the line" than continue in a direction toward God, so she never bugged me with questions of where I was at in my belief at any particular stage.

Sarah had the patience simply to affirm the direction Nicky was headed, knowing that if she was heading down the right road, hanging out with others who were learning to follow Jesus, eventually she would have an encounter with Jesus. I think that's real faith, faith that evangelism is God's business, faith that something good is happening, however slow and confused and inefficient it may appear.

Jesus, bounded and centered

On one level, Jesus seems to model a fairly rigid bounded set. We can even think of them as concentric circles. The largest circle consists of the crowds who follow him, listen to his teaching, appreciate his miracles, and who may or may not one day become his followers. Then there are the seventy, who are fairly clearly identified, and whom Jesus sends on special missions (Luke 10:1-20). The inner circle, of course, are the twelve, and then in the inmost circle are the special three of Peter, James, and John. We could narrow it down even further and suggest that Jesus has a "best friend" out of the three, namely John, "the one whom Jesus loved" (John 13:23).

Yet the boundaries between the sets are not as clear as that might suggest. Start with the obvious fact that one of the twelve is a traitor. He may appear to be inside the line of the twelve, but in his heart he is moving away from Jesus, the center. Then there were the women who traveled with Jesus, who were clearly just as committed to him as were the twelve, and yet were not included in the twelve.

Further, at the banquets that were so much a distinctive feature of Jesus' ministry, there was no distinction between those who were already disciples and those who were, as we would say, checking him out. Nobody was inspecting baptismal certificates at the door. Nobody quizzed the guests as to whether they thought Jesus was Elijah, John the Baptist returned from the dead, or the Christ, the Son of the living God. All were welcome. Yet some people would leave the party eager to know more, while others would leave shaking their heads, dismissing him as dangerous or demented.

These parties were thus a way for outsiders to begin to explore the community. They opened doors for people with varying degrees of interest in Jesus to have a taste of what it meant to be among his followers without making a definite commitment to him. They could feel the atmosphere that existed around Jesus, they could hear the focus of the conversations and sense how Jesus' concerns were picked up (and sometimes misunderstood) by his friends.

The dinner party

I don't know about you, but I love to try and imagine exactly how some of the Bible stories took place; sometimes it's fun to update them and imagine how they might have happened in today's world. As I began to think about this topic of community and evangelism, I found myself reworking the story of Matthew's conversion in my imagination. Some time later, a group of students told me they wanted to reach out to their friends. I said, "What about throwing a dinner party?" And they asked, "How does that work?" What came out was my reworking of the old story. Luke's Gospel tells the story this way:

> He went out and saw a tax collector named Levi, sitting at the tax booth; and he said to him, "Follow me." And he got up, left everything, and followed him. Then Levi gave a great banquet for him in his house; and there was a large crowd of tax collectors and others sitting at the table with them. (Luke 5:27-29)

Now I found myself telling the story as if I were Simon, a friend of Matthew (also known as Levi), the tax collector. He and I had had some shady dealings in the past. Then one day, Matt phoned me and asked me to an impromptu party that evening. I asked him what was going on, and he said something like this:

> All I can tell you is that this morning I was working away at my desk, when there was a knock at the door, and this Jesus guy walked in. I don't know where my secretary was, but somehow he'd got past security and just walked in. Of course, I knew who he was from the pictures in the media.

> Before I could think what to say (after all, what do you say when a prophet barges into your office?), he said, "Matt, I want you to come with me. Right now. Come on!" And I don't know what it was, but there was something about him, his authority, his air of freedom, that I just thought, "You know what? I don't have to stay here a minute longer. I'm going to go. Why not?"

> So I went. We went outside, he introduced me to his friends—John and Peter and the rest—and I've been hanging out with them all day, just discussing God and stuff. He's an amazing teacher, you know, Simon. But I don't want to tell you any more. Just come to the party.

The party is a good party, and Simon manages to watch Jesus without Jesus noticing him. Then Matt calls for silence and invites Jesus to speak. People fall silent and look expectantly at Jesus. A sermon at a dinner party? Doesn't seem quite right, somehow. Let's listen:

Well, first of all I think we should thank Matt for this great party, especially at such short notice. It's been great, and, Matt, thank you for going to all this trouble.

You know, parties like this always make me think of the kingdom of God. There's a kind of life and laughter and good friendship that a party like this brings out that makes me think of heaven.

I don't know how you think of heaven. Maybe for you it's a boring place with everyone dressed in white and looking solemn and playing harps to Victorian hymns all day every day.

But it's not like that: our heavenly Father wants above all that we should find joy in this world by loving him and one other, and by seeking justice and mercy and compassion.

The trouble is (he went on), not everybody accepts God's invitation to the party. And sometimes those God thought were most likely to attend are the ones who make the stupidest excuses, like, "Oh, I've just bought a field and I need to go check it out, as though you wouldn't check it out before buying it." Another says, "Ah, well, I'm terribly sorry. I've just bought a couple of oxen but I haven't actually seen them yet, so I need to go and see what they're like." Another man says, "But I've just got married and I'm off on my honeymoon." (Well, maybe that's a more reasonable excuse.)

But, you know, God got so ticked off at people ignoring the invitations that God said to his servants, "Listen up: just go out into the streets, and grab anyone you can find, I don't care who it is, and get these seats filled up. I'm not going to waste my banquet. The party is open to anybody, whoever they are. They're all welcome."

And so, friends, the fact that you're here tonight is a good sign: you are not far from the kingdom of God.

Jesus' words, along with the startling change in Matt's outlook on life, cause Simon to reflect:

You know, this Saturday, I think I'm going to get the wife to make up a picnic basket and take her and the kids to the park for the day. I hear Jesus is going to be there all day teaching and telling stories, and maybe doing a miracle or two. I can see what Jesus has done for Matt, and I think I should check him out for myself.

What is happening here? Matt has been invited by Jesus into the community of his followers. There he hears the teaching of Jesus, listens in on the discussions, learns the language, observes the way they interact with one another, and is somehow attracted, even though he doesn't fully understand it yet. In this sense, Jesus' community is an open one, a centered set, not a bounded set, and Matt is moving toward the center.

And what of Simon? Things begin for him with a simple invitation to a party. Yet this is a party with a difference. For one thing, this was a party that cut across all social distinctions. There were no ranks of important guests and unimportant guests. All were welcome.[12] He hears a message about God in a totally novel context—a context of celebration and good food and friendship. He hears that the boundary around God's kingdom has been breached, and that all sorts of people (including the non-religious like him) are invited to participate. Almost despite himself, he is attracted. As a result, he decides to take his family and hang out on the fringes of Jesus' community the next weekend. He is moving in the right direction, toward the center. And that should delight the heart of any evangelist.

The question I was left with was this: Can our churches really become the kind of communities that are clear about their commitment to worshiping and following Jesus on the one hand, and yet open to anyone who is curious about faith on the other? Can they be places where people like George and Jen and Nicky and Matt and Simon can take time to discover the reality of Christian faith? That question was going to need some more work.

4.

"So I Send You":

How Jesus Gets Us Involved

"Is there any point to which you wish to draw my attention?"
"To the curious incident of the dog in the night-time."
"The dog did nothing in the night time."
"That was the curious incident," remarked Sherlock Holmes.

"Silver Blaze," Arthur Conan Doyle [1]

I WANTED TO LOOK more closely at the example of Jesus. After all, nobody ever accused him of being a "spiritual flasher." But in a sense he invented evangelism. According to Mark's Gospel, the first thing Jesus did in his ministry was evangelism: "Jesus came to Galilee, proclaiming the good news of God" (Mark 1:14).

That's a pretty basic definition of evangelism—"proclaiming the good news of God." Indeed, the Greek word for good news is *euangelion*, from which the word *evangelism* comes. So what was it that Jesus did in his evangelism that spiritual flashers don't?

I learned what I still count as one of my most profound lessons in Jesus-like evangelism while preparing a sermon. They say the most effective sermons are the ones you've already preached to yourself. Well, this was one of them.

I had been asked to preach at a local church, St. Paul's Presbyterian Church in Ottawa. It was their Missions Week, and I was to preach at the opening service. What to say? I wanted to do a good job. I didn't want to pull out notes of something I had done before. But what did I have to say about missions that was fresh? It was all there in Matthew 28:19: "Go therefore and make disciples of all nations . . ."

I prayed for the help of the Holy Spirit and decided to do some homework. Where were missions in the Bible, after all? As I thought about the way we use the word *mission*, I realized what a confusing concept it is. We speak, for example, of a downtown mission, meaning a hostel or soup kitchen. We use terms such as overseas missions or urban mission. There are organizations such as the Mission to Seafarers. Groups such as Inter-Varsity Christian Fellowship also think of themselves as missions. When I speak for a weekend at a church or for a week in a university, that often is called a mission, too. Then, of course, the general language of the culture adds to the confusion with terms such as trade mission, fact-finding mission, and even suicide mission. No wonder there is confusion.

I checked in my Bible concordance, but that didn't shed a lot of light: the word *mission* is simply not there. However, something from my high school Latin, many years before, reminded me that mission is from the Latin word meaning "to send." I checked the concordance again, this time for sending. This, I found, was much more fruitful.

The gospel of sending

In fact, I made a startling discovery. I found that the idea of mission, of sending, was concentrated in an unexpected place. Indeed, the word was used twice as many times there as anywhere else in the New Testament. I suppose that, if I hadn't checked, I would have assumed that Paul, with his missionary zeal, would be the chief user of the word. Or Luke, with his heart for evangelism among the Gentiles and his account in Acts of the evangelism of the Roman Empire.

Luke actually uses the word only 30 times. That is still more than Matthew (20 times) or Mark (10 times). But the name of the writer most consumed with the thought of mission is John, who speaks of it 60 times. To be honest, I had never thought of John as the Gospel of mission. What was going on here? I began to dig.

The first observation I made is that, while John talks about sending, he doesn't seem to be interested in evangelism. That seemed a little weird. After all, for the other Gospel writers, it's a big theme. Numbers don't tell you everything, but I was fascinated to find another statistical anomaly: Matthew uses words to do with evangelism 16 times, Mark uses evangelism words 18 times, and Luke use evangelism words 20 times, but John's Gospel does not use them at all. Not a single one. Nothing. Silence.

Now John's Gospel often has a unique slant on things, and when John is silent, there's always a reason. For example, "the kingdom" is a major theme in Matthew, Mark, and Luke, the Synoptic Gospels. The numbers this time are Matthew: 54; Mark: 19; Luke: 45; and for John a mere 4. Clearly John is up to something. Scholars have pointed out that while John doesn't talk about the kingdom, he talks instead about eternal life. If we check which Gospel writers talk about "eternal life," the numbers are reversed. Matthew, Mark, and Luke each use the term only twice, whereas John uses it nine times. What is interesting, then (though not relevant right now), is how and why John uses the term "eternal life" that is similar or different from the way the Synoptics use "the kingdom."

You see the point. If John doesn't talk about evangelism but talks a lot about sending, you can bet there is a reason. There is something he's trying to teach us that we would not find in quite the same way in the other Gospel writers. I tracked down every time John uses the word *send*, and here is what I found.

So I send you

First, the most frequent use of the term by John has to do with Jesus coming to earth. In fact, two-thirds of his sixty references are in the phrase, "the Father [who] sent the Son." This passage is typical:

> Anyone who does not honor the Son does not honor the Father who sent him. . . . anyone who . . . believes him who sent me has eternal life; . . . I seek not to do my own will but the will of him who sent me . . . the Father who sent me has himself testified on my behalf. (John 5:23-24, 30, 37)

For John, Jesus clearly is a man on a mission. But why? Why has this captured John's imagination so? Why is it so important to him? I didn't figure this out until later, so I'll leave it for now.

Then I noticed that John has something to say on the question of why God sent Jesus. If asked, I suspect many Christians would answer at once, Well, Jesus was sent to die for our sins, or to model a fully human life, or to take us to heaven. But I was struck by the fact that this is not the sort of language Jesus uses here. He is more likely to say something like, "I have come down from heaven, not to do my will, but the will of him who sent me" (John 6:38).

Jesus' own understanding of why he came was apparently this: he came to do what his Father wanted—constantly, consistently, and in detail.

That would include dying for our sins, of course, but it sounds as though it includes more than that, too. For Jesus, in fact, doing the will of God is such a passionate concern that on one occasion he even forgets to eat: "My food is to do the will of him who sent me and to complete his work" (John 4:34).

My father was an architect, and I think I must have inherited from him an instinct for drawing plans and diagrams. So, as these thoughts crystallized in my head, I reached for a piece of scrap paper and sketched a diagram, like this:

Father > Son > will of God

So what is this will of God that he finds so consuming? The phrase "will of God" can be rather scary (sometimes used to make us feel better about cancer and to justify religious wars), so it's important that the phrases have some content.

The heart of Jesus' conviction is that the will of God is to bring life to the world. "Life" is one of the big themes of John's Gospel. Indeed, it frames the gospel. In the prologue (John 1:1-14) we learn of the Word "in whom was life, and the life was the light of all people"(John 1:4). And the epilogue returns to that same theme: the reason that this Gospel was written, we are told, is "that through believing you may have life in his name"(John 20:31).What is this life? The simplest definition is in Jesus' prayer:"This is eternal life, that they know you, the only true God, and Jesus Christ whom you have sent" (John 17:3).

Life means knowing God and Jesus. I love the way this begins to add up. If God gave life to the world at creation, and if the entrance of sin and evil into the world brought a kind of death, then when God comes again to our world, it is not surprising that God would bring life. If the end of one kind of relationship with God meant death, then it is poetic grace that the coming of Jesus brings a new opportunity for relationship with God.

I added a new step to my diagram:

Father > Son > will of God > life

But in what way does Jesus bring this life to the world? There are twin foci to the way John understands this. First, Jesus speaks on behalf of God, telling people the lessons he's learned from God. Listen to how he explains the importance of words for his mission: "The Father who sent me has himself given me a commandment about what to say and what to speak. . . . What I speak, therefore, I speak just as the Father has told me" (John 12:49-50).

For Jesus, it seems, a crucial part of his task is to talk—to pass on the words he has heard from his Father, words of forgiveness and reconciliation, words of eternal life and judgment. Jesus' mission is at least, in part, an evangelistic preaching mission. I dutifully added that piece to the diagram:

Father > Son > will of God > life > words of God

Sometimes you will hear people quote Francis of Assisi with approval: "Preach the Gospel on all occasions. If necessary, use words." We chuckle when we hear it because the assumption that we can preach by our actions takes us by surprise. Yet, while Francis is right to stress the importance of Christ-like actions (we will come to that in a minute), he is wrong to equate actions with preaching. There are three Greek words in the New Testament that relate to evangelism: (1) the word for gospel or good news; (2) the verb to preach good news (or, to evangelize); and (3) the person who evangelizes (the evangelist).

All three of these items relate to words and to speaking. None of them even hints that actions can be a form of evangelism. I love Walter Brueggemann's assertive way of expressing this:

> At the center of the act of evangelism is the message announced, a verbal, out-loud assertion of something decisive not known until this moment of utterance. There is no way that anyone . . . can avoid this lean, decisive assertion that is at the core of evangelism.[2]

I suspect we like the idea of non-verbal evangelism (oxymoron though that is) because we think (wrongly) that talking about God must be scary and because we believe (rightly) that we have to begin with actions. Nevertheless, words of good news are central to Jesus' ministry, and we dare not give up on them.

There is a second aspect to Jesus' mission, however, that John stresses just as much as words. I first noticed it in the story where Jesus heals a man who was paralyzed for thirty-eight years. When the Pharisees criticize him because he has healed on the sabbath, he responds like this: "The Son can do . . . only what he sees the Father doing; for whatever the Father does, the Son does likewise" (John 5:19).

A similar comment occurs later. Jesus is about to heal a blind man, he says, "We must work the works of him who sent me" (John 9:4). Jesus' mission then is not only a mission of words but also a mission of works. As well as telling people what his Father thinks, he also demonstrates the sort of things his Father does. That, too, is part of his mission.

If we then ask what it is that Jesus' Father does, it is clear from the story: when Jesus heals the paralyzed, or gives sight to the blind, that is precisely the sort of thing he has seen his Father doing. He knows his Father cares deeply about such matters. Of course, the words and the deeds are connected. Jesus says God is love, and he lives the love of God. He cares for people in practical ways, and he tells them in words that he does it because God cares for them. The words and the deeds are mirror images of one another.

In a strange way, this is where John's picture of Jesus resonates with the emphasis of the Old Testament. There, too, words and actions were important. A life filled with the works of God would raise questions for unbelievers, questions that words about God could answer. The difference is that in Old Testament times, the people seldom had better than spasmodic success in fulfilling their calling. In Jesus, God's idea really seems to work.

John talks this way about Jesus speaking the words of God and doing the works of God especially when he's describing Jesus' preaching and miracles. But then it occurred to me: presumably everything Jesus did revealed the character of the Father, not just the public occasions. If you went for a walk with Jesus, or had a meal with him; if you watched while he fixed a broken chair or played with a child—in all those things you would see God. It's just that John never bothers to describe those minor things. Yet Jesus never took a day off from being God incarnate. His mission was his whole life—all of his deeds and words, lived in obedience to God's will.

By this stage, the diagram was getting a bit complicated:

```
                              words of God
Father > Son > will of God > life >
                              works of God
```

Seeing the glory of God

There was one more piece to this jigsaw, and it came as I thought about the effect it had on people to hear and see Jesus doing the will of God. Jesus in reviewing his ministry says to God: "I glorified you on earth by finishing the work that you gave me to do" (John 17:4).

What is God's glory? And what does it mean to glorify God? At its simplest, God's glory is God's character, seen in all its beauty and purity, its love and power. And so to glorify God means to show God's character. God is glorified when people see what God is like.

Jesus seems to be saying to the Father, I have shown people what you are like by the things I have done: the healings, the feeding of the five thousand, walking on the water. All are demonstrations of what God is like, glimpses of God's glory. The effect of Jesus' mission is that God is glorified: in Jesus' works and words, people see the glorious character of God. Thus:

```
                              words of God   )
Father > Son > will of God > life            ) Glory of God
                              works of God  )
```

As a result, Jesus can say calmly and without a hint of arrogance, "Whoever sees me sees him who sent me" (John 12:45). When Jesus does what God wants, the people around actually see and hear God. As Bishop John Robinson once put it, Jesus is "a window into God at work."

This is why people's response to Jesus is so significant. As people are confronted with God in human form, with the view through the window-that-is-Jesus—his holiness, his compassion, his anger at evil, his gentleness with pain—they find they cannot remain neutral. They have a choice to make. Not only a choice about Jesus, of course, but about God. If people don't like Jesus, they certainly won't like God. Jesus understands this. That's why he says, "Whoever believes in me believes not in me but in him who sent me" (John 12:44).

I was excited at the way the jigsaw pieces were falling into place. To be honest, however, John's view of "mission" had not particularly challenged me to this point. But there was one more reference to sending, right at the end of the Gospel, that ended up changing my whole view.

Let me show you how John leads up to it. As this Gospel moves toward its climax, the emphasis in Jesus' teaching moves away from himself and more toward what will happen when he is gone. Jesus hints at this new direction when he announces to his followers that "whoever receives one whom I send receives me" (John 13:20). For the first time, he hints that someone other than himself might be sent, some other person might have a mission from God. Just like the Father, Jesus seems to be planning to send someone.

Throughout this section of John, Jesus is drawing the disciples closer to him. It almost seems that they are being prepared for something. If it didn't seem incredible, it would almost seem they were being prepared to take his place.

Then comes the climax. The words are very simple, as simple and far-reaching as "I do" in a wedding service: "As the Father has sent me, so I send you" (John 20:21).

Now the hinting is over. The challenge is clear. The disciples are indeed to take over Jesus' work. Jesus did the Father's will? Now the disciples are to do the Father's will. Jesus brought life to the world? Now the disciples are to bring his new life to the world. Jesus portrayed the Father by his works and his words? Now the disciples are to portray the Father by their works and their words.

Every condition of my mission, Jesus implies, is a condition of your mission. The way I carried out the will of my Father is the way you must carry out my will. The responsibility I carried for three years is now yours. Jesus was a window into God at work? Now God wants to fill the world with a million windows: the followers of Jesus. This means our diagram now looks like this:

```
                                words of God )
Father > Son > DISCIPLES > will of God > life >               ) Glory of God
                                works of God )
```

I told you earlier that I wondered why this topic was such a passion with John. We can only guess, but I wonder if it is connected with the fact that this Gospel (probably) was the last to be written, and John the last apostle to die. Maybe he was more aware than anyone else of the church's responsibility for the mission of God. The apostles couldn't be looked to for leadership any more. Jesus' mission had passed into the hands of their spiritual children and grandchildren.

What an amazing responsibility. How can Jesus even dream of giving his followers that kind of job? Doesn't he know what they're like? David Reed, a colleague at Wycliffe, heard me explaining this understanding of John's Gospel, and said (tongue in cheek), "Oh, so you're a Binitarian rather than a Trinitarian, are you?" Immediately, I realized he was right: I had made no reference at all to the Holy Spirit. I went back to the concordance, and discovered to my delight that there is one more aspect of *sending* in John. It's not just that Jesus sends his followers: he sends the Holy Spirit to help them do the impossible. These are the two references I found: "The Advocate, the Holy Spirit, whom the Father will send in my name, will teach you everything. . . . When the Advocate comes, whom I will send to you from the Father . . . he will testify on my behalf" (John 14:25; 15:26).

Aha! So for Jesus to send the disciples isn't such a crazy idea after all. Jesus doesn't simply go away and leave the disciples floundering. He returns, now in spiritual form, to help them carry out the job he's given them. That makes all the difference in the world.

                                                          words of God)

Father > Son > Holy Spirit > DISCIPLES > will of God > life >   ) Glory of God

                                                          works of God)

I leaned back in my chair. If this was really Jesus' understanding of his followers' responsibility, then some of our Christian thinking and behaving is way off base. No wonder we have problems with evangelism.

"Ordinary Christians" and "missionaries"

I thought, for instance, of how most churches treat "mission" of any kind as separate from the main work of the church. It is as though the church operates in one place over here, while missions operate somewhere else. There are the normal Christians and there are those involved in mission; there are normal Christians and there are those who do evangelism.

Occasionally the two come together, with varying degrees of discomfort: a special offering for missions, a special speaker, a stack of newsletters at the back of the church, maybe even a special church outreach. But that's not really us, that's them. Yet this was obviously not Jesus' way of thinking. As far as he was concerned, being his follower automatically meant involvement in his mission by word and deed. He was serious when he said, "Follow me." We follow him in mission as much as anywhere else.

Sharon was a student I knew who worked at the peer counseling center in her university, where advice was given on birth control, abortion, and drug use. She found that often the tenor of the advice given by other counselors was implicitly (and sometimes explicitly) anti-Christian.

Mission in the Gospel of John

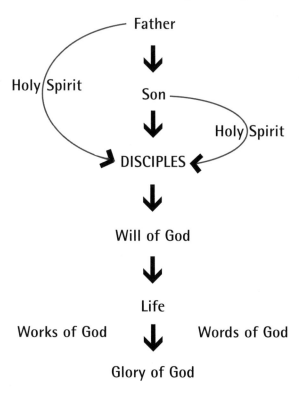

She, however, was universally respected for her gracious but firm Christian stand on issues. She lived and spoke with integrity. At the end of the year, to her amazement, she was asked to stand for election as the coordinator of the center.

That's what it's about, I thought: an ordinary Christian, not on a "foreign mission field," not engaged in "full-time Christian work," not in "the ministry" (so-called), but simply fulfilling her calling to be faithful to Jesus wherever he sent her. Sharon was trying to incarnate the words and works of Jesus in her own words and works. She was a missionary after the pattern of John's Gospel, and evangelism was simply a part of who she was as a follower of Jesus.

"Full-time Christian" versus "secular" work

John Stott has written about how Christians seem to perceive certain careers as inherently more spiritual than others: the most spiritual being the cross-cultural missionary, followed closely by the pastor. Doctors and teachers are close behind but in a slightly lower category. And right down at the bottom of the list in terms of spiritual suitability are the lawyer, businessperson, and politician.[3]

But if all life is God's because God made it, if sin has affected all that God has made, and if God is concerned to restore all of life, then in God's eyes there can be no distinction between secular and sacred. The only distinction is between work done for God and work not done for God. Lawyers can be deeply "spiritual" in this sense, if they understand their work as a calling from God to contribute to God's kingdom. Equally, cross-cultural missionaries can seem "unspiritual" if their work is done for motives of self-glorification.

If our job as followers of Jesus is to glorify God—that is, to show the world what God is like—how will the world see God's character as artist (say) unless God's people are artists and architects and craftspeople? How will the world see God's concern for home and family unless there are homemakers (male or female) representing God in the home? How will the world see that God is a clear and gracious communicator unless there are clear and gracious secretaries (female or male) showing God's character in the office? The list is endless.

In whatever vocation, we are called to bear the image of the Creator. Each one can be a channel for God's glory. Each can be a window into

God at work, a window through which people see the reality of God. Each one can provide a living challenge to come to terms with the reality of God, just as Jesus himself was.

Social action and evangelism

John's ideas also show the way churches have been known to separate evangelism and social action. Someone has said that in conservative churches, individuals may get involved in social action, but the church as a body organizes evangelistic activities. Conversely, in liberal churches, individuals may get involved in evangelism, but the church as a body organizes social action. It's an over-simplification, but there is a grain of truth in it.

I remember doing a week of evangelistic talks on one university campus and noticing one day that there was a sign up to invite students to participate in World Vision's 30-hour Famine. "Are you involved in that?" I asked, knowing that World Vision is a Christian organization.

"Oh no," replied the Christian students, "we're too busy with our week of outreach. That's being organized by the Students' Union."

That's one reason evangelism gets itself a bad name. It talks about love, but too often does little. Jesus' ministry, as we have seen, knew no such division. His mission was words and works. Sometimes, to be sure, it was one more than the other, according to what was needed, but in the overall shape of his ministry both were present. It makes sense, doesn't it? We know all too well that words without works run the risk of hypocrisy; but works without words can be ambiguous.

I thought of a wonderful program my family and I were involved in for many years, called International Christmas. Every Christmas hundreds of students from around the world, studying in Canada, enjoy a Canadian family Christmas away from home. A number of Canadians run each camp, and provide a mixture of winter activities, cultural celebrations, traditional Christmas food, and sheer friendship. Why has it continued for more than forty years now, while other programs have come and gone?

I suspect it's the close-to-ideal blend of words and actions. Our international guests experienced the warmth of Christian hospitality. Each day there was the opportunity to discuss our own religious traditions, and to learn the true meaning of Christmas. And all of this went on in the context of friendship that included the truth and love of Christ. Mission done on the model of Jesus. It never fails. Why would it?

Preaching to myself

That's basically how my sermon looked. Mission is following the example of Jesus, as he invited us to do. Evangelism is speaking the words that
talk about God just as our works show God. We show God's love and we
talk about God's love. Evangelism is the "tell" in the Christian's show-and-
tell. That's what it was for Jesus. That's what it is for us.

I don't know if my sermon that Sunday did anyone else any good. But
it certainly had a deep effect on me. Even if my listeners don't remember
it, I do.

5.

The Jesus Model:

Evangelism for "Normal" People

Christ accepts you as you are—just as you are—because He knows what's really in your heart. And He knows what you can become through Him! This is how we are to love one another: to remember that love identifies, love cares, love accepts. There is no superiority in love. . . . And love is generous.

Rosalind Rinker, *You Can Witness with Confidence* [1]

ONE OF THE MAIN WAYS that children learn is by imitation. Whether it's eating with a knife and fork, beginning to talk, or cleaning their teeth, the first step normally is watching someone else do it. Not that imitation ends with childhood, of course. Even as adults, we watch others operate a computer, drive a car, or swing a tennis racket. Once we've seen someone else do it, then we have a go.

It seems that God invented this imitation idea. Human beings, after all, were made in the image of God, to live out God's character in the world. Just as children imitate their parents, we were made to imitate God.

This is another way of understanding those words of Jesus we looked at in the last chapter. When he said, "As the Father sent me, so I am sending you," in effect he is saying, "I've imitated the Father's words in the things I've said, I've imitated the Father's works by the things I've done. Now you imitate me just as I've imitated the Father."

People like Margaret Atwood and Sandra Tsing Loh find many attempts at evangelism dehumanizing and insensitive. Indeed, I suspect that, like many Christians, that's the only kind of evangelism they've ever known.

The only people who found Jesus' evangelism offensive, however, were the religious folk. So I found myself wanting to know, What did Jesus' evangelism look like? Then perhaps we can learn to imitate him in that, too.

This line of thought pointed me in the direction of one of my favorite stories in the Gospels, the story of "the woman at the well" in John 4. This time I decided to ask of it a specific question: What can we learn about evangelism from Jesus' example in this story?

Jesus and the woman at the well

The disciples have gone into town, and Jesus, wanting some solitude, is sitting alone by a well. As he waits, he sees a woman coming toward him across the hot sand, carrying a water pot in the noonday sun. When she arrives, Jesus greets her and asks her to draw him some water from the well so that he can have a drink. It happens to be a very hot day and he happens to be thirsty. A perfectly human reaction, you might think.

The woman, however, is startled. She's a woman, he's a man. A respectable rabbi wouldn't be seen talking to a woman (even his wife) in public. Normally, you would only make this kind of a request of someone in your family. Yet this rabbi doesn't seem to care about such protocol.

But Jesus' faux pas is worse than this. Jewish readers of that time would have shaken their heads in disbelief after hearing this story. What would they see that we might not see? That in the Jewish scriptures, there is a long tradition of romances beginning by wells:

- Abraham's, servant meets Rebekah by a well, and discovers that she is the one for Abraham's son, Isaac (Genesis 24).
- Isaac's son Jacob in turn meets his wife Rachel by a well (Genesis 27).
- When he flees Egypt after murdering one of the slave drivers, Moses pauses at (you guessed it) a well, and helps seven daughters of a local priest draw water. One of the seven, Zipporah, becomes his wife (Exodus 2).

By talking to a woman by a well, Jesus is thus being indiscreet, to say the least. Then there is the strange fact that he's there at all. Jews usually did not speak to Samaritans, and would go miles out of their way to avoid Samaria. By standards of Jewish orthodoxy, Samaritans were theologically and racially tainted, and a rabbi like Jesus should have known better than to have strayed this close to contamination.[2]

So the woman is curious. She knows he has crossed several big barriers to get to the point of asking this simple favor, and she is suspicious: "How come you're asking me for a drink? Come on, you know I'm a Samaritan. What are you up to?" The underlying questions seem to be: Why are you the person you are? What makes you willing to risk ridicule and rejection from your peers by talking to me? What makes you tick? You obviously march to a different drum . . . what is it?

Then Jesus knows exactly what to say. I suspect the image comes to him in a moment of God-given intuition. It's not a formula. Neither is it the same as anything he said to any other person before or since. His words are for her and her alone. In fact, it is really rather rude of us to eavesdrop. With a twinkle in his eye, he says: "Of course, if you knew who I was, you might have asked me for a drink, because I can give you living water." My guess is that there was a long silence before the woman replied. Let me back up and tell you why I think Jesus' comment took her off guard.

It seems clear that this woman was shunned by the other women of the village. Fetching water was a boring, heavy job, so the women normally did it together (so that it became a social occasion), and in the morning or the evening (when it was cooler).[3] This woman, however, is fetching water by herself and in the middle of the day. The message is clear: the other women simply do not want her around, for reasons we will discover later.

Beyond that I am just speculating, but I have a couple of hunches that would at least make good sense. Let me explain them, and then you can take or leave them as you please.

I suspect that, as she trudges alone across the sand in the heat of the noonday sun, she has already begun to make connections between her thirst for water and her thirst for what she wants from a man.

She must have thought a lot about water, and the frustration of getting it. She has no one to walk with her to fetch the water (which increases the boredom), and she has to fetch it at noon (which increases the effort). I imagine her cursing the necessity for water and wishing there were some other way to quench her thirst.

She must have thought a lot about men, and how hard it was to find a man who would give her what she really wanted. Five men have divorced her (or she has divorced them), and she is uncertain about the future of the present relationship. She wants intimacy, fidelity, tenderness, love; they want a perfect slave. Is there no other way to find what she thirsts for, deep down?

Maybe she thinks to herself, "If only there were another source of water somewhere else, nearer the city, to save all this trudging. Why can't the water last longer? Why do we have to feel thirsty again so soon?"

Maybe she thinks to herself, "If only I could find someone who could love me for myself, someone who could meet my deepest needs, someone who would not reject me when I fail. Why does it never work out? Why can't I just be satisfied with life the way it is?"

If this scenario is at all close to the truth, water and love are closely connected in her experience. After all, because of her marital life, fetching water has become one of the worst things in her life, instead of a leisurely and sociable thing to do. Her frustration at the constant need for water has grown along with her frustration at the constant need for love and intimacy and acceptance. Both love and water cause her incredible hassles.

Neither the water nor the relationship has ever lasted. Neither satisfied for very long. The water kept running out, and the men kept running out, too. Where were they when she needed them? She needed their company, she needed their love, she needed their help and their support.

Her body and her spirit are constantly crying out for satisfaction: trying to slake a thirst that is constantly demanding more, trying to keep body, heart, and spirit satisfied. Where will it all end? Is this all there is to life?

Water: physical or spiritual?

In the silence after Jesus' bombshell, then, questions race around her head: Is he talking about what I think he's talking about? Is he talking about this water, or is he talking about the big question? How does he know the answer? How does he even know it's my question? Is he for real? Who is he anyway?

The woman is intrigued. "Where is this water? If you can give water like that," she deduces, "that would make you even greater than our ancestor Jacob, who gave us this well." Implied: and that can't be true, can it? *Can* it?

Jesus does not give a direct answer to a direct question. Instead, he sows intrigue in order to reap a question. He tells her the living water will stop her thirsting. "The water I can give you is different from this well water.

With my water you'll never be thirsty again. My water will be a constant source of refreshment inside you, welling up to eternal life." They are talking about the same thing (water) but Jesus has added a strange new dimension to it (living).

Again, I imagine the woman thinking furiously: *Can he be talking about what I think he's talking about?* She wants to believe it, but doesn't dare. "Well, sir, in that case, please give me this special water. It would be great never to be thirsty again, and I wouldn't have to keep trudging out here to fetch water every single day."

It sounds as though she has understood Jesus' spiritual offer only on the literal level, but I don't think she's really being as slow as she appears. On the contrary, she is used to operating on these two levels, spiritual thirst and physical thirst, and the problems of satisfying both.

Then the conversation shifts gear. "All right then," Jesus says calmly, "Why don't we discuss this with your husband as well?" Why does Jesus raise the delicate subject of her marital disasters? Perhaps because she needs to see that the thirst she has been hoping to satisfy in human relationships can really be satisfied only by God. If her pitcher is full of ordinary water, she can't have it filled with living water.

Jesus gives her one chance to explain it herself, but she ducks it. "Oh, er, funny you should mention that, but as a matter of fact I have no husband," she stammers.

"That's true," Jesus replies gently, "You've had five husbands, and the fellow you're living with now is not your husband."

Jesus could have worked out—or intuited—why she is there alone in the middle of the day. She was being shunned for some reason, and he might well have guessed that it was to do with her marital status—or lack of it. Knowing there have been six men in her life, however, can only be supernatural. A good psychologist could have guessed at an unhappy marriage, or even two. But no amount of scientific training could train a therapist to know six rather than three, five, or seven! There is a blending here of what we call the natural and what we call the supernatural—although that is not a distinction the Bible knows.

Opinion varies as to what lies behind this exchange: one possibility is that she had divorced five men, and was now living with someone else. If this is correct, then Jesus raises the subject as a "way of bringing the woman's sin into the open"[4] and offering her forgiveness.

A second possibility is that five men had divorced her and someone else had taken her in, perhaps out of pity. In this case, Jesus is helping her face her pain and find in him and his living water the source of healing.[5] Finally, some combination the first a and second may be possible.

Either way, the woman's history was a source of anger, shame, guilt, and confusion for her. And in a "city" the size of Sychar, maybe as small (by our standards) as five hundred people, everybody would know her story, and a significant number of the population would have been involved personally in her history. No wonder this is a hornets' nest!

Her response? "Thank you, Jesus. You're right. I really have been wasting my time on things that don't satisfy." Not exactly. I imagine the woman gulps and doesn't know where to look. "Well, you're obviously a prophet. Er . . . maybe you can tell me something that's always bothered me: do we have to worship in Jerusalem, as you Jews say, or is it okay for us to worship at the mountain here?"[6]

Basically she tells him, I can see you're a religious expert. Maybe you can solve a question that's been bothering me for years. Should we be Lutherans or Baptists? You're offering me the fulfillment I've been frustrated at not finding all my life? That's great. But don't we have to decide first whether we should baptize people when they're babies or only when they're adults? Come on, Jesus, these are serious issues.

Jesus seems to go with the flow. His graciousness seems endless. We might have been tempted to say, "Hey, don't avoid the issue! Do you want what I have to offer or not?" Instead, Jesus says, in effect, "Yes, that's a very good question. But the fact is that God doesn't care about denominations. The outward form of worship is really not that important. God cares first and foremost about your heart: do you really want to know God or not?" Eugene Peterson in *The Message* translates this saying: "Your worship must engage your spirit in the pursuit of truth. . . . Those who worship God must do it out of their very being, their spirits, their true selves, in adoration" (John 4:24).[7]

The woman seems to miss the personal implications of his statement. She decides it is time to wrap up this unusual conversation. "Well, all these questions are very difficult, I think," she sighs. "But one day the Messiah will come, and then he will explain all these puzzling things to us." She implies: *So let's drop the subject now, okay?*

But the conversation is not over. One day I would like to make a movie about this story. I find it very visual and very dramatic. What happens next is a line to make a film producer's mouth water. She says, "Oh well, the Messiah will explain all these things." Jesus replies, "I who am speaking to you . . . I am the Messiah." How does he say it? Does he draw himself up to his full height and pronounce the words with Charlton Heston-like authority? Perhaps. In my movie, however, he hardly moves. Maybe he leans forward a little to catch her attention again. His body tenses a little. I suspect a slightly mischievous smile comes over his face (after all, did he expect this? I don't think so). He says, quietly but clearly, "I am he . . . the one you are talking to." Then there is a silence. The camera moves to her face: incredulity, then dawning understanding.

Educators talk about the "Aha!" principle, that moment when you find the last piece that goes in the center of the jigsaw puzzle and see what the picture is all about. At this moment, the woman in effect says, "Aha!" Something clicks. She sees that it is all true. It is because he is the Messiah that he is not embarrassed to ask for a drink and to speak to a Samaritan woman. It is because he is the Messiah that he knows all about her. It is because he is the Messiah that he knows her question and he knows the answer. Of course. It all makes perfect sense.

Just then the disciples return. A pity, really. I would love to know how she would have responded to his declaration if the disciples hadn't come back just then. Would she have fallen at his feet, saying, "My Lord and my God" a couple of years earlier than Thomas? Maybe she would simply have covered her mouth with her hands and been speechless with astonishment and perhaps joy.

Instead, the focus shifts. As Jesus turns to the disciples the woman hurries back to Sychar to tell those in the marketplace about the man "who told me everything I have ever done." She has discovered what she was thirsting for all those years, though she never knew it: the living God to be her lover, her husband, her helper, her satisfaction. After all, that's what the living water is: God—nothing more, nothing less.

As I came to this story afresh, with my head full of new insights about evangelism from the Old Testament and about mission in John's Gospel, some things struck me that I had not noticed before.

Jesus is open to God working through him

If we ask how Jesus came to be in conversation with this woman, there are two theories. Theory number one says that, early that morning, as he spent time in quiet and prayer, God the Father gave him his instructions for the day:

> Go through Sychar. It's very important that you aim to arrive at noon. When you arrive, sit and wait at the well. Soon a solitary woman will arrive to fetch water: I want you to speak to her. Don't immediately talk about the Gospel to her, just ask for a drink. Make sure you treat her with respect. When she says to you . . .

In this scenario, Jesus simply does as he is told, and the story unfolds in detail as God planned it.

Maybe there are some people whose relationship with God does function that way, and whose opportunities to speak about faith come that way, too. I'm not like that, and most Christians I know are not like that. If that was really how Jesus did it, and how I have to be, I'm a non-starter.

However, there is a second possible scenario. As Jesus prayed that morning, he said to God the Father:

> Help me to live for you today. Help me to speak your truth and live your love wherever I am and whoever I meet. Oh, and there is one decision I need your special wisdom about: there are two ways I could go to Galilee—through Samaria or round Samaria. It seems to me that it would make a stronger statement about how big your kingdom is if I went right through, because it would show the Samaritans that your kingdom is for them, too.

And God said, "Great!" So Jesus and the twelve traveled through Samaria until, around noon, they were feeling hungry and thirsty so they stopped by a well.

While Jesus was there, he saw a woman coming out from the town carrying a water-pot. This puzzled him: *Why would a woman come for water without any friends and in the middle of the day? Did she not have any friends? If not, why not?* Jesus was rather thirsty. He would ask her for a drink of water and see what happened.

I guess I'm not making a secret of which interpretation I prefer. You may ask, Why bother with this distinction? Why does it matter? It seems to me important because it is common to view Jesus the first way—and, I believe, quite wrong. Also, I have come to the conviction that to see Jesus this way makes life both easier and more challenging.

That may sound paradoxical. What I mean is that following Jesus becomes easier on the second model, because it means that, if we don't get a detailed sheet of instructions from God each morning, we are not spiritual failures. At the same time, the second model is also more challenging for this reason: as we try to live a life that is pleasing to God, and as we do what comes naturally (sitting down because we're tired, waiting for lunch, asking for help), we may also find ourselves unexpectedly in a position to do significant ministry.

That sends tingles down my spine. The chances of God spelling out what I should do in detail during a day seems extremely remote; the chances of God using me as I commit my way to God . . . well, that could actually happen.

Often I have to travel by train. Being pretty introverted by nature, I try to find a seat by myself or, if I am forced to sit by someone, I choose the person who looks least likely to want to talk. God, I find, is not impressed. More than once, the person I thought most likely to leave me in peace with my book is the very person who wants to talk to me, and with whom I get into serious conversations about spiritual issues. I imagine God saying, "Well, you did say that you wanted to serve me today. Remember? Didn't you want me to take you seriously?"

Jesus acts naturally

Jesus initiates the conversation by asking for a drink of water. I used to think, How clever of Jesus, how subtle. What a good way to establish a relationship! Certainly it is one way that relationships begin, but now I find myself doubting that it was meant as a subtle move on Jesus' part. It was simply the natural reaction of a thirsty man on a very hot day.

Of course, there is more to it than that. Even under those conditions, many men in Jesus' day would have found another way—any other way—to get themselves a drink, rather than ask someone else . . . especially a woman. So it is significant that Jesus is not afraid of making himself vulnerable by asking a woman for help. Jesus has no false sense of pride.

He is able to be vulnerable because his strength and his identity come from being in love with God and knowing God loves him. Thus even something as "natural" as asking for a drink of water flows out of his sense of who he is.

The same is true of his choice to go through Samaria, not around it. Jesus is just doing what comes naturally to him as God's person. He knows that God doesn't care about the taboos that say some people are kosher to talk to and others are not, and Jesus doesn't care either. He doesn't consciously choose to hurdle the social barriers. He simply doesn't notice they're there in the first place.

I find this helpful because evangelism often seems like a fantastic, superhuman effort, requiring hours of prayer and fasting, the study of encyclopedias of information, and a sustained effort to be nice to everybody. As we watch Jesus, however, we see that evangelism flows out of who he is. As he does what comes naturally to him, people sit up and take notice, and ask him questions.

Surprising though it may seem, the same is true of us. What comes naturally to us as Christians is distinctive and attractive to those around, even when we are not aware of it. This struck me when my friend Dave, a year after coming home for a meal with my family, commented, "I will never forget holding hands around the dining table and thanking God for our food." Frankly, saying grace is not a big deal in our family. Sometimes, it is perfunctory and formal. Sometimes we forget. But something that is perfectly normal in a Christian home can make a disproportionate impact on someone who is not used to it.

I suppose I could have said, "Aha, Dave is coming for a meal, and he is not a person of faith, so tonight we'll say grace. I'll spend an hour preparing it, and Dave will be really impressed." Of course it sounds ridiculous. It would be totally counter-productive: nothing would turn Dave off Christian faith more quickly. The whole point is that it is normal and taken-for-granted.

Our usual reaction to this way of thinking is to say, "I'm sure that isn't true in my life. There's nothing at all that would impress anyone as different about my life." Frankly, we are not always the best people to judge the impression we make on others.

I'm sure that the Christians Nicky got to know did not consider themselves "super Christians" in any sense. But what she saw in them was very significant:

As time went by, I started to notice that Sarah and the other Christians in the residence seemed to live by some kind of code that was different from everyone else. . . . They were all so kind and friendly, quite the opposite of what I expected from religious people. . . . I discovered that actually they failed from time to time, but I was more impressed by their readiness to own up to failure and to start again with new enthusiasm.

If we have been trying to follow Jesus for any length of time, trying to obey him and let his Spirit direct our lives, then there will be things that are different about us, even though we may not be aware of them. If we deny that, we are not being modest. Rather, we're implying that the Spirit of Jesus hasn't been doing a very good job.

Of course, one thing Jesus' Spirit does in our lives is to change what counts as normal. The things we think of as "normal" are simply the result of repeated choices we have made that have slowly become part of our character. Some of those may be good and health-giving; others may be self-centered and destructive.

As we follow Jesus, we begin to make different choices. We choose to give rather than hold back, to apologize rather than tough it out, to pursue partnership rather than competition, to take risks rather than playing safe. All sorts of things. And the more we do that, the more our Christ-like choices become "normal," the more our character changes to be like his.

This is why Augustine, a bishop of the early church, could say, "Love and do what you like."[8] If we are learning to love and follow God, then "what we like" will change to come into line with what God likes. Hence, Jesus was thinking like God in deciding to go straight through Samaria; Jesus was feeling as God does in treating the woman as a full human being. Jesus loved God with all his being . . . and could do what he liked.

This story shed a whole different light on evangelism. No trace of the spiritual flasher here. Instead, we find relationship, good conversation, openness about spiritual matters. Certainly there is a challenge, but it seems appropriate to the context. In this chapter, as elsewhere in the Gospels, I was struck by Jesus' God-driven humanity. Here, finally, is an evangelist worth imitating. But there was more in this story.

6.

Process Evangelism:

On a Scale of 1 to 100

I remember once encountering a zealous Christian. His brow was furrowed, he seemed anxious and impatient, and he sounded angry. Then he told me God loved me. I couldn't help noticing the difference between his message and his style.

Rebecca Manley Pippert, *Out of the Saltshaker* [1]

I N THE STORY of the woman at the well, there are several occasions when Jesus might have been more direct than he is. Here are some ways the conversation might have turned:

Opportunity 1: The woman arrives, and Jesus says, "Good day, Madam. I am the Messiah and you are a sinner. The time has come for you to repent and believe in me."

Opportunity 2: Her question: "How is it that you, a Jew, ask a drink of me, a Samaritan?"

The direct answer: "Because I knew that would get your attention, so that I could tell you how much God loves you. Let me introduce myself."

Opportunity 3: Her request: "Give me this living water."

The direct answer: "I happen to know you've had five husbands and the man you're living with now you're not married to. If you want this living water, you'd better repent of your sins and clean up your act right now."

Opportunity 4: Her comment: "The Messiah will explain all this to us."

The direct answer: "I who am speaking to you am he. Confess your sins right now and believe the gospel."

I don't have to tell you things did not happen this way, or that it is better they did not happen this way. At best, the woman would have quietly grabbed her bucket and left. Her response could have been stronger. She might have lashed back, saying, "No way—I can't stand you religious freaks." Result? Neither of them would have received the water they needed. No more evangelism that lunchtime.

Jesus' failure to be pushier is not a case of wimpishness or deviousness. It is typical of Jesus' overall approach to life and shows care and respect.

Safeguarding people's freedom

For one thing, Jesus wants to engage the woman in conversation, not preach her a sermon. There are contexts where sermons are appropriate and expected, and situations where they are inappropriate and offensive. One-on-one meetings fall into the latter category. In one-on-one contexts, the give and take of dialogue is polite and respectful. Speeches on the part of one person overrule the other person's right of free speech. They demonstrate lack of appreciation for the individuality of the other, and constitute a form of verbal power tripping.

Yet there is a deeper reason that Jesus is so indirect. He wants to give the woman freedom to express her interest in spiritual questions, but not force such a conversation on her. It's a delicate balance. He longs for her to respond to his message, but also respects her dignity as well. It's the same balance the philosopher Pascal was trying to express when he said that God has given us sufficient evidence that if we want to discover God we may, and if we wish to avoid God we may do that, too. So he speaks in an intriguing way: "You can give me one kind of water; but there's a better kind that I could offer you."

She immediately starts to question: "Who are you? What water are you talking about? Where do you get it?" The fact that she asks the questions tells you this is not "flasher evangelism." He's not preaching or being pushy: he's just answering questions.

I find this encouraging. In order to evangelize, I had better not have religious speeches ready memorized for the first suitable occasion that comes along. I don't even (in the first place) have to be specially bold and articulate in raising questions of faith. In fact, such things may be counterproductive.

Rebecca Manley Pippert understands this. In her classic book on evangelism, *Out of the Saltshaker,* she describes an occasion when, in talking with a friend about faith, she began to feel she was saying too much. She stopped and said:

> "Look, I feel really bad. I am very excited about who God is and what he's done in my life. But I hate it when people push 'religion' on me. So if I'm coming on too strong, will you just tell me?"
>
> She looked at me in disbelief. "I can't believe you just said that. I mean, I cannot believe you honestly said that," she answered.
>
> "Why?" I asked.
>
> "Well, I never knew Christians were aware that we hate being the recipients of a running monologue," she answered.[2]

It's the same thing as happened with the woman at the well. Because Becky is not pushy, because she gives the other person space to say no to the conversation, and because she arouses curiosity in her friend, the conversation can in fact go ahead. Jesus' style precisely.

This is an art I would like to cultivate. I know an eleven-year old in whose home the only Christian influence is the Narnia stories of C. S. Lewis. Some time ago, we were discussing a strange comment of Aslan's (the lion who is a Christ-like figure in the books) at the end of *The Voyage of the Dawn Treader.* As the children in the story reluctantly prepare to leave the magic land of Narnia and return to our world, Lucy protests sadly: "We shan't meet you there. And how can we live, never meeting you?" To which Aslan replies, "But you shall meet me, dear one. . . . There I have another name. You must learn to know me by that name." [3]

I asked my young friend, "Do you know Aslan's name in our world?" She looked startled. Clearly the thought that this story might have something to do with real life was a new one. "No," she replied, mystified. Then, remembering Lewis's reluctance to let people vivisect his stories by "interpreting" every point, I said, "Oh, it's really important to discover what Aslan's name is in our world." And then I stopped, and the conversation moved on to other things.

To be honest, I don't know if I did the right thing. Should I have gone a step further and explained how Aslan is like Jesus? Or was it enough to raise the question and leave it with Margaret to pursue for herself? I think my response was the right thing to do. It was at least an attempt to sow intrigue in the way that Jesus did in this story.

Jesus treats people with respect

There were three good reasons Jesus "should" not have respected the woman at the well: (1) she was a Samaritan; (2) she was a woman; and (3) this particular woman was on the garbage heap of the marriage market and was therefore doubly unsuitable company for a respectable man.

The wrong race, the wrong gender, and the wrong history. But Jesus hurdles those three major barriers to come face to face with her. And what does he do first? He asks her a favor: "Give me a drink." He makes himself vulnerable, puts himself at her mercy. Another mark of respect.

When she says, "He told me everything I did," I suspect it is not just the supernatural aspect of the conversation that impresses her, but the fact that he knows and still respects her. Many in the city of Sychar knew the same "everything," and had probably stopped respecting her a long time ago. C. S. Lewis says:

> It is a serious thing to live in a society of possible gods and goddesses, to remember that the dullest and most uninteresting person you talk to may one day be a creature that, if you saw it now, you would be strongly tempted to worship. . . . You have never talked to a mere mortal.[4]

That is the basis for respecting people: they are in the image of God. That is what Jesus saw and affirmed in this woman. Recently, I met up with an old friend by the name of Deb. She told me the story of an evangelistic encounter where she had not felt respected. I asked if she would e-mail me the story, so I could pass it on to you. When the e-mail came, it was headed, "Still angry after all these years." This is the story she told:

> I was at one of the food places in the university, got a tea or something and sat down. Soon after, someone came over, asked if I was alone, and if she could join me. It seemed odd, as there were plenty of other available tables, but I said "sure" and she sat down. (I wondered if maybe she was lonely, or maybe she thought I was lonely—I'm not sure.)
>
> I don't know how we got from that to her making her evangelistic speech, but it happened very fast, and with little or no opportunity for me to tell

her I didn't need it, that I was already a believer. She certainly didn't ask before launching in.

So there she was, well-launched, and me thinking, "She doesn't know the first thing about me." It felt pathetic and infuriating—as if I was just part of her weekly quota, a notch in her belt. I was angry for a long while afterward, I guess because it was a kind of assault and aggressive. Now, looking back, I just shake my head and think even more how misdirected and damaging that approach is—and how lucky it was me she assaulted—at least I took the hit, rather than someone else.

And the other thing I think about, and even now it's not without tears, is the foolish, damaging life/relationship choices I was making at the time (the consequences of which are so much clearer these fifteen years later), and how desperately I needed help from someone who *truly* cared. Of course I'm not blaming that on her, but for me the contrast makes her actions all the more troubling. I did need help—but not hers. Hers felt deeply uncaring. She didn't give a damn about me: all she cared about was her little project.

A *project*, not a *person*. The verbal message (God loves you) was contradicted by the non-verbal message (you are another project). There was no equality in the conversation, no interest in the other person's faith journey, no concern for her pain. In other words, no respect.

One of the nicest compliments I was ever paid was by a student who had recently become a Christian. Tobi wanted me to meet her sister when I was out in Winnipeg, and encouraged Stacy to meet me by saying, "John's religious . . . but he's safe." Religious . . . but safe. Of course, there is a sense in which finding out about Jesus is never safe, because he challenges us to the very roots of our being. But in another sense he is always safe—indeed, we are never truly safe without him—and as we represent him we should be known to be safe, too. Because we respect the other person.

I was speaking to a conference about this issue once and, at the end, a woman came to me in some distress, and said, "Now I understand why my family won't become Christians." Six months earlier, Tammy had dramatically become a Christian. She had immediately felt it her duty to urge her family to do likewise, threatening them with hell fire in order to facilitate the process. To her surprise and dismay, it didn't work. In fact, the family members (understandably) dug in their heels and were on the verge of cutting off communication with her. They had felt assaulted, certainly not respected.

Tearfully, Tammy asked, "What can I do?" There was only one thing I could think of: "You need to phone them as soon as you can and apologize, not for what you believe but for your attitude." We prayed together, for Tammy, for her family, and for God's grace to be active in the situation.

Later on, I met Tammy's sister, who was by now inquisitive about Christian faith. I asked her to tell me about the phone call. "Did Tammy apologize?" I asked.

"Oh yes," replied Julia, "she apologized for about half an hour!" With that apology, the barriers came down. The family felt Tammy's love again. They felt the freedom to ask their own questions and to move toward God at their own speed. Shortly after that, Julia became a Christian. Respect had meant giving her space to work things out for herself without pressure.

That leads on to another aspect of this story that has turned out to be one of my most fruitful lessons in evangelism ever.

Jesus respects natural processes

Jesus said on one occasion that evangelism is like sowing seed (Mark 4:1-20, especially verse 14). Paul, picking up on the same imagery, added that some people (like his colleague Apollos) are good at watering the seed (1 Corinthians 3:6). Dr. Robert Bruce was a pioneer Christian missionary in Iran at the end of the nineteenth century, and he took the image a step further. He once wrote to his friends:

> I am not reaping the harvest; I scarcely claim to be sowing the seed; I am hardly plowing the soil; but I am gathering out the stones. That, too, is missionary work, let it be supported by loving sympathy and fervent prayer.[5]

In the story of the Samaritan woman, there is a situation of reaping. Jesus says to his disciples, "Look around you, and see how the fields are ripe for harvesting" (John 4:35). This is not an abstract spiritual command. Jesus is simply saying, "Hey, look over there!" Presumably they look in the direction he points. What do they see? John has already observed that "the people were coming out of the city toward him." Presumably what the disciples see is the approaching crowd, perhaps even swaying like a crop in the wind, all ready to welcome the Messiah. The harvest is coming to the reapers!

Sometimes this saying, that "the fields are ripe for harvest," is taken out of context to suggest that, anywhere in the world at any time, the harvest is always going to be ready. To me, that makes utter nonsense of the imagery and sets us up for disappointment. Even Jesus did not always reap. At Nazareth, after all, there was little harvest for him because the people were too hard-hearted (Mark 6:1-6). Presumably there were too many stones, or nobody had broken up the ground.

Certainly the fields are white sometimes. At other times they're brown earth because the shoots haven't begun to show yet. At other times they're green because the crop is growing but still isn't ripe.

Here at Sychar there is a harvest. And Jesus makes it clear why that is. "Others have labored," he says, "and you have entered into their labor" (John 4:38). The thousand-dollar question is: "Who sowed at Sychar?" Maybe it was disciples of John the Baptist, who brought his message of the coming Messiah, which the woman obviously knew. Perhaps it was a rabbi who, like Simeon, was waiting for the hope of Israel, and taught the people to do likewise.[6] Maybe the woman had a grandmother who prayed faithfully for her.

In my movie version of this story, at some point during this revival at Sychar, the someone (I haven't yet decided who—but it would be quite moving if it were the grandmother, don't you think?) would come up to Jesus, and say, "Thank God you've come. We've waited and wept and prayed for this day for so long." I picture Jesus taking her hands, and saying, "So it was you. I didn't know who it was, but I knew there had to be someone."

Nobody short-circuits God's natural processes. Even Jesus is subject to them. On this day, this woman is ready to become a follower of Jesus. Presumably, six months earlier this conversation couldn't have happened. The harvest wasn't ready.

Moving in a Christ-ward direction

For many years, I worked at a Christian summer camp. Sometimes the counselors were too eager to share their faith with their campers, and the campers, eager to please their counselors, were all too ready to make a "Christian commitment." Then, not surprisingly, once camp was over, and the campers went back to their home environment, all signs of faith evaporated.

These days the camp orients its counselors to the spiritual work of the camp like this. They suggest that everyone in the world is on a continuum of 1 to 100 in terms of their getting to know God. No one is at 0 because all human beings know something about God, even if they try to suppress it (Romans 1:18-22). Equally, nobody is at 100 because that is in the next world, when we see God face to face and know as much about God as it possible for a human being to know. Suppose, too, that 50 is the point when a person realizes that Jesus is the key to this business of getting to know God, and they begin to follow him.

```
•————————————————————•————————————————————•
1                        50                      100
```

Much evangelistic effort goes into trying to get people to cross that line from 49 to 50. But it is clear that there is little point in talking to someone as if they are at 49 if they are only at 17. What the person really needs is an invitation to move to 18. Of course, this makes the whole thing sound very mechanical. The way God draws us is much more relational, and our response is much more devious and messy than this image suggests. (In *Traveling Mercies*, for example, Ann Lamott describes her own journey to faith as being like that of a frog jumping haphazardly from one lily pad to another!)[7] Nevertheless, you get the point: coming to faith is a gradual process, and Christ-like evangelism will respect that.

A survey in 1990 revealed that, of those who came to Christ in Canada in the 1980s, "half of the respondents said they heard the gospel at least ten times or more before they made their decision."[8] A survey in England revealed that most Christians said it had taken four years for them to come to faith—and, of course, that is only the part of the process they were aware of.[9] The process actually began "before the foundation of the world" (Ephesians 1:4). God is not in a hurry.

In fact, if Christianity is indeed a centered set more than a bounded set, where direction counts more than position, what is important is not the "number" a person is at but the direction they are facing, and the focus of evangelism should be encouraging people in a Christ-ward direction rather than looking for a crossing-the-line experience.

Not that such an experience is not important, but its significance may be psychological more than theological. Robert Brow suggests "that faith may be strengthened by making a decision. Some of the greatest preachers have been used to bring people . . . to a more vital faith by persuading them to take a first step of faith." [10]

Many people, of course, have never had a crisis of conversion, and yet are clearly part of God's family and continue to move steadily "beyond 50" and toward Christ.

In the camp context, therefore, counselors encourage campers to take "yes-steps" toward God. In two weeks at camp, exposed to Christian people and Christian teaching for the first time, a child may simply learn to feel gratitude to God for our amazing world—and move from 1 to 20. Another child who has learned nothing about faith beforehand may learn that the world belongs to God and that our job is to look after it well. A third may come from a home where no one ever says, "Sorry," and learn at camp how apology can restore relationships.

None of these spiritual lessons is "the Gospel" in a full sense, and yet each prepares the ground for hearing the message of "the Gospel." If I am truly grateful to God, then when I hear of "love so amazing, so divine" in the hymn, "When I Survey the Wondrous Cross," I will understand that it "demands my soul, my life, my all." If I understand that this world is God's, then an understanding of sin as flouting the Creator's instructions is not likely to be far behind. If I have learned the value of apology, the message of repentance and reconciliation to God will make a lot of sense.

William Abraham suggests that evangelism is "that set of intentional activities that is governed by the goal of initiating people into the kingdom of God for the first time. . . . It is more like farming or educating than like raising one's arm or blowing a kiss." [11]

He is right. After all, farming and education are two images directly from the pages of the New Testament: sowing and reaping on the one hand, and Jesus as rabbi on the other. We might add that evangelism is not only a set of activities, but that there is usually a wide variety of different Christians involved in those activities, each contributing a different piece to the process.

Stuart's story

Stuart began to think seriously about faith through the influence of a Christian economics professor. The professor didn't say much about his faith (though he didn't keep it secret either), but the student noticed that he remembered everybody's names, and that he was always willing to give extra time and attention to any student who needed it. Then he got to know a student called Tim, who just happened to be an enthusiastic new Christian and who shared his faith in a spontaneous and non-threatening way. Tim introduced Stuart to me, and I invited him to an "Agnostics Anonymous" group where people of faith and people of no faith were thoughtfully discussing the biography of Jesus together. People started praying for Tim. Shortly afterward, he started attending a church where a friend of mine was pastor.

Six months later, over lunch in a smoky student pub, Stuart asked me, "So how do I become a Christian?" I told him as best I knew how. He went and talked to Tim and told him he had decided to become a follower of Jesus. Each person had a part to play. Each person did what they were gifted to do. No one person was "the evangelist" for Stuart. And, as he moved toward faith in Christ, sower and reaper rejoiced together. Once again, evangelism works as an expression of the whole Christian community.

I suspect it is because evangelism is a process that courses for teaching the faith have become so popular in recent years. Thirty years ago, it was possible to hold a single "evangelistic meeting" for people to hear the message of Christ just once, and to respond there and then. In some parts of the world, it is still possible. But the reason people respond instantaneously is that a seed has been growing invisibly for some time. I know, for example, that in my own life, when I heard the invitation to follow Christ, I already knew the outline of Christian belief and I was familiar with Bible stories, and so the message made sense immediately. The field had been well prepared.

Now, however, fewer and fewer people have that kind of background, and so evangelism has to start "further back" and to be prepared to take longer in order to nurture the process. This is, I believe, one reason for interest in such programs as Alpha, where Christian faith is taught over the course of several weeks or months. This gives people time to reflect on what they hear, to ask their questions in a friendly atmosphere, to make friends, and to watch Christians in action.

One reason I appreciate Nicky's story, I suppose, is because the process is so clear. When she met Sarah, she wasn't even sure she believed in God. But Sarah shared her life with her: "We spent a lot of time getting to know one another and having a good laugh." She went to her small group: "During these meetings I would say absolutely nothing. I would simply listen. Sometimes I would be intrigued or confused, and at other times I was amused."

She observed people's lives: "I scrutinized those around me to see if they really were living a life that was true to what they believed." Nobody pressed her to participate more. Then she went to a week of special meetings. After this, two Christian leaders met with her (and only her) once a week for two months and "as I grew comfortable with them, I began to ask lots of the questions I had been wondering about." She tried praying: "I remember lying in bed, praying, asking God that, if he did exist, would he do this, this and this." By Easter she felt the confidence to stand up in church and thus make her faith known.

So many things contribute to the process of people figuring out what they believe about Christian faith. Each person, each event, each experiment, in however small a way, helps that process of moving toward faith in Christ that we call evangelism.

And the dance goes on

I realized that John 4 had been tremendously fruitful in shaping my understanding of evangelism. The importance of listening, of patience, of respect, for starters: none of them characteristics of the flasher, but all of them present in Jesus. One of the characters in Brian McLaren's book *A New Kind of Christian* sums up what I felt I had been learning:

> I think of [evangelism] like a dance. You know, in a dance, nobody wins and nobody loses. Both parties listen to the music and try to move with it. In this case, I hear the music of the gospel, and my friend doesn't, so I try to help him hear it and move with it. And like a dance, I have to ask if the other person wants to participate. There's a term for pulling someone who doesn't want to dance into a dance: assault. But if you pull someone in who wants to learn, and if you're good with the music yourself, it can be a lot of fun.[12]

I guess I was growing to like the way Jesus danced, and I wanted to be that kind of dancer myself. But Jesus was not the only dancer in the New Testament. I turned the pages to discover how his followers fared as they made their first moves in the dance of evangelism.

7.

A Healthy (Church) Lifestyle

The confessing church . . . knows that its most credible form of witness (and the most "effective" thing it can do for the world) is the actual creation of a living, breathing, visible community of faith.

Stanley Hauerwas and William Willimon, *Resident Aliens* [1]

THE FIRST THING that struck me in the world of the Acts of the Apostles was how different it is from the world at the time of the four Gospels. What it means to be a follower of Jesus changes significantly as the Gospel begins to move away from the world of its Jewish origins and into the Gentile world. It was still a matter of "As the Father sent me, so I am sending you," but the world into which the disciples were sent was increasingly different from the world into which Jesus was sent.

Right from the beginning there are distinct differences. For starters, Jesus no longer is present in his physical body, to be consulted and to hold their hands. And, two, partly as a result, the Christian community takes on a new significance. Now the Spirit has come and they interact in new ways. They come to be called "the body of Christ," hardly a term that would have suited them before. And they have to learn to act as such.

In these ways the world of Acts is actually closer to our world than that of the Gospels. In our case, too, Jesus is not present in the flesh, and the Christian community has to learn to operate like the limbs of Jesus' body. Thus, I realized, Acts might shed light on the subject of evangelism in some ways the Gospels don't.

To my surprise, the first thing that struck me in Acts was not the early Christians' evangelism at all. Oh yes, it is dramatic—three thousand converted on one occasion (Acts 2:41), five thousand on another (Acts 4:4)—yet to me, it was the quality of their life as a church (or churches) that stood out. So what was the connection between that and the effectiveness of their evangelism? Here is what I noticed.

The early Christians' sense of togetherness

People in Acts seem to be drawn to Christ in part by the warmth of the Christian community. As I read the stories, it became clear to me how one early observer could say, "See how these Christians love one another!" [2]

All the believers lived in a wonderful harmony, holding everything in common. They sold whatever they owned and pooled their resources so that each person's need was met. They followed a daily discipline of worship in the temple followed by meals at home, every meal a celebration, exuberant and joyful, as they praised God. People in general liked what they saw (Acts 2:44-46; 4:32).

The New Testament has several images for the Christian community. It pictures believers as:

a body	(1 Corinthians 12:12)
an extended family	(1 Timothy 3:15)
a building with many stones	(1 Peter 2:5)
an army wearing the whole armor of God	(Ephesians 6:11)
a loaf of bread	(1 Corinthians 10:17)

Personally, I doubt whether these images were revealed wholesale from heaven: "This is how thou shalt describe the church." More likely they arose from simple observation of how the Christians functioned: "You know, these people are as tight with one another as the stones in a building. That's amazing!"

How are community and evangelism connected? Someone has said that much evangelism is like a bodiless arm. The arm reaches out, but there is no warm, healthy body for the new Christian to belong to. This is the lone ranger evangelism George Hunter was taught, the kind of evangelism that produces "decisions for Christ" but few church members. In these stories in Acts, however, people are invited not to enter a private relationship with God but to become part of Jesus' new community.

The community dimension of the church has been expressed in different ways down the years. The medieval period saw the rapid expansion of monastic communities. The eighteenth century Wesleyan revival revolved around a network of thousands of tightly knit small groups. The 1960s saw hundreds, perhaps thousands, of intentional Christian communities spring up. Sometimes large numbers of believers sold their own properties and

moved into large homes or residential complexes together, sharing everything in common. The 1970s saw more modest efforts, in particular a
greater emphasis on extended households. One family we know, with two
children of their own, invited a single mother with a small child, and an
elderly man with no living relatives, to join their household. Such
arrangements were not uncommon.

Today, many Christians have experienced the warmth and intimacy of
a home study group, usually meeting once a week, and sharing life
through such activities as picnics or house-decorating parties. The form
Christian community takes will vary according to the culture, but there
has to be some tangible expression of community if evangelism is to be
effective.

Often when I ask Christians what it was that influenced them to
become Christians, they will credit the influence of a Christian community. In this respect, Nicky's story is a classic. Its truth is reinforced by the
findings of a survey in England, which revealed that 15 percent of men
and 24 percent of women said a group or community of Christian friends
was the main factor in their finding faith; 39 percent of men and 40 percent of women said it was a supporting factor. One respondent said:

> They seemed to be so different. When I was in their presence I felt differ-
> ent than when I was with other people. I realized that I did not have what
> they had. They had a different outlook and happiness in whatever they
> were doing. [3]

That's the effect of authentic Christian community.

Early Christians had a profound experience of prayer and worship

As I worked my way through Acts, I was struck by the worship of the
first Christians. God seemed to be very immediate and real to them. Their
worship was often spontaneous and had remarkable effects on them and
those around them. More significantly for my purposes, time after time,
there appeared a pretty direct link between prayer and worship on the one
hand and evangelism on the other. In fact, it seems to have been worship
more than anything else that led to bold proclamation. My first example
was not hard to find. On the Day of Pentecost, the disciples are praying

and worshiping, the Spirit comes upon them, and Peter preaches his first evangelistic sermon. Coincidence? I don't think so.

I turned the pages. In chapter 4, after Peter and John are released from prison, instead of retreating to lick their wounds and wonder where they went wrong (which I could imagine myself doing), what do they do? They take time to worship and to pray (Acts 4:23-24, 31). Then the Spirit comes on them and they go out to evangelize yet again.

Clearly there is a connection here. But what is it? I began by thinking about worship itself. What exactly is it? Worship has a wide range of meanings in the Bible. At the heart of all its expressions, however, seems to be something like this: that worship is an appropriate response to who God is. After all, an appropriate response to a good meal is to eat it with enthusiasm and gratitude. An appropriate response to a lover's touch may be an embrace or a kiss. An appropriate response to the cry of a child is to reach out. So with God: when we become aware of who God really is, the appropriate response is to turn and yield our whole being, heart and soul and mind and strength: that is, to worship. [4]

So what then is the connection between worship and evangelism? Worship focuses our attention on God, and the God of Jesus Christ is a God who reaches out in care and evangelism. Thus the closer we come to this God, the more we are drawn to share in the evangelistic heart of God.

The opposite is a disturbing but logical possibility: if worship does not lead to an increase in concern for evangelism, then something is missing in that worship. It hardly matters how beautiful the worship is, how faithful to its tradition, even what sense we may come away with of God's presence. If the worship actually puts us in touch with the God who is Father of our Lord Jesus Christ, one effect it will have on the worshipers is to make them more evangelistic. Worship that does not lead to evangelism is as deficient as evangelism that does not lead to worship.

Someone has said that Christian faith is centrifugal. [5] You remember the principle that describes the way water flies off a wheel as it goes round. The more we come close to the heart of God, the more we are spun off "away from" God into the world in the name of God. That certainly seems to be what's going on in Acts. As they come close to God in worship, they are spun off into more evangelism.

Whatever form worship and prayer take, they need to be there at the heart of our community's life. Otherwise evangelism becomes a horizontal exercise, a merely human activity.

People in Acts experienced the supernatural

Awe came upon everyone, because many wonders and signs were being done by the apostles. (Acts 2:43)

In his writing of Acts, Luke takes miracles for granted. David Watson points out that Luke is so accustomed to displays of the supernatural that in Acts 19:11 he even refers to some of them as "extraordinary" miracles.[6] Apparently most miracles no longer surprised him. They were too ordinary.

Frankly, talk of the miraculous makes many people today nervous, especially in mainline denominations. This is true of the man who said to his pastor, "Oh dear, I do hope nothing supernatural ever happens in our church!" Some will argue that we should not expect miracles today, whether ordinary or extraordinary. It is true that miracles are not distributed evenly, even through the Bible. They occur strangely clustered together, particularly around those times when God was doing something new in the world—during the times of Moses and Elijah, and during the times of Jesus and the Acts.

Even when the pages of the Bible contain no miracles, however, they demonstrate the reality of the presence of God in other ways. In the book of Esther, for instance, God is hardly even mentioned. Yet at the heart of Esther's story is the way God saves the Jewish people, exiles in Persia, from likely annihilation, in answer to concerted prayer—and the boldness of Esther. Is it a miracle? Not in the generally understood sense. Is it a dramatic reminder that God is actively involved in the world? You bet it is.

So I can't say that miracles are essential for the credibility of the message of the gospel. But I would say this: that God should be clearly present among us in one way or another, if not by miracles then by answers to prayer, and if not by answers to prayer then by something else. If the heart of the gospel is "Emmanuel, God with us," it ought to show.

How then does it show if there are no miracles? A thousand ways. Here's just one: A pastor in the south of England used to tell the story of two women in his congregation. One came to him to say that she had been diagnosed with cancer and to ask the church's prayers. The church prayed and she was dramatically healed.

A second woman came, with the same story. Without knowing why, the pastor hesitated. "Before I ask the church to pray, let's pray about it privately for a week, and see what God tells us." During the week, the pastor became convinced that the woman would die. "How on earth am I to tell her?" he wondered. But when he went to visit her at the end of the week, she opened the door with a big smile, and said, "It's okay. He's told me, too." That woman did die, but her dying was a testimony to what it means to die in the faith of Christ.

In the first woman's case, the reality of God was seen in a miracle. In the second woman's case, God's glory was seen in her suffering and death. But both are legitimate expressions of the reality of God.

Novelist E. M. Forster referred to "poor little talkative Christianity."[7] We are known in the secular world, it seems, for talking a lot and doing little. Especially is this dangerous in a society that is saturated with words. There should be something about our life as a Christian community that simply cannot be explained in human terms, something that says that this God thing is more than words. It may be miracles, whether ordinary or extraordinary. It may be startling answers to prayer. It may be a style of life—or a style of death—that is refreshingly different. People should comment about us: When these Christians talk about God, it's for real!

Put it this way: before the discovery of Pluto, astronomers knew it must be there because of the behavior of the planets they could see. They had worked out that only an invisible planet would explain the data. The same should be true of us—that our behavior and our experience make sense only if there is a powerful but invisible body exerting an influence on us.

The early Christians were involved in social caring

The practical caring of the early Christians was outstanding. None of them was allowed to be in need. Some, like Barnabas, even sold off their personal property to meet the needs of others. Undoubtedly, one of the reasons the early church grew so dramatically was that its love was so real and so compelling. As Jesus was sent to show the Father's love for others, so Jesus' followers knew themselves to be sent to love.

How are evangelism and social action connected? John Stott has suggested that there is an equal partnership between the two.[8] After all, as we saw in chapter 4, both are authentic expressions of the life of Jesus. Yet the two do not simply operate in parallel, independently. In practical terms, it is the caring that gives credibility to our words, just as the words explain the significance of our actions.

Our lives are the proof that our message is true. If there is no congruity between our words and reality, then there is no reason on earth why our words should be believed. If our words say that God is love, then our actions should speak love as well.

Social action to express the love of God may be on an informal, personal scale or it may be communal and organized. Christians have been known to organize everything from food banks to housing co-ops, from literacy centers to suicide hotlines. One group of Christian students I heard about replaced all the possessions, including the lecture notes, lost in a student rooming house fire.

A Christian businessman in Indonesia collected money from his business acquaintances and then "called the men of the community together and said, 'My Christian friends want you to have this money to build your mosque.' He then spent six months helping them to build the mosque." [9] Such things prepare the ground for the gospel and give it credibility. When the man later began a Bible study, many people were interested. No wonder.

A student fellowship at Queen's University in Kingston, Ontario, used to operate the secondhand book exchange every September. This effort served the campus by providing the inexpensive textbooks that students needed. The book exchange also served the wider community, giving thousands of dollars to local and global charities. In the second term, the same group put on an evangelistic outreach event. Both were expressions of their Christian faith. But the fact that the book exchange came first created an environment where the Christians were respected, appreciated, and trusted, and their message was taken seriously.

People in Acts had an alternative culture

Derek Warlock, Roman Catholic bishop of Liverpool, England, once defined culture as "the way we do things round here." There are longer, more sophisticated definitions of culture, but that one is difficult to beat. As the early church got going, Christians found that their way of doing things was not how other people did things. Indeed, they had their own way of doing things "round here." Often the two cultures came into conflict.

One result was that the early Christians frequently found themselves on the wrong side of the law. Peter and John were put in prison for preaching about the discredited pretender Jesus (Acts 4:3). Later on, Paul was given a hard time because he deprived a group of businessmen of their profit from a demonized young woman (Acts 16:16ff.) At Ephesus, Paul's preaching threatened the economy of the whole city. The artists who carved statues of the pagan goddess Diana realized that if people turned away from idolatry, they were out of business, so they instigated a riot (Acts 19:23).

These things should not particularly surprise us. The kingdom of God and the kingdom of this world will always be at loggerheads. Where God's values of compassion and justice are preached and practiced, there will be a clash of cultures with those who want to "do things round here" a different way.

A friend of mine named Paul was a top student at Yale University. In his summers, he used to be a camp counselor, working in a Special Needs program for disabled young people, earning two dollars a day. For two summers he was responsible for Glen. Glen was in his mid-twenties but had the mind of an eighteen-month old. Glen could not speak, walk by himself, go to the bathroom alone, or clean himself. My friend Paul helped him with all those things. Sometimes Glen needed to be bathed several times a day. Usually Paul communicated with him by singing songs to him.

Was that a good way for Paul to spend his summers? It didn't make him any money, didn't stretch his mind, didn't further his career prospects. It didn't make sense by any standard of our culture. Paul did it, of course, simply because he loved God and loved people. A counter-cultural summer experience.

Another friend of mine spends her time working with street people. If you met her in a different context, you would classify her as a refined, educated Englishwoman, which she is. But her vocation is to spend time on the streets and befriend people who are homeless—to mend the holes in their socks, to help them find their way around various aid agencies, to listen to their stories, to teach them to read, and to talk to them about Jesus. Her career goal is to live in one room with as few possessions as possible. Crazy? Only by the standards of a culture that does not know the love of Jesus.

People in Acts had a world vision

Geography is probably more significant in the book of Acts than in any other book of the New Testament. For the first seven chapters of Acts, the first followers of Jesus operate mainly in Jerusalem. At the end of chapter 7, however, Stephen dies, the first martyr of the Christian community. Persecution breaks out against Jesus' Way, and most of the believers scatter throughout Judea and Samaria. Thus the Christian faith begins to ripple outward in a way that will eventually affect the whole world.

When Paul becomes the central figure in the narrative, that movement receives a powerful new impetus. Paul goes as far as Rome, but even that does not satisfy his wanderlust (Acts 19:21). He still wants to go to Spain (Romans 15:28) and even to lands beyond there, wherever that may be (2 Corinthians 10:16).

Why is this important? Simply that, without this kind of vision, there would be no Christians today outside the Middle East. I would not be writing this book and you would not be interested in reading it even if I were! A healthy church will always have a world vision. There is some-thing about the presence of the Spirit of Jesus that presses people to look beyond themselves, beyond their community, to the ends of the earth.

I think of the small churches I have known that have a world map in the foyer, showing sister churches, or photos of denominational mission-aries, around the world. Churches whose young people are sponsored by the congregation to go on short-term missions overseas, or to interna-tional conferences, and report back to the congregation when they return. Churches where some members take early retirement from their jobs to offer their expertise and years of experience to developing nations for a few years before "really" retiring. And churches where it is assumed that a generous chunk of the outreach budget will always be earmarked for work overseas.

I cannot think of a single church like this where there is not an equal passion for evangelism. The two go together naturally. When a church's heart beats with concern for the rest of the world, it is likely to have a heartbeat for evangelism also. Conversely, when a church has a vision for evangelism, that vision is likely to spill over into passionate interest in world affairs. Fundamentally, both are a reflection of the heart and the vision of a God who made the whole world and who is always reaching out to others.

The early church believed in teaching and preaching

It is the Day of Pentecost. After forty days of waiting, the disciples finally encounter the Holy Spirit. They speak in languages they have never learned, and they begin to praise God loudly in a very public and rather embarrassing way. In fact, some amused passers-by assume they must have been drinking. Peter's response is interesting. It goes something like this: "No, we're not drunk. It's too early in the morning for that! What's really going on here is that God has sent the Holy Spirit, just as the prophet Joel promised centuries ago." Then he goes on to explain about Jesus. There is no need to round up an audience and persuade them to come hear the preacher. People are already curious and wanting the answers he's ready to give.

Evangelistic preaching in Acts is often like this: the Christians have to explain what on earth is going on. In the very next chapter, Peter and John are used by God to heal a lame man, and once more they have to spell out what has happened and why. Preaching answers the questions raised by their life.

In recent years, I have often given evangelistic talks in the context of dinner parties or dessert parties (evangelism can be difficult for those on a diet). As I have done that, I have been struck by how very different that experience is from giving a lecture in a huge, impersonal lecture theater. At the dinner party, by the time I speak (usually between main course and dessert), people have had a taste of the reality of Christian community. There has been friendship, laughter, and joyful servanthood, as well as good food and drink. When I begin to speak, I feel in a sense that all I have to do is say, "Let me explain to you what you've just experienced. Jesus once said that the kingdom of God is like a party . . ." My words are simply interpreting the reality that people have already experienced, helping people know how to "read" the party, if you like.

Actions often need to be interpreted by words in this way. The story is told of a Christian man who felt that it was better to share his faith through actions rather than by words. Six months after he had made this resolution, a colleague accosted him at the water cooler. "You know, Pete, there's something different about your life, and I reckon it must be something to do with your religion." Pete beamed. It had worked. "Let me guess," Jeff continued. "You're a vegetarian, right?"

In Acts, there is a basic assumption: words are necessary, words are a part reflection of who God is. Yet this is combined with great flexibility. The assumption of Jesus is that words are central to God's communication to the world, and that God's people are sent to speak them. Just how that happens takes almost as many forms as there are people to hear the words.

Does preaching and teaching work these days? My experience has been that time after time people will approach me after a talk and say things to the effect of, "Wow, I didn't know Christianity was like this. This is really neat. Tell me more." Time after time, people with no religious background will come to an Agnostics Anonymous group, and keep coming in spite of busy schedules, because it is dealing with real questions of life and spirituality and death. Don't let anyone tell you words have outlived their usefulness. Words are still integral to our humanity and, if they are connected to vitality and integrity, they can still come with the power of God.

The Old Testament dream come true

I had read the book of Acts before, but never with the question about evangelism in mind. I found I was struck by the way that their evangelism emerged from the matrix of a rich spiritual life. More than that, having done that survey of evangelism (or lack of it) in the Old Testament so recently, I could not help comparing the life of the church in Acts with God's intention for the life of the people of Israel in the Old Testament. It even seemed to me that all these marks of the church in Acts are marks of the Old Testament community of God at its best. They, too, had a strong sense of caring for one another in community. They, too, had worship at the center of their community life. From time to time, they, too, experienced God's supernatural intervention. Their culture was a different way of doing things from that of the world around. Their prophets reminded them of God's worldwide strategy, and taught them that God communicated in words as well as actions.

What happened in the book of Acts, it seems, is not really new. Christians who try to model their church life and evangelism on that in Acts are following in a long tradition that reaches back way before the time of Jesus.

8.

Cross-Cultural Communication:
Paul in Athens

Tell All the Truth but tell it slant

Emily Dickinson, opening line of poetry

I N SPITE OF WHAT I HAD LEARNED SO FAR, I found there was still
a nagging dissatisfaction. The people Jesus spoke to, for instance, were
familiar with the subjects he talked about—sheep and shepherds, sowing
and reaping, and kings holding court and throwing banquets. Even Peter's
listeners on the Day of Pentecost were impressed by the way he quoted
the scriptures: their reaction seems to have been, "If that's what the scriptures say, then I guess he must be right."

But the people I know are not like these people. They are not
impressed by quotations from the Bible. They know more about black
holes in space than about shepherds in first-century Palestine. They are
more likely to be impressed by royal, or presidential, sex scandals than by
tales of kingly majesty and authority. If they try to call up mental files on
Jesus or salvation or the authority of the Bible, their minds draw a blank.
Even if that information was ever there, it was deleted long ago. Because
of this, I cannot begin sharing faith with them in the way Jesus or Peter
could. The gulf seems too wide.

Then I found a story buried right in the heart of the book of Acts that
gave me a clue. At this point in Acts, Paul is center stage. His life has been
following what is for him a familiar pattern: *preach—interest—opposition—
driven out of town—go on to the next town.* But because he has a pastor's
heart, he is concerned for the early Christians, the fledgling churches, he
has been forced to leave behind in the places he has been. He can't go
back himself without risking more riots, so he sends his fellow travelers
Silas and Timothy back down the road they have just walked, in order to

care for the new believers. And the place Paul waits for their return is the city of Athens.

What does he do? Among other things, he does a little sightseeing. Athens was famous then as now for its historic architecture. And, as Paul looks, he sees some interesting things. In particular, he is struck by the Athenians' deep concern for spirituality.

Of course, being Paul, he gets into conversation about questions of spirituality with everyone he meets. Luke tells us first that Paul argues "in the synagogue with the Jews and the devout persons" (Acts 17:17). For Paul, that's normal. With them he can begin on familiar ground. On that scale of 1-100 from chapter 6, many people probably are at 40: they already understand the nature and character of God, the reality of sin, the need for costly atonement, and the promise of a Messiah. Paul's experience was that that mind-set was a fertile seedbed for the gospel.

Athens, however, is not Jerusalem, and Paul also argues with the Gentiles "in the marketplace with those who happened to be there." In particular, he debates with philosophers of the Stoic and Epicurean persuasions. His listeners respond to his message in two ways. Both have something to teach us about communicating the Christian message to people who know nothing about Christian faith, who have no "Christian memory."

On being an intellectual magpie

The first lesson, it seems to me, concerns a rude name the people of Athens call Paul. It is translated in different ways: "babbler" (New International Version, New Revised Standard Version); "charlatan" (New English Bible); "parrot" (Jerusalem Bible); and even "airhead" (*The Message*). In other words, the Athenians are not impressed! The word meant "seed-picker" or "persons who had acquired mere scraps of learning." [1] My guess is that Paul was using material from poets and philosophers, historians and dramatists to illustrate his points. In this respect, anyway, he is not being very original, and some of his "scraps of learning" must have sounded familiar to them already. This is interesting because, as we will see, Paul does indeed pick up ideas from various non-Christian and non-Jewish sources. To that extent their criticism is just.

As I thought about this, I remembered an evangelistic book from my student days. It was *Jesus Spells Freedom* by Michael Green. [2] As a young

Christian I had read it and been dazzled by Michael Green's range of material. There were quotations from Nabokov's *Lolita*, Shakespeare's *Macbeth*, the musical *Jesus Christ Superstar*, Albert Camus, the Roman poet Ovid, King Crimson, Jimi Hendrix, and Bob Dylan. "Scraps of learning," if you like. But a powerful way of intriguing an audience.

I remember being intoxicated by the realization that the Christian message wasn't just about "religious stuff." It could hold its own in the cultural world of music and philosophy and literature and drama, and had something powerful to say to all of them. Of course, some of Green's quotations connected better with the 1960s than with the start of the twenty-first century! But that's okay. Probably if we knew what "scraps of learning" Paul had demonstrated that day, they wouldn't mean a whole lot to us either—but, as we will see, they were obviously just right for his listeners back then.

Michael Green was doing the same thing Paul was doing: being an intellectual magpie. The nickname may not have been intended as a compliment by the intellectual snobs of Athens, but for evangelists, it is a compliment. It means they're doing something right.

What's in a name?

The Athenians' second response shows how deeply they misunderstand his message. They say, "He seems to be a proclaimer of foreign divinities." Who are the divinities they think Paul is talking about? Luke gives us a clue in the sentence that follows: "This is because he was telling about the good news of Jesus and the resurrection" (Acts 17:18). The new gods were Jesus and resurrection! The Greek word for resurrection is *anastasis*, from which we derive the woman's name Anastasia. It was not uncommon for Greek and Roman gods and goddesses to have their divine partners, so here, obviously, was another couple of gods to be added to the list: Jesus and his wife Anastasis.

We may laugh at their misunderstanding, but only because we are familiar with the word *resurrection*. If we are at home in the Christian story, the word will come with memories of the crucifixion and burial of Jesus, the sadness of Easter Saturday, the women at the tomb early on Sunday morning. On a broader canvas, the word may make us think about life after death, God's creation of a good physical world, the wages of sin being death, the resurrection as God's "seal of approval" on Christ's work, and even the final resurrection and judgment. All that is associated with the word *resurrection*—for anyone who happens to know the story.

But the Athenians did not know that story. Indeed, they had their own story and naturally tried to fit the word *resurrection* into their own understanding of the world—with results we have just seen.

When my colleague Joe Mangina was at Yale University recently, he found himself walking behind two undergraduates as they passed a stone archway with these words carved into it: "The dead shall be raised." One of the students pointed the words out to the other, whose response was immediate and heartfelt: "Yeeugh!" Why? Because for her, presumably, the words were part of yet another story, a story where zombies and "the night of the living dead" are more real than the story of God's new creation.

I'm not sure if Luke intends us to laugh at the Athenians' misunderstanding. Maybe he does, though it would be a wry kind of laughter. But all humor is based on truth, and the truth underlying the humor here is actually a sobering one: we cannot assume that our words will be understood unless we share a context with our listeners.

Fortunately for Paul and the Athenians, he has a fuller opportunity to explain what he means. Paul's listeners take him to where they always held their debates and discussions, the Areopagus. "Your teaching," they tell him "is startling." (The Greek word implies *alien* or *very foreign*.) "Tell us more." When people outside the faith say, "Please tell us more," something good is happening.

Paul, I am sure, takes a deep breath. Where to begin? These, after all, are people who know nothing about, or at least are not drawn to, the austere religion of the Jews, with its strange prohibition of idols and its strict moral code. One thing we know for sure: the Old Testament is not going to be a central part of his presentation. Even for an experienced speaker like Paul, this is a formidable challenge.

Paul on Mars Hill

Paul begins carefully: "Athenians, I see how extremely religious you are in every way. For as I went through the city and looked carefully at the objects of your worship, I found among them an altar with the inscription, "To an unknown god" (Acts 17:22-23).

What is this altar? Fortunately for our understanding, historical references to such altars do exist.[3] What is even more interesting, history gives us a story of how such an altar might have come to be on Paul's tourist itinerary.

The story is told by Diogenes Laertius, a Greek writer from the third century B.C. [4] Six centuries before Christ, a terrible plague decimated the people of Athens. According to legend, the city elders asked the advice of Epimenides of Crete, who told them that in spite of all their sacrifices to the gods, there was only one god who could help them. He explained how to make a sacrifice to this Supreme Creator on specially erected altars, and the plague ended instantly. Maybe the altar Paul came across that day was one of the last of these.

No one knows, of course, whether the story of Epimenides' advice is true, but it would not surprise me if it were. It would be a particularly dramatic illustration of the fact that God is at work in every culture. It would be a vivid reminder that every nation has places where God's handiwork is apparent for those who have eyes to see, places where the reality of God becomes clear in the fabric of daily life, if people will only see it. Every culture has its altar to the Unknown God.

Paul then goes on, announcing, "There is a connection between your Unknown God and the God I know. The very thing you confess you do not know is exactly what I do know." This is either breathtaking arrogance . . . or simply a statement of fact. How can Paul say such a thing?

Finding the anknupfungspunkt

The Germans have a word for what Paul does here: he finds the *anknupfungspunkt*. This word isn't as threatening as it sounds, once you break it down. A *knupf* is a button, *knupfung* is "buttoning," and *anknupfung* is "buttoning on." The word *punkt* has the same origin as the English word point. So *anknupfungspunkt* becomes the point of buttoning on, the point where the button goes through the buttonhole.

Think of it this way. The good news of Christianity is like a precious button that will fit into the buttonhole in a person's life and understanding. The trick is to link together the button and the buttonhole—in other words, to find the *anknupfungspunkt*. At this point in Paul's sermon, he finds that point (the altar to the Unknown God) and the button (news about the Unknown God) goes perfectly into the buttonhole. [5]

Behind this approach to evangelism is a particular understanding of God. Sometimes Christians assume when it comes to talking to a friend about God that the other person knows nothing about God, has never experienced God, indeed that God has never taken an interest in that person until that minute. Paul's approach to evangelism assumes the opposite: that God is already involved in people's lives, trying to catch their attention, nudging them, intriguing them, making them aware of the spiritual issues of life. One of Brian McLaren's characters says this:

> Whenever I get to know individual non-Christians—I mean really get to know them—I am completely convinced that I find God already there and at work in their lives. It doesn't matter if they're way-out New Agers or even atheists.[6]

I remember, before I learned this lesson, spending time with a group of students in an Agnostics Anonymous group. During an early session, I spent some time telling them the traditional arguments for the existence of God. To my dismay, they were not impressed and managed to poke holes in all of them. "But," I appealed to them, "haven't you ever *experienced* God?" Immediately the atmosphere in the room changed. "Well, of course," they replied, laughing incredulously at my naïve question. And one by one they told stories of experiencing God in one way or another. God clearly had bypassed their heads and communicated directly to their hearts. The buttonhole was there, where I was too obtuse to think of looking, until my friends graciously brought it to my attention.

That was what Paul discovered at Athens: God had already been at work in that culture, preparing the buttonhole for the button. As this idea dawned on me, I realized, too, that looking for the *anknupfungspunkt* was not just Paul's idea. This is exactly what Jesus was doing in that story of the woman at the well (chapters 4 and 5). Her thirst and his offer of living water were an exact match between buttonhole and button. God had already been active in the woman's life, making her aware of her need for lasting satisfaction. What Jesus did was simply to bring to fruition what God had already been doing.

My mind went further back. Of course, this connects with Genesis chapter 3, where God goes looking for Adam and Eve. Evangelism is primarily God's passion, not a human invention. Any involvement we may have in evangelism can only be as apprentices to God. Paul here models what it means to be a coworker alongside God. God had created the buttonhole through the fact of the altar to the Unknown God and the events that led to its building. Starting with that God-given buttonhole, Paul proceeds to show them the God-given button.

It is as though the Athenians, while worshiping many gods, still have an outline sketch of the one true God. They know that (1) this God exists, but (2) they don't know much about this God; (3) yet (perhaps) the God they don't know is the God who stopped the plague. What Paul does is to fill in that outline, to add detail and perspective and color—and to draw some very practical conclusions.

Could this be the right way to understand this passage? I went to one of my favorite Bible commentators. The name John Calvin, I know, has some negative connotations, even for Christians. "Isn't he the guy who taught about predestination?" they ask. But there is more to Calvin than that. My experience has been that often Calvin is the only one who answers the very question that has driven me to the commentaries. So I checked what he said about this story. This was his answer: "[The Athenians] were convinced that there was some divinity: their . . . religion was merely requiring to be corrected." [7]

In a sense maybe this is always the heart of the gospel, to answer the question "What is God really like?" Everything else flows from that. This Unknown God, Paul declares, is the Creator (Acts 17:24) and Sustainer of everything that is (17:25). As such, God is also the rightful Ruler of the world (17:26). Now, so far, the content of Paul's sermon would not be unfamiliar to his audience. F. F. Bruce explains why: "Here are combined the Epicurean doctrine that God needs nothing from men [sic] and cannot be served by them, and the Stoic belief that He is the source of all life." [8]

At this point I began to wonder, "Is Paul here not in danger of diluting his message?" Surely the whole point of Christian faith is that it is not something we can work out for ourselves. Rather it is a message revealed by God through Jesus Christ. Then I recalled a line from Steve Podborski, a Canadian skier who won a gold medal at the Winter Olympics in Calgary. In an interview after the race, he said: "I knew I was ahead, because all the way down I was on the verge of falling." If Paul appears to be "on the verge of falling" here, it is only because he is "ahead" in his efforts to communicate with the Athenians. Maybe good communication always involves risk.

Then Paul's sermon begins to get more personal. In spite of this God's greatness, the Creator is close to us. As we seek for God, in fact God is close at hand (Acts 17:27). Paul seems to imply that it really isn't difficult to find God. What you need is an interpreter, someone to say, "This is what your experience means. Here is evidence of God's greatness and goodness; here are signs of God's involvement in your life. Let me tell you more." Maybe Paul says this in part because it's what he had been thinking as he walked around. These people are feeling after God, but they haven't found God. Here in their altar to the Unknown God is a sign of God, and yet they don't realize the implications.

Then he backs up his point in a very original way. He quotes from their own Greek poets (Acts 17:28): probably Aratus (from the third century B.C.) or Cleanthes (even earlier), and Epimenides (from the sixth century B.C, the same man whose name crops up in the story of the plague).[9]

Paul . . . quoting pagan writers? It seems to come naturally to him, though he seems to expect his listeners to be surprised ("even some of your own poets"). For Paul, finding truth in secular poets should be expected. After all, it's consistent with his belief in God as Creator and what he's just said about the accessibility of God. Paul realizes that wherever people seek for truth, there is a toehold for the gospel. Often it's a culture's poets who highlight truth about God, if they are faithful to truth and to the world around them. To find glimpses of God's truth and beauty in the most unlikely places is part of the fun of being a Christian.

How do the Athenians respond to this foreigner quoting from their poets? We don't know. But as I thought about this and tried to imagine the faces of Paul's listeners, I remembered an experience of my own.

I was once speaking at a Christmas camp for overseas students who could not go home for Christmas. (I described this camp in more detail in chapter 4.) This particular year, there happened to be a large number of Nigerian students, sent by their government to study in Canada. Most of them were Muslims and, while they were friendly, when it was the time of evening when I told the Christmas story, they sat together at the back and their body language said, "This is not for us."

I wondered for several days how to draw them in, and consulted books on Islam to understand better where they were coming from. To my surprise, I discovered that the Koran calls Jesus the Word of God, just as John's Gospel does. The next evening, when I talked about Jesus, I mentioned as casually as I could that Christians consider Jesus to be the Word of God, "as the Koran also says," and what a helpful description of Jesus that is. The look on my friends' faces was fascinating. Suddenly they were a part of what was going on. "This guy talks our language," they seemed to be thinking. "This is not a totally alien thing he's talking about." Using their language brought us closer and made fresh conversation possible.

I suspect that when Paul tosses out those quotations from the poets, his listeners change, too. Perhaps they lean forward in their seats. They catch one another's eyes and nod. "Maybe this guy is okay after all. He's obviously more cultured than we thought."

When evangelizing, Christians sometimes talk about "building bridges." In this story, for example, they might argue that Paul is constructing a bridge between his world and that of the Athenians. A bridge built out of the Unknown God concept, plus common concepts of God and quotations from the poets. A bridge he can cross to carry the freight of the Christian message. I confess I don't resonate with this kind of talk as I once did. I think it is because I dislike the sense of distance it suggests between "believers" and "unbelievers." I fear it is precisely that sense of "us" and "them" which actually encourages the impersonality that makes flasher evangelism possible.

The imagery of *bridges* also implies that all the good stuff is on our side, and none on the other, and that our job is transport all the good stuff across to the other side. Paul in this story is doing precisely the opposite. In effect, he is saying, "Hey, there's good stuff in this culture. It resonates with my understanding of faith. Let's explore these connections."

By Acts 17:30 he feels confident enough of his relationship with the audience that he introduces some of the specific teachings of Jesus, things that cannot be learned merely from philosophical reflection or even from their poets:

> God . . . commands all people everywhere to repent, because he has fixed a day on which he will have the world judged in righteousness by a man whom he has appointed, and of this he has given assurance to all by raising him from the dead. (Acts 17:30-31)

This transition follows perfectly logically: If we are agreed that this is what God is like—Creator, rightful Ruler, close to each one of us—and if the Athenians have not responded to God appropriately, then this has consequences. Up to now, the Athenians appear to have thought of God as purely an interesting philosophical proposition. Now, says Paul, you need to start treating God as a moral and practical reality to be reckoned with.

I suspect that in spite of the relationship Paul has established, these words still felt emotionally jarring to the Athenians, and maybe to Paul, too. As a result, there is a mixed response to Paul's lecture. Some people scoff, others want to continue the discussion another time. A few turn to Christ, and no church is founded that we know of.

Did Paul make a mistake?

Suddenly I stopped and scratched my head. All this was very gripping, but was it right? What about the message given for all time, to be handed down without dilution or alteration? Isn't Paul getting carried away with all this cultural stuff? And after all, it didn't work, really . . . did it?

Wasn't there a school of thought that said Paul made a big mistake at Athens? According to this theory, Paul found a poor response to his message because he had not stuck to "the simple gospel" and flirted with different methods. Then, as a result, he vowed never to preach that way again. After all, he went on from Athens to Corinth (Acts 18:1), and it was there he "did not come proclaiming the mystery of God to you in lofty words of wisdom. For I decided to know nothing among you except Jesus Christ, and him crucified" (1 Corinthians 2:1-2).

Could that be right? Is he criticizing his own approach at Athens in turning from "lofty words of wisdom"? Was his approach at Athens all a mistake? Time to think about the content of his message in Athens. Was it biblical? Was it faithful to the model of Jesus and those other evangelists who had gone before him?

I began by looking up the cross-references in my Bible. Surprise! Within eight verses in Acts 17, he actually made indirect reference to no fewer than eleven Old Testament books—and one Apocryphal book for good measure.[10] Whatever else he had done at Athens, he had not thrown out the Bible. It was in his intellectual and spiritual bloodstream. That was a good start. Were there any other ways that Paul might be defended?

It is often said, and rightly, that you can't prove the correctness of the message from the number of converts. People will put their trust in God as a result of evangelism but (recalling Jesus' parable of the sower) not necessarily, not always, and perhaps not permanently. So the fact that Paul got a small response at Athens isn't a measure of the validity of his approach.

For this audience, in fact, a meager response is just what one would expect. This was a clearing-the-stones-out-of-the-field exercise, not a reaping exercise. Unlike the people Paul met at the synagogue, these Athenians did not have much of a foundation of understanding of God and God's ways. On our scale of 1-100, Paul probably helped them move from 5 to 15, not from 45 to 50.

I looked again at Luke's account of Paul's visit to Corinth, and suddenly a light went on. To whom was Paul speaking in Corinth when he said that he was determined to talk only about the cross? In the first five verses, Jews are referred to four times. Specifically, he was "testifying to the Jews that the Messiah was Jesus" (Acts 18:5). That explains his change of emphasis: it was a different message for a different audience, not a mis-calculation of strategy.

Relating to the culture

As Western culture moves away from its Christian orientation, an Athenian kind of evangelism becomes increasingly important. When I became a committed Christian in my teens, I already knew the stories of Jesus and the basic claims of Christian theology. The gospel simply filled the Christ-shaped gap in my formal Anglican background. But fewer people today have that basic information in their minds when they hear the gospel. They are people without a "Christian memory." So the starting point has to be different.

Like Paul, we need to understand our culture: its questions, its doubts, the points where it feels the effects of separation from God. Like Paul and like Jesus before him, we need to be on the lookout for an *anknup-fungspunkt*: the place or places where God is already at work, seeking to catch people's attention.

We often assume that evangelists need to be people who are very eloquent with words. In this story, however, the first thing Paul does is not to talk at all—it is to look. Hence his sermon begins with "as I went through the city and *looked carefully* at the objects of your worship" (Acts 17:23). He has learned a lesson from Jesus, who observed a woman coming across the sand toward the well where he was sitting, and who chided his disciples to lift up their eyes and look. Sharp eyes are more important than an eloquent tongue.

Every culture has altars to the Unknown God. This has come home to me in trying to explain the Christian message to students. My conclusion has been that God is indeed creating many an *anknupfungspunkt*, and in the most unlikely places.

For instance, cartoons are a big part of our culture (the humor section of my local bookstore occupies the same amount of space as the religion section). Humor is based on an unspoken agreement about the nature of reality, a common ground where the reader identifies with the cartoonist and the characters. You may remember Bill Watterson's popular comic strip *Calvin and Hobbes*, for instance. The characters regularly discussed questions such as these: Does God exist? What is the purpose of life? Is there life after death? Why is the human race in such a mess?

Movies, too, express much of what is going on in our world, as well as helping create it. One of my presentations for students is called "The Gospel according to Jim Carrey," because many of Jim Carrey's films raise questions of personal identity, social structure, freedom, and of how to overcome human problems. These are questions to which Jesus has strong and authoritative answers.

At the same time, I need to remind myself that as I become immersed in culture, I also need to be immersed in the scriptures. This way, however much our culture shifts, I have an intellectual and spiritual anchor. That way, what I bring to culture is God's message. I am a citizen of two cultures.

The incarnation principle

Ultimately it is Jesus, not Paul, who is the key to this question of culture. What we are talking about is basically the principle of incarnation. God embraces our culture and submits to our limitations. As Jesus, God adopts our way of dressing, eats our food, speaks a particular language, uses certain cultural images, and dies a first-century Roman death. When we attempt to incarnate our message in new dress, we are basically following his example.

Jesus also taught, and demonstrated, the principle of death and resurrection. Culturally nuanced presentations of the gospel (the only kind there is) are meant to give life in their time, but then they die. As far as we know, he never preached it again: it died, and Paul's gospel, like its subject, was resurrected in a new form.

9.

Kingdom Risks:
Boldly Following God's Spirit

The tendency to avoid challenge is so omnipresent in human beings that it can properly be considered a characteristic of human nature. But calling it natural does not mean it is essential or beneficial or unchangeable. It is also natural to defecate in our pants and never brush our teeth. Yet we teach ourselves to do the unnatural until the unnatural becomes itself second nature.

M. Scott Peck, *The Road Less Traveled* [1]

THERE WAS ANOTHER THEME that grabbed my attention in the book of Acts. At first, it made me uncomfortable, and yet it was clearly linked so intimately to the early church's evangelism, I tried to look it in the eye. It was the theme of risk. In a sense, it had been there all along. Some people would argue that creation itself was a risk on God's part. Certainly for God to choose fallible people like Abraham and Sarah would seem to us like a risk (although, come to that, there were no infallible people around). In human terms, for Jesus to come to earth was a risk, Jesus choosing the twelve was a risk, and so on. But now it became clear to me that evangelism was inevitably linked with risk.

The theme emerges in the first chapter of the book. In the first sentence of Acts, Luke explains to Theophilus that in his gospel he described what Jesus began to do and teach, as though now he will simply tell what Jesus continued to do and teach (Acts 1:1-2). Part of what Jesus continued to do is to inspire his followers to take the good news to new geographical areas. Yet for them, as often for us, geographical boundaries are not always the most difficult to cross.

At the beginning of Acts, Jesus and his followers already have different ideas about the best way to proceed. Listen to their last conversation in Acts 1:6-8. They ask, "Is this the time when you will restore the kingdom to Israel?" In other words: "Lord, this is really exciting. This really is the end of the world now, isn't it? Everyone is going to see that you're the king any minute now. Right? Right? Remember that conversation we once had about who would sit at your right and your left, Lord? Remember that? Do you think that . . ."

Their focus is the present, on Israel, and on what Jesus will do. When Jesus replies, however, his focus is different: "You will be my witnesses in Jerusalem, in all Judea and Samaria, and to the ends of the earth." He seems more interested in the future ("you will"), in the ends of the earth (not only Israel), and in what the disciples are going to be doing (being witnesses). Clearly a little tension is in store. They are looking for comfort and resolution, but he is pushing for risk and ambiguity.

The risk of leaving the nest

The church's evangelism begins in Jerusalem, and for a time everything goes well. Thousands of people are converted and form the nucleus of the first church. Even those who do not actually become disciples are impressed by the lifestyle of this new group (Acts 5:13). Clearly, God is active in their midst.

Then the tide begins to turn. First, there is an internal crisis: a couple called Ananias and Sapphira commit a sin that Peter calls "lying to the Holy Spirit" and are struck dead (Acts 5:1-11). Then outside forces begin to trouble them. Some of the apostles are put in prison, though it is not for long and they emerge triumphant (Acts 5:17). Third, suspicions of racial or cultural discrimination surface. As the community cares for poverty-stricken widows, some suspect that the Jewish widows are getting a better deal than the Greek widows (Acts 6:1). This, too, is dealt with sensitively by the appointment of a cross-cultural deacons' group to look after that ministry. To most observers, these are signs the honeymoon is coming to an end.

Then an unbelievable tragedy happens. Stephen, one of the brightest of the fellowship, is opposed for his preaching, is brought to trial, preaches an inflammatory sermon, and is put to death by stoning. He is the first martyr to the cause. (I imagine some asking, Why did he have to be so blunt? What a waste of a promising young life. Which, on one level, it was.) The effect of this disaster is that everybody takes off out of the city, with the exception of the apostles, who stay at home base (Acts 8:1).

To them, it must have seemed like an unmitigated catastrophe, the destruction of all they had seen miraculously built up. Surely God was with us, yet where is God now? Probably the Holy Spirit saw things differently. While the disciples may have feared that this was the beginning of the end for the church, the Spirit knew that this was only the end of the beginning.

The risk of going to people who are different

If Jesus' first area of concern had been Jerusalem, his second was Judea and Samaria (Acts 1:6). You will remember that he himself had had an unexpectedly warm welcome in parts of Samaria (John 4:1-42). Now at last, after seven chapters in Jerusalem, the narrative moves on to phase two of Jesus' dream: the Samaritans (Acts 8:5-8).

The Samaritans had been considered theological and ethnic mongrels since 722 B.C. You remember from the story of the woman at the well that Jews and Samaritans had no dealings. Now the rumor reaches Jerusalem that Philip has gone and preached in Samaria, and that some Samaritans have become believers in Jesus, yet without receiving the Holy Spirit. Imagine the conversation once the reports have arrived:

No Holy Spirit? What do you mean, no Holy Spirit? They simply can't be real believers. Becoming a disciple means receiving the Spirit. Receiving the Spirit means becoming a disciple. Doesn't make sense.

To be honest, I'm not convinced that Samaritans can be disciples anyway. Always was something strange about them and their religion, everyone knows that. What do you think, Thomas?

Well, I remember at least one Samaritan city where the people truly turned to the Master. Come on, Andrew, you have to remember that, too, surely?

But there is definitely something fishy going on here, I'd say. And yet you know Philip. He's a good guy. I can't see him screwing up. You think he'd simply forget to tell them about the Spirit? Get real!

You know what? Someone better go and check it out. Peter, why don't you go? You won't stand for any nonsense. And take John with you. You make a good team.

So Peter and John go, as representatives of the true church, because what is going on is unorthodox, and they needed to check it out. Even after three years of hanging around with Jesus, watching him break one religious rule after another, they are still nervous when it comes to breaking their own religious rules. Commentators still disagree as to why the Samaritans did not experience the Spirit when they believed. Personally, I put my money on the theory that God is drawing the church leaders' attention to the newness in the situation. The Holy Spirit is concerned to rub their noses in it: "Notice what's happening here. Never forget it. You know what this means, don't you? The gospel is for all people, even Samaritans!"

More than that, the fact that the apostles go ensures that afterward they have no one to blame but themselves for the fact that there are now Samaritans in the church. They cannot distance themselves from what has happened, and pretend it was all someone else's mistake. By going to see for themselves, they are compromised. They are forced to take ownership. And in case we have any doubts as to whether they have learned their lesson, the last sentence of Luke's story underlines that they have: "Peter and John . . . returned to Jerusalem, proclaiming the good news to many villages of the Samaritans" (Acts 8:25). They share the good news with the marginalized Samaritans. Wonders never cease.

The risk of being inefficient

This incident with the Holy Spirit is not the only strange thing to happen to Philip in Samaria. He continues to have a fruitful evangelistic ministry in one of the Samaritan cities. Hundreds are coming to faith. Dozens are getting healed. Demons are fleeing in terror. (Acts 8:5-13) A little scary, but also intoxicating.

Then one morning, Philip announces that he has to leave. To go and preach to bigger crowds? Not exactly. In fact, just the opposite. He is going to take a walk into the desert. To our eyes, and doubtless some of theirs, too, it looks thoroughly irresponsible. People are depending on him. The harvest is ripe, and surely it may start to rot if left. What about the crowds of sick and distressed waiting for his touch? What about the crowds lined up since before daybreak, waiting to hear him preach? What is he up to?

Imagine the scene. The previous day has been a long one of preaching, counseling, and healing, and Philip is saying his bedtime prayers:

> Lord, this is amazing. It's so exciting to work alongside you. I feel as though my words are inadequate, and yet somehow your Spirit makes them communicate to people. Thank you so much. Same again tomorrow, Lord?

> No? . . . You want me to do what? . . . No, honestly, Lord, I'm not telling you your job, but that is a desert road. . . . Yes, I know you know that. . . . No, I didn't think you hadn't noticed. I just thought . . . Oh, nothing. . . . Yes, of course I'll go. . . . No, you're quite right. There are others who are good preachers who can look after things tomorrow. . . . No problem, Lord. Talk to you in the morning.

So Philip goes off by himself into the desert, not sure what is going to happen and probably feeling a little foolish. He looks all around. Nobody there, just as he feared. Then he spots a small cloud of dust on the horizon, quickly coming closer.

A cart? A cart! "Lord, is this it?"

"Start running, Philip."

So he does. . . . The Finance Minister of Ethiopia has identified himself with the Jewish religion, although we cannot be sure to what extent. He may have been a Jewish proselyte. In any case, he has fulfilled a lifelong ambition by worshiping and offering sacrifices at the temple in Jerusalem. It has been wonderful.

Still, he finds himself left with questions that nobody has adequately answered, questions that still bother him. The trip home seems a good time to work on those questions: no cell phone, no secretaries, no meetings. He pulls out the precious scroll he's bought in Jerusalem, unrolls it, and looks again at that mysterious saying: "Like a lamb that is led to the slaughter . . ." (Isaiah 53:7). He's seen lambs led to the slaughter in the temple. It was a poignant sight. But here is a man who is to be sacrificed as a sacrificial lamb. Who can this be?

Deep in thought, he suddenly is aware of a face alongside the cart. He wonders, "Who is this guy and where has he sprung from?"

The stranger asks, "Do you understand what you are reading?"

How long has he been there? Has he heard him reading the words of the prophet? He must have done. The Ethiopian shrugs: "How can I unless someone helps me make sense of it? If I give you a ride, will you tell me what it means?" Philip nods. Before the Ethiopian can order the driver to slow down, Philip has already scrambled in.

Sometimes we have a sense that certain encounters take place by divine appointment. As the Ethiopian man unburdens himself to Philip— "Who is this man? Why does he die? Why does God hurt him this way? What has this to do with sin?"—Philip's mind is probably buzzing— "What if I hadn't come? What if I'd pretended not to hear? Lord, thank you, thank you so much."

Evangelizing the Ethiopian is too easy, not so much taking candy from a child, more like giving candy to a child. Or maybe it would be a more biblical metaphor to say that the labor is over by the time the midwife gets there; all she has to do is stand there and receive the baby.

Maybe the Ethiopian would have liked to return to Jerusalem after his conversion. There, after all, he could have sat at the apostles' feet and asked questions to his heart's content. What an opportunity for a new believer! Plenty of time to return home later. But no. He goes home, the first and (for a time at least) the only Christian in his whole nation. Philip the risk-taker, it seems, has delivered a spiritual child with the same spirit.

The risk of physical danger

Chapter 9 of Acts introduces us to another risk-taker. Ananias is a respectable, law-abiding citizen, a responsible member of the new church, everyone's favorite greeter on Sunday mornings. He is still enjoying the honeymoon of his new relationship with God. Only one thunder cloud looms on the horizon—an evil man named Saul—but he is far away in Jerusalem and not exactly an immediate threat. Ananias remembers to pray for his brothers and sisters in Jerusalem.

Then God comes to Ananias, not as at first with a message of love or forgiveness, not even to warn Ananias of danger but rather inviting Ananias to walk directly into danger, to go looking for that thunder cloud. Imagine Ananias's reaction when God tells him Saul has become a follower of Jesus, and, what is more, that Ananias will be Paul's personal spiritual advisor.

So Ananias goes out, pretending not to hear his wife calling, "Honey? Where are you off to so late?" He leaves his house, closing the door thoughtfully behind him, knowing he might never open it again, and deliberately goes to pay a visit to the one man in the world who wants to kill him.

But as he approaches the street where Saul's staying, he wonders how to begin. "Excuse me, sir. May I have a word with you, Mr. Saul?" By the time he is knocking at the door of Judas's house, however, he knows what to say. In his best Sunday greeter's voice, the voice that makes everyone feel welcome, he begins, "Brother Saul." And Saul, who had had a vision of a man called Ananias, is relieved he has come.

The obedience of Ananias plants seeds that, down the road, will produce a flowering of evangelism all over the ancient world. Ananias is never heard of again in the New Testament. But it is right that he should be honored in its pages as the greeter who went out of his way to welcome the man who wanted to kill him. Too bad there aren't any churches dedicated to St. Ananias the Risk-Taker.

Later, as a group of Jesus' followers are meeting in Jerusalem, this same Paul comes knocking at their door, claiming to have become a Christian (Acts 9:26-28). Is he for real? They are scared, and understandably so. But one man, Barnabas, goes out to talk with Paul.

He listens patiently, occasionally asking a question for clarification, nodding and smiling. Does he really believe Paul's story? We don't know for certain. But he seems to prefer the possibility of being taken in by Paul to that of turning away a genuine new believer. So he takes a risk. Then he returns to the house. With his arm around Paul's shoulder, he cajoles the Christians into letting them in to listen to his story. It's a tense moment.

Could Barnabas be wrong? Maybe it is a clever trap, and they will all get killed. God isn't telling. But if Barnabas is right, the church will receive its most dynamic and passionate apostle ever. Perhaps. Barnabas gambles—and wins.

The risk of breaking the rules

One day, Peter goes to the roof of a house at lunchtime to pray (Acts 10:9). There he has a strange vision. A huge sheet is being let down from heaven, and in the sheet is a whole zoo-full of exotic animals.

A voice tells Peter, "Kill and eat!" But the animals are the kind considered "unclean" in Jewish law, so Peter protests: "Lord, you must be joking. You know my wife runs a kosher kitchen. How could I touch that stuff?"

But the voice is persistent and encourages Peter to eat, saying, "What God has made clean, you must not call profane" (10:15). Then he wakes up. What a weird dream! There is a sound of talking down by the front gate. Someone is asking for him. Uh-oh. Is it possible that the dream has something to do with these visitors? You've got it, says the Spirit. There are three men looking for you, and I want you to go with them. Just do it, Peter. I've brought them here.

Peter discovers that the three are Gentiles. For some reason, Peter isn't surprised. Taking six fellow-believers from Joppa, presumably for moral support, he goes with the visitors. Sure enough, when they reach their destination, it is the home of a Gentile by the name of Cornelius. A good man, certainly, a man who worships the God of the Jews, but, all the same, a Gentile and a Roman soldier.

There is still enough of Peter's safe religious upbringing to make him feel horribly uncomfortable in the home of Cornelius. Nevertheless, he does what he has come to do. In spite of feeling uptight and alien, he tells the story of Jesus. And to everyone's amazement, the Spirit falls on the eager listeners in Cornelius's house—according to Peter later, just as the Spirit had come on the first disciples on the day of Pentecost.

What should he do next? Only one thing is appropriate: he should baptize them. He is still careful, however, asking, "Does anyone know any just cause or impediment why these people should not be baptized?"

Yes, it does sound like a wedding service. And just as in a wedding, you always hold your breath for a second, just in case someone does object. For Peter, it is a more real possibility than at most weddings. After all, what he is about to do will shock most of the Jerusalem Christians. Should he do it? How can he not? Nobody protests, not out loud at least, and so he goes ahead and does it.

The day of reckoning comes on his return to Jerusalem in the next chapter: What on earth have you done? Is it true that you visited in the home of Gentiles, and even had meals with them? Now, I am sure, he is glad he had that vision three times as he recounts it "step by step" (Acts 11:4ff).

For the time being at least, the opposition is silenced. The only voices to be heard are those praising God for this exciting new development. And Peter is a different man, with a bigger understanding of who God is, and of what it means to follow Jesus. As Brian McLaren comments, an "evangelistic encounter always has the potential to transform the evangelizer as well as the evangelized." [2]

Without this bold policy move, the church would have stayed safe, but probably died after a few years, absorbed back into mainstream Judaism. Because of this step, however—although it spelled danger—the Christian community was free to move beyond its ethnic and religious roots, and to adapt to every new culture it came into contact with.

But Peter and James could only delay the tide of fear, not turn it back. For the circumcision party (as they came to be called) are always alive and well. Indeed, I suspect they are embryonic in the heart of every sinful human being, not least in those of us within the church. We speak on their behalf every time we argue against opening the doors of the church to let the world in, every time we refuse to see the evidence of God's activity before our eyes, every time we say no to the risk the Holy Spirit offers us.

Risk and evangelism

The fact seems to be quite simply that the kingdom of God does not progress unless Jesus' people are prepared to take risks. This is true in everything that concerns the kingdom; not least is it true in the realm of evangelism.

I know in my own life that growing in evangelism has inescapably meant taking risks. Let me tell you about the time when this question of risk first confronted me head-on. I had been on staff with Inter-Varsity Christian Fellowship for eighteen years, mainly doing Bible teaching, pastoral work, and leadership training with student groups. Near the end of that time, however, I felt a deadness and boredom creeping in. I tried to shake it off, but nothing helped.

Then I read M. Scott Peck's *The Road Less Traveled*. What struck me was Peck's thesis that we grow only through change, that change means leaving behind what is familiar and comfortable . . . and that it is risky. I knew that was speaking to me. I was doing my job well enough, but the heart had gone out of it. I was not changing, not growing, taking no risks. There was no urgency to my praying. I almost felt I could have done my job as well if God had not existed. Something had to change.

For reasons I am not sure of even now, I decided I would deliver a series of lectures entitled "Ten Myths about Christianity," and I would do this in a "high traffic area" of the university where I did most of my work. The Baker Lounge was located between the students' union on one side and the student pub on the other, with the main information desk near by, and the faculty club in front of me. Hundreds of students walked through every lunchtime. It did not feel to me like a safe place to give a Christian talk! With one or two students' help, we booked the space, set out publicity, arranged two rows of chairs, and I did it.

Not many people stopped to listen. I don't know of anyone who became a Christian. Not many Christian students took an interest. But for me it was liberation. Fresh life began to seep into my Christian life, into my relationship with God, and into my ministry in general. Maybe God was telling me something.

The following year, a high school group I was working with were discussing what they could do as a major outreach event in the school. I ran over some things I had seen other groups do. I ended by saying, "Or you could do a debate." As soon as those words were out of my mouth, I knew what was going to happen. They loved the idea. I could even suggest an atheistic speaker who would enthusiastically argue the non-existence of God. But what about a Christian speaker? They discussed for a few minutes, but I knew what I had to say. I could almost feel the Holy Spirit breathing down my neck, saying, "Well . . ?" Finally, I surrendered. "I suppose maybe I could do that." That settled it.

More than five hundred students attended the debate. I looked and felt more confident than I really was. I wouldn't say I won (and I'm sure my opponent wouldn't say it either), but I was aware that none of the Christians felt I had disgraced them. That was good enough for me. With some trembling, I said, "Okay, Lord, what's the next risk?"

What happened next was not immediately relevant to evangelism. It concerned my role as supervisor of the staff in the local area. One of the staff, the one I had spent more time with than any other staff member, burned out. I felt very responsible and guilty and offered IVCF my resignation, which was graciously refused.

I was pretty sure God was telling me that the managerial role was not for me in the long term. Maybe it was time to leave Inter-Varsity. After so many years, that would certainly be a risk. Or maybe there was another role within IVCF that I could fulfill. There were two things people told me I could do particularly well: one was to teach the Bible to Christians, the other (from my experience with the "Ten Myths" and the debate) was to explain the gospel to those with no church background, but I couldn't do both. I had to choose.

Maybe because of my positive experience with risk-taking up to that point, I chose the latter. My supervisor said, "We may not know for five years whether this will work or not." I was grateful that he had the faith to wait that long! However, I was invited to speak at two evangelistic missions in different universities the following year, four the year after, and six the year after that. The risk was bearing fruit.

Your risk in evangelism may not be like any of the above. Yet there will undoubtedly be risks and, if we are taking risks in following Jesus in general, some of those risks will involve evangelism because Jesus longs for people to come to faith.

I have found it a useful test to ask, "Where is my Jerusalem? Where do I feel comfortable and useful and unthreatened?" For me, it was my job, the ministry I had carved out over many years. Not that there is anything wrong with Jerusalem, but Jesus is unlikely to be satisfied with that.

Where is my Samaria? Who are the people who in my book are not quite kosher? They probably strike me as being okay in some ways, but in others I just don't feel comfortable around them. Sometimes these are people of other races; as Christians, we often feel that way about other denominations.

Finally, who are my Gentiles? Who are those people with whom I feel I have nothing in common, around whom I would probably feel thoroughly uncomfortable? Their lifestyle is very alien to me. I can't ever imagine being friends with people like that. I can't imagine what common ground we might have.

Then I find myself asking: Who is my circumcision party? What are the voices, either internal or external, that say: Don't do it. I've never done that before. I'm not comfortable with that. They're too different from me. It's too scary.

The Acts of the Apostles continues to be written today. The Acts of Jesus have not stopped. He continues to press us into new areas of discomfort and growth and influence for the kingdom. We might as well give in graciously. And, as I discovered, there is one other additional resource to make those risks more manageable.

Risk management and the Spirit of evangelism

One thing I couldn't help noticing as I thumbed through the book of Acts was the powerful presence of an invisible actor with very few lines: the Holy Spirit. Some have even called this book The Acts of the Holy Spirit, so clearly does the shadow of the Spirit brood over every page. Not least, the Spirit's influence seems to hover over all evangelistic activity in the book.

I noticed, too, what was at first a strange description of what the Spirit does in people's lives: the Spirit fills people. Of course, in our day, the term has also taken on a specific meaning within the Christian community. To be "filled with the Spirit" refers to a particular (usually) dramatic experience, often accompanied with supernatural phenomena such as speaking in tongues. Is that what Luke was referring to in Acts?

When I tried to think about the language of "filling" apart from the charismatic movement, that also seemed strange because it suggested an unfamiliar image of what a human being is: an empty cup or pail waiting to be filled. I was not used to thinking of people that way.

Luke makes it clear, however, what he means by the term. In other places in Acts, he describes people as filled with such things as jealousy (Acts 5:17), joy (13:52), or rage (19:28). What is the common thread here? The word *filled* seems to mean to be given over to something or to be under its control. Imagine, for instance, those people filled with rage: their thoughts and words and actions are all given over to that one emotion. Their whole being is controlled by their anger.

Presumably, then, by talking about being "filled with the Spirit," Luke is talking about how someone comes to be completely given over to the work of Jesus, whether they are doing works of compassion or speaking words of the gospel. Clearly in his mind, evangelism and being filled with the Spirit are inseparable. So how do we get to be filled?

Children's sermons are always the most memorable. I remember a sermon about the fullness of the Spirit that I have never forgotten, because it was for children. Well, sort of.

Andrew, the assistant pastor, placed on a table in the middle of the church a pitcher of water and several cups of different sizes. First he picked up the smallest cup, and poured water into it till it was full. The children watched with bated breath to see if it would overflow. The preacher knew what he was about, and to their delight it did.

Then he said something like this: This tiny cup is ourselves when we first realize that Christianity means giving as much as we know of ourselves to as much as we know of Christ. At first, we may not know much about Jesus; we may not know a lot about ourselves either, but that's okay. Jesus fills as much as we offer with his Spirit.

Then, said Andrew, we grow. Often, in the school of Jesus, we discover areas of life where we have not been living as Christians—maybe we don't always tell the truth, or maybe there are people at our school we are not very kind to. He probably gave some adult examples, too: our business practices or our sexual morality, maybe religious hypocrisy or buried resentments.

We discover, in a word, that our cup has become bigger, and that we are no longer full. At this point, Andrew poured the contents of cup one into the next size up. Sure enough, it wasn't enough to fill it.

As soon as we hand over those other areas of our lives to Jesus to learn his way in those areas, Andrew went on, the Spirit flows into those places and our lives are full again. He picked up the pitcher, and filled cup number two to the top—and a little bit more. The children giggled appreciatively.

But Andrew also wanted to make a point about evangelism. He went on. Maybe as we learn more about God, we learn that God wants to reach out in love to others, and to make us partners in the family business. We're not sure we want to do that.

What's happening? Once again, the cup of our lives is bigger, and we find ourselves no longer full. Then—you guessed it—Andrew poured the second cup into a third, larger again. When we yield that newly discovered part of our lives to Jesus, he went on, and are willing to try to learn from Jesus how to reach out to others, then he fills us again. Once more the pitcher filled up the half-empty cup.

To be honest, I forget how often the pitcher topped up a half-empty cup. It hardly matters. I expect that all throughout my life God will draw attention to those areas of my life that are not given over to God. God will continually invite me to set aside my own priorities and pursue the Spirit's priorities instead.

Filled with the Spirit as a way of life

My study of Luke and Acts had made it clear that being filled with the Spirit was not always an overwhelming experience, as it was on the Day of Pentecost. It could equally be a way of life: a thumbnail description of Barnabas's character (11:24) includes the statement that he is "filled with the Spirit," as if this is the case most or all of the time. Is this a sudden and dramatic "filling" or a daily and consistent "filling"? Luke seems to affirm both.

Then I thought of times how I approach my preparation for an evangelistic talk. I pray as I begin my preparation, I pray if (or when) I get stuck in preparing the talk, I pray over the crucial parts. I pray for the help of the Spirit, for my choice of Scriptures and illustrations, for an introduction that grabs people's attention, for an ending that encourages people to think more about Jesus but does not pressure them. I pray, often with some of the other leaders, before I give the talk. And when I speak, I am aware that my thoughts, my words, and even my body language have been concentrated on helping people understand the Christian message.

Or I think of times when, over the lunch table or over coffee, conversation has turned to questions of belief and Christianity in particular, and again, everything in me is bent on making things clear and helpful and persuasive.

That sounds suspiciously like the times in Acts when it is recorded that so-and-so was filled with the Spirit. I may not always have been aware of it, just as I am not always aware that there is gas powering my car, but the power of the Spirit was there just the same. I could not have done what I did otherwise; indeed, I really wouldn't have wanted to.

I don't say this with any sense of boasting. I only describe it because I suspect many Christians have had this experience at one time or another. Times when our whole being was deliberately given over to serving Jesus in word or deed. Times when we may not even have been thinking about the Holy Spirit, and yet on reflection, without the Spirit how would we ever have done what we did?

This is not to say that we do not have to think about being filled with the Spirit, or to ask daily to be filled with the Spirit. Of course we do. That regular commitment creates an attitude of openness in us so that, when we need the Spirit, or rather the Spirit needs us, we are available.

If we set ourselves daily to be available to the Spirit, there will also be times when we are aware of what I can only call special nudges. I remember once traveling on the train from Ottawa to Toronto, and deliberately ignoring the businessman in the seat beside me because I was so engrossed in what I was writing (and yes, I confess it, I was writing something about evangelism). I had probably prayed that morning to be open to the Spirit, but had changed my mind by the time I got on the train.

On the return journey that evening, however, as I was lining up for the train, I had the impression that the Spirit was saying over my shoulder, "So, what about this time?" And I felt I had no choice but to answer (with some reluctance: I like my privacy), "Yes, you are right, I am your servant, your student. Whatever you want is okay."

I sat down in the first free seat I came to. (It's much easier to take the risk with the Spirit's help.) As I settled down, I glanced apprehensively at the book my neighbor was reading. It was *A Beginner's Guide to Buddhism*. I sighed. However, we then talked for four hours, about God, Jesus, Buddhism, faith, his Christian friends, how God communicates with us. I even told him my story of how I came to be talking to him. I have a feeling the Spirit of Jesus was there, smiling at me.

10.

What Is the Gospel?

The old lady . . . hesitated, fumbling with her umbrella; then, taking sudden courage, she took a step toward Richardson, and went on, "You'll excuse me, sir, I know it's old-fashioned, and you quite a stranger, but—are you saved?"

Richardson answered her as seriously as she had spoken, "I believe salvation is for all who will have it," he said, "and I will have it by the only possible means."

"Ah, that's good, that's good," the old gentleman said. "Bless God for it, young man."

"I know you'll pardon me, sir, " the old lady added, "you being a stranger as I said, and strangers often not liking to talk about it. Though what else is there to talk about?"

"What indeed?" Richardson agreed.

Charles Williams, *The Place of the Lion* [1]

A WORD KEPT RECURRING as I read and reread the New Testament: the word *gospel*. I did a quick count: there were at least 75 uses altogether. I realized that if I wanted a fresh view of evangelism, I would need to do some work on the word *gospel*. After all, it's no good saying, "Evangelism is sharing the gospel," unless we know what the gospel is.

A simple gospel?

Where to begin? Some would say that's easy. The gospel is John 3:16— "For God so loved the world that he gave his only Son, so that everyone who believes in him may not perish but have eternal life."

Well, it's a wonderful verse. But it seemed to me that it's not that easy. For one thing, there seems to be no indication that John himself ever thought this statement was more important than anything else in his Gospel. Nor does he give any clue that John 3:16 was the gospel any more than twenty other verses in his writing.

Others would say, "The place to start is obviously where New Testament writers themselves actually claim to be stating the gospel." And in fact there are a couple of those. For example, Paul writes to the Corinthians:

> I would remind you . . . of the good news that I proclaimed to you . . . that Christ died for our sins in accordance with the scriptures, and that he was buried, and that he was raised on the third day in accordance with the scriptures. (1 Corinthians 15:1-4)

Paul points to Christ's death for sins and his resurrection as the heart of the gospel. Then, writing to the Romans, he begins with this greeting:

> Paul . . . set apart for the gospel of God . . . the gospel concerning his son, who was descended from David according to the flesh, and was declared to be son of God with power according to the spirit of holiness by resurrection from the dead, Jesus Christ our Lord. (Romans 1:1-6)

Again, a statement of "the gospel": the gospel is about Jesus, who is a descendant of David and yet Son of God.

So far, so good. But, of course, those two statements are very different from one another. It is true that both focus on Christ, and both mention his resurrection. But one stresses forgiveness of sins while the other foregrounds Jesus' royal descent. The first says twice that Christ's work was "according to the Scriptures," so is it an essential ingredient of the message to say that Jesus fulfilled Scripture? On the other hand, the second talks about him being descended from King David: is that indispensable to the gospel? If we then throw John 3:16 into the mix, other elements get added that are not mentioned in the other two statements: God's love, believing, eternal life and so on. You see the problem. It is obviously important to know what the gospel is, but how to find out exactly what it is?

One of the nice things about teaching in a seminary is that there are experts around to give advice on any branch of theology. I decided to ask Terry Donaldson, who teaches New Testament at Wycliffe College, what I should read on this, and he pointed me in the direction of a writer named James Dunn. I headed off to the library.

Dunn, I discovered, says the reason we have a problem pinning down the gospel is that every time the message is spoken in the New Testament, it's spoken to different groups, in different situations, and not least in different cultures. So of course it's going to be different, and of course you're not to going to find just one form of the message:

> One can sometimes say in a particular situation, in response to a particular challenge: This is the gospel, there is no other. . . . But if the New Testament is any guide, one can never say: This particular formulation is the gospel for all time and for every situation.[2]

John Stott illustrates this, listing seven different New Testament explanations of the gospel. Each is presumably more helpful than another for a particular audience. Thus the gospel is:

Sacrificial—the shedding and sprinkling of Christ's blood.

Messianic—the breaking in of the age of God's promised rule.

Mystic—the receiving and enjoying "eternal life," being "in Christ."

Legal—the righteous judge pronouncing the unrighteous forgiven.

Personal—the Father reconciling his wayward children.

Salvific—the heavenly liberator coming to the rescue of his oppressed people and leading them out into a new exodus.

Cosmic—the universal Lord claiming universal dominion over the powers.[3]

So is there a center, a form of words of which we can say, "Aha! This is it, the gospel"? It was beginning to look as though the answer was no. Yet even Dunn, having argued so strongly for flexibility, still insists that there is nonetheless a basic outline of the gospel. He isolates three main emphases: the gospel is about Jesus, the gospel always invites a response, and the gospel brings benefits. [4]

1. The gospel is about Jesus. It is true, says Dunn, that there are different ways of thinking about Jesus and of describing Jesus:

- Paul emphasizes that Jesus is the resurrected and reigning Lord.
- John emphasizes the majesty and authority of Jesus as he walked this earth.
- Peter emphasizes that Jesus fulfilled Old Testament prophecies about the Messiah.

But one way or another, all talk of "the gospel" centers on Jesus, his life, death, resurrection, ascension and coming again. Three times, Luke says that the apostles "preached Jesus" (Acts 5:42; 8:35; 28:31) when he might just as well have said they "preached the gospel." In a sense, there's no difference. That's the heart of the matter. Frankly, if there is no Jesus, there is no good news.

My friend Harold Percy tells the story of a pastor who said to him, "We don't like to talk much about Jesus in our church. We find it a bit embarrassing." To which Harold promptly replied, "If you go to the hardware store and ask for a wrench, do you expect them to be embarrassed to talk about wrenches?" Another minister said, "But at seminary I was taught not to talk about Jesus." Yet if we can't talk about Jesus, what on earth does it mean to be a Christian community, as opposed to some other kind of religious community?

2. The gospel always invites a response. There are two words that focus the response the gospel calls for: repentance and faith. Repentance, unfortunately, can sound heavy and gloomy: "Repent: the end of the world is at hand" sort of thing. In fact, the word *repent* simply means "change your mind" or "turn around."

Repentance means turning away from other paths and turning toward Jesus, and so it's actually a very liberating thing (which is not to say it's an easy thing. C. S. Lewis says, "Repentance is no fun at all"[5]). We get to turn away from things that would destroy us, and experience God's new life instead. That's good news right there! Repentance, it would seem, is actually a great gift of God in itself.

Faith, for many people, is a weird quality that only religious folk have and that normal people don't. Because the word *faith* so often is misunderstood, I often prefer to use the word *trust* instead. A child putting his hand in his mother's hand to cross the road is exercising faith: he trusts her. That's the kind of faith God invites us to: to put our hand in the hand of Jesus.

3. The gospel brings benefits. Every time someone in the New Testament explains the gospel, they inevitably talk about the benefits of faith, and how Christ meets the deepest human needs. Typically they talk about the forgiveness of sins and the gift of the Holy Spirit: the past is pardoned, and we are empowered to face the future. But there are also gifts such as the gift of joining God's family, the gift of reconciliation with God, or the gift of new life. One way or another, say the writers, if you trust Christ, blessing will follow.

This summary was helpful to me: the good news is about Jesus, who brings the blessings of God, but we have to repent and believe—in other words, we have to say yes to him. Dunn's outline does not tell me in detail what the gospel is, because that will change with circumstances. Still, it does give me a simple template to work with. It combines form and flexibility.

Still, as I thought about it, it seemed like there was an element missing from this outline. After all, surely all of these three points assume human need? Jesus comes, not just for a friendly visit, but because human beings are in need. The reason Jesus asks for repentance and faith, a drastic change of mind and heart, is because we have a need to change direction. And even Dunn's discussion of the blessings of the gospel assumes that we need those blessings. The shorthand for what seems to be missing is the word *sin*—not *sins* (plural) in the first place, but *sin* (singular).

What's the difference? Sin is the state of not acknowledging God. Sin is thinking our lives belong to us, to live as we see fit, thinking that the world is our own to make use of in whatever way we like. Sin is the state of a world that organizes itself as though God were irrelevant. Sins, on the other hand, specific acts of breaking God's laws, are merely the symptom of which sin is the disease.

Of course, there are other effects of sin in our world, including brokenness, sickness, and death. Not that there is necessarily a direct cause and effect link, say, between sin and sickness. Jesus addressed that issue very specifically (John 9:1-3). Nevertheless, the reason we suffer these things is because this is a world where sin exists. It's like living in a world where pollution is running rampant. Those who suffer the worst consequences of pollution are not normally those who cause the most pollution. Yet the reason they suffer is still the pollution.

It seems to me that the idea of sin, with all its different expressions and all its varied consequences, needs to precede Dunn's three points—Jesus, repentance and faith, the blessings of the gospel—in order to explain why they are necessary in the first place.

But even with this four-point summary, I was not entirely satisfied. Something else Terry said in an e-mail kept me thinking:

> One more recent development that should be mentioned is the idea of the gospel as a "story." Since it is of the nature of a story that the same story can be narrated in different ways, the diversity in the New Testament versions of the "gospel" may be less of a problem if we conceive of the gospel as a narrative rather than, say, a set of doctrines.

As I thought about this, I realized he was right. Any summary of the gospel, no matter how succinct, is not the same as a story. It may be a useful summary of the story, but it's not the whole of it.[6] After all, when Jesus comes to be the heart of the gospel, his coming is the climax of a story that has been going on for centuries. If we miss the big picture of Jesus' coming—the mountain of which this is the peak—I think we sell Jesus and the gospel short, and as a result we sell people short.

The wider context of a three-point or four-point gospel is, in a sense, the whole story of the Bible, from beginning to end. In the Introduction I mentioned N. T. Wright's suggestion that we think of the Bible as being like an unfinished Shakespeare play.[7] I decided to try playing with this image, and described the acts of the play like this:

> In Act 1, God creates a beautiful world with intricacy, diversity, vitality, and love. It is fresh and alive. At the heart of the world are human beings, male and female, made to reflect like a mirror image the character of the Artist who made them, with love and creativity. They live in a dance of perfect harmony with the Creator and with one another, and with their environment.
>
> In Act 2, however, things go horribly wrong. Human beings try to play God. They behave as though they're the center of the universe. They treat

the world as though they were the landlord, although they're only the tenants. They step out of God's cosmic dance and get out of step with one another and with the environment—and, most importantly, they get out of step with God. Instead of love binding the world together, now the loudest voices are those of self-centeredness and anger.

At this point, a lot of artists would simply give up on their work of art and start over. Fortunately for us, God is more patient than some! Instead of trashing this world, God decides to restore his work of art to its original glory and—what's even better—God invites human beings to become apprentices in this restoration project.

In Act 3 God starts with one couple, Abraham and Sarah, telling them that through their descendants "I will make you a great nation . . . and in you all the families of the earth shall be blessed" (Genesis 12:1-3). The story of this nation, Israel, is told in the Old Testament.

In Act 4, God's restoration project reaches a crucial stage. God takes center stage in the drama of human life. It's as if Shakespeare should write himself into the play *Hamlet* and become one of the characters in his own creation.[8] That way we can see what God is like in a way we can relate to, and we can learn what God's dreams are for us and for the world. This character in the play we call by the name Jesus.

Jesus dies for our sins, conquering all the powers that have ranged themselves against the authority of God,[9] and is raised to life again on the third day. He returns to heaven and takes the place of highest honor.

Act 5 is different in that it has not yet been written. Rather, it is being written, in our time, by the choices we make, by our every action and our every word. Our job as human beings is to play our part, whatever it may be, in the great story, faithful to what we know of the beginning and the end of the story, but with individuality and creativity, with courage and with flair.

And there is Act 6. The Bible doesn't tell us a lot, but it does give tantalizing glimpses of the end of the story when Jesus will return, and the earth will be restored to its original beauty and then some. "It's the redemption of the world, the stars, the animals, the plants, the whole show."[10] God will then give to each what their hearts have most deeply desired, whether that is to know God face to face, or to avoid the reality of God.

This is the final act—although, as C. S. Lewis says at the end of the Narnia stories, this is "only the beginning of the real story . . . the beginning of Chapter One of the Great Story which no-one on earth has read." [11]

This telling of the story, the big canvas on which Jesus is the central character, puts any summary of the gospel in a broader perspective. Jesus does not appear like a fairy godmother out of the blue to grant our deepest wishes if we will trust him. His coming and his gospel are the climax of what God has been about all through history, in every age and every culture.

The good news is not that God meets our needs, even the genuine spiritual needs for forgiveness of sins and the Holy Spirit. The good news is not simply that God rescues individuals from hell and gets them into heaven. [12] That's far too narrow and self-centered a view to count as "the gospel." The gospel is far bigger than that.

The good news is that God has not given up on us and this world. God is determined to make a brand new world out of the mess we have made of the old one. In a sense, the gospel message is the whole Bible because this is its major theme: from beginning to end, God acting in our world for redemption. The narrative climaxes in the story of Jesus, his life, death, resurrection, and ascension for us—of course—but that's what it is, the climax, not the whole.

This understanding means that repentance is not some arbitrary and unpleasant process God dreamed up to make us miserable. It is the invitation to throw our lot in with the Grand Story of the universe, and to give up on anything less. If the gospel is this big, it also means that "faith" is not a peculiar religious quality. It is deliberately steering our canoe into the current of God's river.

Terry's clue about the narrative nature of the gospel had made me think about "the big picture." In turn, that pushed me to look back at the New Testament in a fresh way. Maybe there were other places where "the gospel" was being explained but I had never thought of them that way before. I turned to a passage I often read to my class at the start of a new term. Suddenly it took on new meaning. I like how Eugene Peterson has rendered it in *The Message*:

We look at this Son and see the God who cannot be seen. We look at this Son and see God's original purpose in everything created. For everything, absolutely everything, above and below, visible and invisible, rank after rank after rank of angels—everything got started in him and finds its purpose in him. He was there before any of it came into existence and holds it together right up to this moment. And when it comes to the church, he organizes and holds it together like a head does a body.

He was supreme in the beginning, and—leading the resurrection parade— he is supreme in the end. From beginning to end he's there, towering far above everything, everyone. So spacious is he, so roomy, that everything of God finds its proper place in him without crowding. Not only that, but all the broken and dislocated pieces of the universe—people and things, animals and atoms—get properly fixed and fit together in vibrant harmonies, all because of his death, his blood poured down from the Cross. You yourselves are a case study of what he does. (Colossians 1:15-20)

I had never thought of this as a passage that explains the gospel before. But there's Dunn's focus on Jesus, unmistakably: "from beginning to end he's there." There are the consequences of sin and the blessings of trusting Christ: "all the broken and dislocated pieces of the universe . . . get properly fixed and fit together." And the response is implied in the fact that the Colossians are a "case study of what he does."

The Gospel is not just John 3:16. At least, it is John 3:16—when that verse is set against the backdrop of the whole story. And that makes it a big Gospel, much bigger than "me and Jesus in heaven." It's about God's great purpose for the world. It's about you and me being invited to be a part of what God is doing in the world, to play our part in the ongoing drama.

As I thought about this, and began to talk with students about this "big view" of Christian faith, a new image for Jesus came to my mind, not to replace the old ones, of course, but to provide a fresh starting point for those whom the old images no longer touch. I found myself putting it something like this:

Among all the Oscars, there is one they never give, and I think they should, and that's for casting director. So much depends on getting the right actors for the right parts. In the story God is writing about our world, it is as though Jesus is the casting director. And whenever anyone comes and says to him, I'd really like to be a part of God's story, Jesus smiles and says,

"You're welcome. I have just the part for you. It will stretch you. There will be adventures you could never have imagined. Sometimes it will be hard, but it will bring you joy. And it will be the right part for you, the part for which I made you in the beginning." [13]

What is the gospel for you?

I have learned over the years that I am more of a teacher than an evangelist, even though a big chunk of my ministry has focused on evangelistic speaking. One thing that teachers know is that you have to teach students at their own level. You don't give high school material to kids in kindergarten; you don't send undergraduates to take courses at a Ph.D. level. More than that, students will respond to new material out of their own experience. A child from a home full of books will probably respond more readily to the idea of reading in class than a child who knows only TV. And so on.

My experience with evangelism has been that people's first response to the Christian message is often not at the point I would expect. What they notice and are drawn to is a reflection of what they understand about God already, or of what has happened in their own lives to that point. In theological terms, their response may be at kindergarten level, but, frankly, who cares? It's a beginning, and that's what's important.

I think of a wonderful woman who was my secretary for some years. Her father had died in World War II while her mother was pregnant. So Phyllis Ann was born and grew up without a father. Then, as a child at a Christian camp, she heard that God could be a Father to her! That for her was the best good news there could ever be.

Or take Peter, a student at Bishop's University in Quebec, who told me how, as a first-year music student, he had been studying the music of John Cage, which reflects the view that the universe is random. As Peter studied, he realized that he simply could not believe that the universe operated only by chance. Yet if it was not chance, then that might suggest the existence of a rational mind behind the universe. Eventually that line of thought led him to believe in God and in Jesus Christ.

Now reverse these discoveries. What happens when you say to Peter: "Do you realize that you can address God as your father?"

"Well," he replies, "that's important, of course, and I'm grateful for it, but I can't honestly say it's the most wonderful thing I've discovered."

You see, it doesn't excite him in the way discovering the Maker of an orderly universe did.

"And Phyllis Ann, do you realize that the God you relate to is also the Creator of the universe?"

"Well yes, sure," she replies. "It's great, but, to be honest, for me it's not very personal. But the fact that this Creator is also my daddy. Now that is incredible!"

What's happening here? Is the gospel different for these two people? In one sense, of course not. There is only one God, only one Christ. Whether we prefer John 3:16 or Colossians 1, the good news about this God, this Christ, is for all people equally. Yet the way these two people were drawn to that gospel is certainly different. Each person was drawn by a different facet of the good news. Someone else may be drawn by the reality that Jesus has conquered death. For another person, the good news is that God is the healer who can put together broken and fragmented lives. For a third person, the good news is that Jesus is the missing key to understanding truth. . . . And so the stories go on.[14]

I suspect that if we could have conducted some personal interviews with the first Christians, and asked them, "How has Jesus been good news in your life?" their answers would have been equally diverse:

What if you could have asked Peter: "What is good news about Jesus for you personally?" I imagine his eyes would fill with tears and he might say, "The Lord forgave even my betrayal."

"And Thomas, what about you?" "No question: he was patient with my doubts, and convinced me that he had conquered death."

"Matthew?" "Jesus loved me when nobody else would, and gave me a new start."

"Mary of Bethany: what was good news about Jesus for you?" "I don't know if you will believe it, but he taught me as a disciple, even though I am a woman."

"What would you say, Bartimaeus?" "He noticed me, he called me, he gave me my sight, and he let me follow him."

"And Zacchaeus?" "He said that, in spite of all I'd ever done, I could still be a part of God's great plan for the world."

Each one has a different story. The goodness of God is so great, and God's delight in the individual so boundless, that Jesus is good news to people in unique ways.

It is true of course that the apostles preached what we might call the macro-gospel—Jesus as God's ultimate communication to humankind, his death for our sin and his triumph over death. But at the same time, individual believers undoubtedly talked about what I would call the micro-gospel, telling how the breaking in of God's kingdom had touched them personally and brought good news to their situations.

I suppose this is one reason I would like to ban the use of the word *evangelism*. In the early days of the Christian community, nobody said, "Hey, I really think we should do some evangelism. Where do we begin? What should we say? Could someone please get us some training?" Rather, those first disciples had something to say to people about what Jesus meant for them and had done for them. So Jesus came first, as the focus of an adaptable message, not a concern for evangelism. The message was real, personal, joyful, and contagious.

I sometimes wonder if we talk too much about evangelism and not enough about the message—the evangel—that is the good news. For Christians to talk about the gospel is a sign of health; to talk about evangelism is a sign that something is wrong. David Watson says something similar: "Having to stress the Great Commission, and having to urge people to witness, is not a sign of spiritual life, but a sign of spiritual decadence." [15]

If, like those first disciples, we had an authentic and personal message, I suspect many of our problems in evangelism would solve themselves. In fact, I have noticed several times recently that churches that are growing because people are finding faith there do not use the word *evangelism*. Jesus is real to them, so they talk about Jesus, not about evangelism. They no longer need the scaffolding: the building is up.

A personal gospel?

In that conversation with the woman at the well, one of the many startling things Jesus says is that "we worship what we know" (John 4:22). He makes a similar but even stronger statement in the previous chapter, during the discussion with Nicodemus: "Very truly, I tell you, we speak of what we know and testify to what we have seen" (John 3:11). There is an important secret of evangelism here: true evangelism has an authentic message. We must always speak what we know. A second-hand message in evangelism does not ring true.

May I ask a personal question? What is the gospel according to you? In other words, in what way has Jesus been good news in your life? How has the breaking in of God's kingdom to this world touched your life? Or, to put it less dramatically, what is it about God that keeps you hanging in as a Christian despite all the hassles? When so many are giving up on church as bad news, what is the good news about church that feeds your soul?

Whatever that kernel of good news is in your life, it is crucial to your ability to evangelize. You may not feel able to communicate the macro-gospel to anyone, but you can certainly say something about the micro-gospel. You do not need to be eloquent, you certainly don't need to be aggressive, and I promise you don't need to learn special sales techniques. All you need, at the heart of things, is a story—your story of why you think Jesus is good news.

You might not be sure right now how to answer that question. That's okay. If this is a new thought, it may take a few hours or a few days before it dawns on you. You could of course ask God what it is! I suspect you'll be delighted when you realize, and it will be a key to your involvement in evangelism.

Macro and micro together

I like to think of the macro-gospel as a circle: there is the sum total of God's communication of good news to the world throughout history and culminating in Jesus Christ, his life, death, resurrection and ascension. The micro-gospel is like arrows coming at that circle. People are drawn for different, often personal, reasons. These include:

* Victory over death
* Meaning in life
* Forgiveness
* Healing from brokenness
* Knowing the Creator

How the Gospel Impacts Us:

The Micro and the Macro

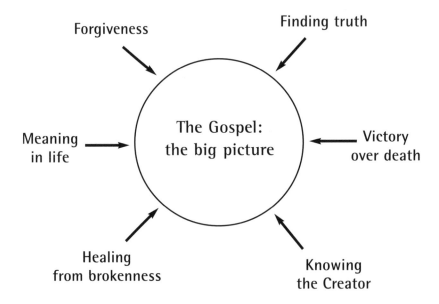

The macro-gospel alone can seem abstract, impersonal, and remote (God has a plan for the universe). The micro-gospel alone becomes narcissistic and individualistic (God exists to meet my needs). But the two together represent, I believe, the balance that exists in the Bible itself. We need both. More than that, we need to become comfortable with both.

Let me put it like this. One way to understand spiritual growth is to say that it means moving beyond the point at which I join the circle, to understanding the rest of the circle, the bigness of this plan of God into which I have been drawn. God is kind enough to meet us where we are, but, fortunately, God is kind enough not to leave us there. And those who are leaders in the church, in particular those who are pastors, teachers, and evangelists, will be the more effective the more they understand the bigness of the circle and how the macro-gospel speaks to "all sorts and conditions" of people.

At the same time, nobody, least of all church leaders, can afford to get so involved in thinking about the macro that they forget the micro. As my own understanding of the "big picture" gospel has evolved over the years, I am aware that my grasp of the micro-gospel has changed, too. (Asking people what is the gospel for them has at least served to help keep me honest!) So I am aware that, when faith first came alive for me when I was a teenager, there was a strong sense of discovering what the religion I had been brought up with was all about: that was good news. Later, I had an overwhelming experience of forgiveness of sins: the good news was now something new. Then there was the good news of risk and growth I talked about in chapter 9. But if you ask me what is the gospel for me today, I would have to say that it is the reality that God "makes all things new." I have known it in my marriage, in my work, in friendships, and in my experience of Christ.

I am reminded of the words of Aslan to Lucy in *Prince Caspian*. Lucy has returned to the magical land of Narnia after some time away, and once again meets Aslan the lion, the Christ figure:

"Aslan," said Lucy, "you're bigger."

"That is because you are older, little one," answered he.

"Not because you are?"

"I am not. But every year you grow, you will find me bigger." [16]

And that, too, is good news.

11.

Translating the Message

Translation it is that openeth the window, to let in the light; that breaketh the shell, that we may eat the kernell; that putteth aside the curtain, that we may look into the most holy place; that removeth the cover of the well, that we may come to the water.

Preface to the Reader, *King James Version* of the Bible (1611)

I REMEMBER DRIVING back from a week of outreach at Cornell University. I was reflecting on the week with James, a friend who had come with me. Among other things, we got to musing whether the gospel could ever be expressed in a way that was not limited by any culture. After some thought, we settled on "God loves you." Surely that's close to the heart of the gospel and also can communicate to almost anyone? But then we realized there were four problems with those three words.

1. For a start, the word *god* has a thousand meanings. I remember explaining to a neighbor that part of my job was helping students figure out what they believe about God. "Which god?" he asked. It was a very appropriate question.

2. Then there is that troublesome word *love*. It has multiple meanings. C. S. Lewis wrote a book called *The Four Loves*, so, when we say God loves, which one are we talking about?

3. And then there is the difficulty of *you*: Is that singular or plural? "You" as an existentialist would understand it? A New Age you? A socially constructed you? The "you" you are "on the inside"? Do "you" even exist?

"God loves you," far from being a "simple gospel," turns out in fact to be highly complex and requiring a great deal of definition. (The fourth problem, in case you are curious, was the fact that "God loves you" is English, which, though spoken around the world, is by no means universal.)

With this in mind, how does one communicate the Christian message? The answer, in a word, is translation. I decided this was an area where I needed to do some work. As I thought, and read, and discussed with people, I came to the conclusion that translation is on the one hand very difficult, even dangerous, and on the other hand, an opportunity— an opportunity for adventure, learning, and joy.

Learning from cross-cultural missionaries

After a lifetime of working as a cross-cultural missionary in India, Lesslie Newbigin returned "home" to Britain, only to discover that it was now an unfamiliar culture to him as a Christian just as much as India had been when he first went there. He drew the obvious lesson: that those who want to live and speak as Christians in the West today need to learn from the experience of overseas cross-cultural missionaries,[1] not least because they have had to learn this lesson of translation from language to language, culture to culture.

One of the most dramatic stories I have ever heard of cross-cultural translation is that of Don and Carol Richardson. In the early 1960s, they were Canadian missionaries to the Sawi people of Borneo. They tell their story in the book *Peace Child*. [2]

After making friends with the Sawi and learning their language, they arrived at the point where Don could tell the story of Jesus to the men (this was a patriarchal culture). The story didn't provoke much response until he told the part of the story where Judas betrays Jesus with a kiss. Then:

> About halfway through the description I noticed they were all listening intently. . . . At the climax of the story, Maum whistled a birdcall of admiration. Kani and several others touched their fingertips to their chests in awe. Still others chuckled. At first I sat there confused. Then the realization broke through. They were acclaiming Judas as the hero of the story.[3]

What the Richardsons did not know until that point was that, among the Sawi people, "treachery was idealized as a virtue, a goal of life."[4] Thus when he told them the story of Jesus, they were struck, not with the heroism of Jesus, but with the ingenuity of Judas, betraying his master with a kiss, and with the gullibility of Jesus. In fact, they used the phrase of Jesus, "tuwi asonai man," which means "to fatten with friendship for an unsuspected slaughter," like a wild pig that is tamed and well fed until the time for a feast arrives. The Richardsons had no idea where to go next. They only knew that "mere recitation of the gospel would not be enough." [5]

Shortly afterward, however, the Sawi went to war with a neighboring village. The Richardsons urged them to make peace, and even threatened to leave the village, taking their medical supplies and skills with them, if the war did not end. The leaders finally agreed. But how would the warring parties be able to trust one another? How could they ever know that the peace was not another effort at "tuwi asonai man"?

The Richardsons then witnessed the peace-making ritual. In a dramatic ceremony, the two villages exchanged newborn babies, each a "peace child" to the opposing side. These children were the guarantee of peace between the two communities. As long as the peace child lived, the peace was assured. If the peace child died, there would be trouble, and, of course, for someone deliberately to kill the peace child would be to launch the communities into another bloody war.

It dawned on the Richardsons that this event put into their hands a fresh way of explaining the gospel: an *anknupfungspunkt*, in fact. Don began once more to explain the story. God wants us to have peace with him, and God has given us his own son Jesus as a guarantee of his desire for peace, as the ultimate Peace Child. When the peace child came, however, we killed him. Yet God brought him back to life, and now he can never die, as the eternal pledge of God's love. Now the Sawi understood. Now Judas was seen no longer as the hero but as the villain of the story, because he had betrayed the peace child. The people began to put their trust in Jesus, God's peace child.

What the Richardsons were doing in explaining the gospel this way was exercising the ancient Christian art of translation, taking the words of Christian faith from one language and one culture and transposing them into another. You see, I think, why I say this task is one of adventure, learning and joy.

Translation central to Christian faith

I decided I wanted to know more about the art of translation since it seemed so crucial to evangelism. Dr. Grant LeMarquand, a friend who teaches mission, suggested I start by reading Lamin Sanneh, a Gambian now teaching at the Yale School of Mission. I did and found myself enthralled.

In *Translating the Message* [6] and other books, Sanneh argues that translation is absolutely central to Christian faith. Christianity thrives when people translate it into other cultures and languages, and withers away when its followers refuse to do so.[7]

Sanneh's thesis, however, is that Christianity is by its nature translatable, and that effective evangelists learn to translate both language and culture. When Christian faith is thus translated, Sanneh argues, it puts power into the hands of the recipients, and tends to take it away from those who brought it: "When one translates, it is like pulling the trigger of a loaded gun: the translator cannot recall the speeding bullet." [8]

As a result, he sees the African independence movements of the 1950s and 1960s and the overthrow of European colonial powers as the direct fruit of the people having the Bible in their own language. He believes it is significant that the most dramatic growth of the Christian church happened after the days of colonization. Across Africa, between 1964 and 1984, numbers of Christians grew from 60 million to 240 million.[9] Through the work of translation, Christianity had become for Africans an African religion.

This is powerful stuff. To be honest, my musings about why "God loves you" was not a universal statement seemed fairly frivolous by comparison. Translation is actually a demanding business with far-reaching effects.

Barriers are shattered

What might this mean for us, if indeed we are cross-cultural missionaries to a post-Christian West? What would a church look like that saw itself as a mission station rather than a maintainer of the status quo?

Recently, I received an e-mail message from Bert Hopkins, an old friend in Ottawa. He told me of a recent visit to the city by a group of young Christian people who ministered to schools and homes in his community. But the section of his message that particularly struck me was this:

> In expressing their message in the schools, the group used music and dance forms immediately understood by the students. Their success was shown by the spontaneous explosion of post-assembly conversations with the students all over the auditorium and on the stage.

It is widely understood that expressions of the gospel must appear in someone's culture—be it Bach chorales, American gospel music, Scottish
metrical psalms, Gregorian chant or country and western music. Whereas
most Anglo-Saxon Christians (me!) would regard hip-hop, rap and break
dancing as utterly alien to Christianity, this group showed me how it can
be converted into a tool to reach out.

Hip-hop and rap are African-American cultural forms. There was a time
when they did not exist; there will come a time when they won't exist—
but that is also true of my culture of Anglican psalm chants. These kids
jerked me out of my provinciality.

This accounts for the group's amazing capacity to engage a modern culture
by doing it better than the secularists. When Ray Perkins (one of the
group) dances, gravity momentarily ceases and the barrier between him
and the unchurched is shattered.

There it is again: missionaries doing amazing things to communicate
the timeless message of Jesus in ways that are totally in sync with the culture, such that "barriers are shattered." Only this time the culture is
contemporary Western culture.

Not that these young people are deliberately imitating missionaries, of
course. They would probably be very surprised at such an idea. Nor, from
their point of view, are they translating. They are speaking their own language, not a second language. Rather than imitating missionaries, they are
actually imitators of the one who came and identified with our culture in
order that we could hear and see the message of good news: ". . . though
he was rich, yet for our sake he became poor, that by his poverty we might
become rich" (1 Corinthians 8:9).

The meaning of the cross

Let me tell you of an example, an issue I struggle with in translation,
a place where I try to take a missionary's risks, and undoubtedly get it
wrong sometimes: explaining the cross of Christ. I am often reminded
when I am speaking on a university campus of Paul's words about his first
visit to Corinth: "I decided to know nothing among you except Jesus
Christ and him crucified" (1 Corinthians 2:2).

To Christians, the cross of Jesus Christ is the clearest picture human
beings have of the heart of God. It is also the means by which our sin is

forgiven, we are reconciled to God and we become God's children, with all that implies for time and for eternity. In a sense, the cross is the center of space and time, the hinge on which all history turns. So, in any explanation of the Christian message, this is crucial (pun intended).

But how does one explain this to the average unchurched North American? It is not enough to repeat like a mantra, "Christ died for our sins." Novelist A. S. Byatt makes that clear when she says, "I rejected the atonement on the grounds that I did not need it, or want it. . . . God had sent his only begotten son into the world to die 'for' us, but the story did not make it at all clear what 'for' meant." [10]

Aye, there's the rub. People may know something of who Jesus was. They certainly know what it is to die. They probably also know that Jesus died by crucifixion. Maybe they even have a vague sense that "sin" is something to do with wrongdoing. So what is it that is so difficult about this sentence? What makes it difficult is that little word for, the word that connects the two great realities of Christ's death and our sin. What on earth does "for" mean? To the world outside the church, "Christ died for our sins," far from being one of the most electrifying truths in the world, is in fact one of the most unintelligible statements in the world.

I decided to go back to the apostle Paul's letters, and see what I could learn from his example of preaching about the cross. One passage in particular helps me think about how to translate the cross. Often, when I am in the middle of a university mission, when I get some time to myself, this is a passage I turn to for encouragement and focus: 2 Corinthians 5.

Different metaphors, common meaning

One of the things I love and am inspired by here is precisely Paul's fluidity in this business of translation. Within just a few verses, he seems to be able to move without hesitation from one cultural language to another to describe the cross. In verse 15, for example, he uses the language of resurrection: "And he died for all, so that those who live might live no longer for themselves, but for him who died and was raised for them."

Here, God is the giver of new life. God raised Jesus from the dead, and now, as we come to Christ, we also die and come to life again. We die to our old self-centered way of life, and we are resurrected to a new life in which we learn to love God and love our neighbor.

Then, in verse 19, Paul switches to a different metaphor, this time from the world of relationships: "in Christ, God was reconciling the world to himself, not counting their responses against them."

This is no longer *resurrection* language. The language here is that of alienation and reconciliation. It is *relational* language. We have been alienated from God by our pigheaded lust for independence. God is now a lover whose beloved has gone off with someone else, and he is hurt and angry. In the death of Jesus, Paul says, God is seeking to get back together with us, to be reconciled with us.

Finally, in verse 21, Paul changes to religious language—a language of sin, righteousness, and sacrifice that is reminiscent of the Old Testament: "For our sake [God] made him who knew no sin to be sin, so that in him we might become the righteousness of God."

God is now the Holy One who cannot be approached without suitable atonement for sin. Christ died for our sin in the same way that a sacrifice was offered for the sin of the worshiper. But the miracle is that God has provided the only really effective sacrifice ("God made him"). Paul deduces that, as a result, we are restored to right standing ("righteousness") with God. As I followed Paul from one picture to the next, I noticed that the three have a strong family likeness.

Each talks about humankind being in the wrong or in need:
- We experience a kind of death.
- We are alienated.
- We need forgiveness.

Each one also speaks of Jesus as the key to the problem:
- Jesus was resurrected.
- In Christ we are reconciled.
- Christ became sin for us.

And each talks in terms of an exchange; Christ gives us something, and we give Christ something:
- We give Jesus our death, he gives us his resurrection life.
- We give him our alienation from God, and he gives us his relationship with God.
- We give him our sin, and he gives us his righteousness.

Paul, the experienced cross-cultural missionary, moves effortlessly from resurrection language to relational language to sacrifice language. He is used to translating basic theological concepts into different languages, making use of different metaphors of redemption in his listeners' worlds. He is, I suppose, culturally multilingual.

So here is my question: How can I communicate the truth of what Christ did on the cross to audiences who know little or nothing about the Bible or Christian tradition? What would it mean to say to them, "Christ died for your sins"? [11]

Complementary images

One insight that has helped me is to remember that no one picture conveys the whole truth. I remember when we moved into our present house, we took photographs of it from different angles to send to our family in Britain. It was not a perfect representation of our home, of course, but it was the best we could do. Probably on the receiving end there was some puzzlement: *Is this the back or the side? How does this piece fit with that? How do you get from this room to that one?* You can imagine the problems. The difficulty is how to represent a three-dimensional object in two dimensions.

Still, we do not give up on photographs. We simply understand that they do not (cannot) tell the whole story, we make allowances accordingly, and we use our imagination. Candid photos may convey truth, but they can never show the whole truth.

What Paul is doing is to send us word-photos to help us understand the death of Jesus. They are metaphors, struggling to convey an immense and wonderful mystery. Because the death of Jesus is such an important thing, there are many ways to understand it, yet none of them is enough by itself.

Leon Morris, who wrote a 400-page book about the cross, admitted the same:

No theory has universal acceptance and it is probable that none ever will. Christ's atoning work is so complex and our minds are so small. We cannot take it all in. We need the positive contributions of all the theories, for each draws attention to some aspect of what Christ has done for us. [12]

If we are wise, we will not say, "Well, that image is inadequate" or "I don't see how that fits together with the others." Rather, we respond, "If I knew what God knows, I suppose I would see how the pieces fit together, how the two-dimensional descriptions add up to make three. I understand that my mind is limited, that human language is limited. So I will treasure these photos, because they are all we have. I may speculate about the reality beyond the words, other truths that the metaphors suggest, but my speculations can never replace the images. Indeed, my speculations will be nothing more than new images, though I may not realize it." [13]

Thinking this way is, frankly, a relief. There is no way of talking about the cross that is absolute and timeless. Paul obviously experimented with different ways of telling people about the truth of the cross. What I may be able to do, then, is to find an image, or a couple of images, that act like a photograph, so that a person in contemporary culture says, "Wow. So that's why Jesus died. I'd never thought of it that way before."

Nicky describes how she was first struck by the atonement:

> After a while, the song, "You Laid Aside Your Majesty," began having great meaning for me. I didn't understand it, but I was amazed at the idea that even if I had been the only person on earth, Jesus would have come to die for me. I didn't know exactly why he would need to, but I did know that it was a demonstration of love. That in itself meant a lot to me and made me want to worship him.

At this point, she has not grasped the whole of the atonement (as if any of us can), but she has been grabbed by one aspect of its truth: the cross means the love of Jesus for her. And from that beginning point, she can go on (indeed, she has gone on) to a much fuller, broader understanding of the cross. But all of us have to begin somewhere.

Imagery of the lawcourt

When I was a student, the predominant image of the cross I heard about in preaching and lecturing was that of the court of law. It went something like this:

God is the judge. We are on trial for our rebellion against the rightful ruler of the universe. There is no doubt that we are guilty. And because of the heinousness of the crime, the only fitting punishment for our rebellion is death. Yet the judge cares for us and does not want us to die. So he graciously steps down from the bench and offers to die in our place so that we can be acquitted. Thus the judge remains just (since the penalty is paid) but also shows his love (since we are forgiven).

Now I would say that is only one image, one way of telling the story. For me and my generation, back in the 1960s, it seems to have worked. Now the culture has changed, and the image does not resonate in the same way. In fact, I counted at least five cultural obstacles to a contemporary Westerner's understanding of that image. The picture assumes the following:

- There is such a thing as objective right and wrong, independent of my personal views of right and wrong.
- I am responsible to God for my actions, not simply to myself.
- A judicial system can reliably administer justice. [14]
- Punishment that is intended as retribution (rather than therapy or a means of rehabilitation) is appropriate for wrong doing.
- The death penalty is appropriate for some crimes (at least, this is a problem in nations like Canada that have abolished the death penalty).

Is there then a different way to tell the same story? A way that equally tries to hold fast to the truth of the Bible's images and yet resonates with people who have grown up in contemporary culture?

The cross and the prodigal son

Clark Pinnock and Robert Brow are two writers who have experimented with a fresh way of thinking about the cross that I think works well. They call it a "relational model" of the cross. Here is how they summarize their idea:

Suffering love is the way of salvation for sinners. Jesus takes the pain of divine love on himself in solidarity with all of us. . . . God elects to defeat his enemies by turning the other cheek. . . . On the cross God absorbs all

the hurt our sins have caused. . . . Not lashing out, not retaliating, not holding out for satisfaction, God simply loves. The pain of the cross is the cost
to God of restoring the broken relationship.[15]

In fact, I believe Pinnock and Brow are simply following Paul's example. Paul uses his three different images, knowing that each will make
sense to a different audience. Pinnock and Brow are doing the same thing,
trying to be faithful to the data while translating it freshly for a new audience. But are they being faithful to the Bible or are they moving too far
away from traditional formulations of the meaning of the cross?

For many years Kenneth Bailey was New Testament Professor at the
Near East School of Theology in Beirut, Lebanon. During his time living
and teaching in the Middle East, Bailey did extensive research into the
sociological background of many New Testament stories. What is relevant
here is his explanation of the story of the prodigal son in Luke 15. He
comments on the paradox of this story: if, on the one hand, this story is
Jesus' summary of his message—that God welcomes us back whatever we
have done—and if on the other hand the cross is supposed to be central
to Christianity—why is there no cross in this story? Bailey comments:

> Islam claims that in this story the boy is saved without a savior. The
> prodigal returns. The father forgives him. There is no cross, no suffering,
> no savior. . . . But not so. The cross and incarnation are implicitly yet
> dramatically present in the story. More than this, the going out of the
> father and his visible demonstration of suffering are the climax of the
> parable. . . . The suffering of the cross was not primarily the physical
> torture but rather the agony of rejected love. In this parable the father
> endures this agony all through the estrangement. . . . Is not this the story
> of the way of God with man [sic] on Golgotha?[16]

This is relational language. "The agony of rejected love . . . estrange-
ment . . . suffering." This strongly suggests that Pinnock and Brow are
honoring a strand of teaching that is at the heart of Jesus' message, not
introducing some new, soft, half-hearted message. In a world that values
relationship but knows the pain of broken relationships, it seems to me it
is images of relationship—joyful, broken and restored—that will best help
to explain the atonement to people in contemporary Western culture.

In trying to explain the gospel to students, I am always looking for cultural connecting points, or *anknupfungspunkten*, images that the Holy Spirit might use to bring insight to someone trying to understand Jesus. Les Casson is a friend from Queen's University in Ontario who has been on the cutting edge of helping students with spiritual issues for some years. She suggested this movie image for a relational understanding of the atonement: [17]

What's Eating Gilbert Grape? is the story of a dysfunctional family— a mother, two sons, and two daughters. The mother, played by Darlene Cates, has not stirred from the couch in front of the TV for years, and is painfully overweight as a result. The younger son, played by Leonardo DiCaprio, is a mentally challenged thirteen-year-old whose main joy in life is climbing the water tower in the little town where they live, so that the fire department frequently has to come and rescue him. Finally, however, the police get tired of dealing with him, and decide to lock him in a cell to teach him a lesson.

His mother, Bonnie, decides to do something about it. With great difficulty, she gets up from the couch, calls for her coat, and, for the first time in years, leaves the house. She goes to the police station, and demands, "Give me my son!" with such passion and authority that the police, breaking all regulations, release him into his mother's care. As they leave, however, Bonnie supported on both sides and walking only with great difficulty, a crowd forms. They stare at her, giggling and whispering behind their hands. One man takes a photograph. But the mother doesn't care: she has her son.

It would actually be possible to read this story in traditional legal terms. Arnie breaks the law and suffers the due punishment. His mother, innocent of any offense, chooses voluntarily to endure suffering on his behalf, in order that Arnie can be acquitted of the charges against him. The picture could be improved only if she were imprisoned in his cell instead of him.

There is also a way to read the story through the relational lens. Arnie and his mother love one another. Yet Arnie's actions have hurt his mother. Like the father in Luke 15, she has a choice. She could say, let him suffer, he has brought it on himself, it will teach him a lesson. He has hurt me—

he deserves to be hurt. She could in that way bounce the hurt back onto him. Instead, she is willing to bear the shame and humiliation it costs in order to get him back. And the great hug with which she greets him is like the hug the father gave the prodigal son.

"Anyone hurt by evil can seek revenge or can, through suffering, forgive." [18] In human terms, God was faced with a similar choice. We have done wrong—to God, to ourselves, and to God's world. God could have allowed us to feel the full effects of his righteous anger. Like Arnie, we would have had no grounds for complaint. That would only have been justice.

But, like Bonnie, God decided to take the other alternative: to suffer and forgive—to allow the hurt to stay with him—not to bounce it back onto us, but to substitute himself for us. And in the cross of Jesus we see the effect that our sin has on God. Why is there no cross in the story of the runaway son? As Bailey hints, there is a cross, but it is not a visible one. The cross is the suffering in the heart of the Father who allows himself to be hurt, even to be killed, rather than visiting that pain on the child whom he loves.

Does the relational model have the same theological value as the "court of law" model? Does it communicate with the same degree of truthfulness and faithfulness to the Bible? It is not a full description—none is possible—but I believe it does. The story needs to be told in a way that is appropriate for each culture, whether it is Old Testament sacrifice imagery for first-century Jews or the Peace Child analogy for the Sawi people or the relational model for contemporary Westerners.

But to find such images, we need all the gifts of the missionary—the flair for translation, the love of different cultures, the ear for metaphor, the eye to spot redemptive analogies, and the inspiration of the Holy Spirit. Paul models what it means to be flexible but faithful, faithful but flexible. My prayer is that we may learn to be both.

12.

Hell and a Loving God:
Does It Add Up?

Light grew. He began to walk. . . . He wished to escape the light. It was desirable that he should still be left alone. He did not trust the light to let him alone. It was desirable that he should be free to make pictures for himself and tell himself tales. He did not trust the light to let him do it. . . . The light still gently spread.

Charles Williams, *Descent into Hell* [1]

I N ANY DISCUSSION OF EVANGELISM, at some point the question of hell is almost bound to come up. I suppose, as I worked my way through the Bible story, it was in the back of my mind. However, as often happens, it was a personal conversation that focussed my thoughts.

Graham would not have called himself a Christian, but many of his friends were Christians. He was thoughtful and open to questions of faith and doubt, and at some point Jesus' teaching about hell was brought to his attention, probably without a lot of subtlety, as is so often the case.

We sat on the dock at camp as the afternoon sun slowly went down, and talked about God, and Jesus, and faith. Finally, Graham said:

What my problem comes down to is this: it seems utterly unfair of God to decide whether to send me to heaven or to hell on the basis of a choice I make about Jesus in one split second of my life. Isn't God interested in what I do with the rest of my life, either before or after?

I'd never thought of the problem quite like that before, and it set my brain racing. Some of what follows is the substance of what Graham and I discussed that afternoon, although, to be honest, it has evolved and changed some since then.

First, I told Graham, some things are just as much a problem for Christian believers as for non-believers. Hell is one of these. Most people who are not Christians, but hear about the idea, understand it as a threat: "Believe or else! Accept my infinite love or I'll torture you for eternity." They want to ask, What kind of a choice is that? Isn't there some kind of third option?

But believers, too, have a hard time, because it is difficult to reconcile the idea of hell with God's love. (It was news to Graham that Christians might struggle with this idea.) Personally, I remember being relieved to discover that even C. S. Lewis wrestled with the concept. In *The Problem of Pain*, he admits, "There is no doctrine which I would more willingly remove from Christianity than this, if it lay in my power. . . . I am not going to try to prove the doctrine tolerable. Let us make no mistake: it is not tolerable."[2]

Maybe we would find it palatable for really evil people (setting aside the vexing question of what is "really" evil). But even then it seems extreme. Is there really no hope of redemption for a Hitler even after several million years in hell? Well, maybe not. Maybe we can let Hitler go, if God insists.

The doctrine also suggests, however, that sincere, kind people also go to hell if they don't believe the right things. This includes followers of other religions, who presumably also believe the wrong things. This seems too harsh.

"So why believe in hell at all?" asked Graham.

Other people might add, "Why believe anything that makes you uncomfortable?"

C. S. Lewis argues that the serious follower of Jesus must start with these facts: "it has the full support of Scripture and, specially, of Our Lord's own words; it has always been held by Christendom; and it has the support of reason."[3]

The first is easy to establish. I reminded Graham of some of the references. Take Matthew's Gospel, for instance. Jesus warns that, under certain conditions, we "will be liable to the hell of fire" (Matthew 5:22). Or, again, if we compare our deeds now with the consequences in the afterlife, "it is better for you to lose one of your members than for your whole body to be thrown into hell" (5:29).

Jesus uses different images to describe hell: "fire" (13:42); "outer dark-ness" (8:12; 22:13; 25:30); the place of "weeping and gnashing of teeth" (8:12; 13:42; 13:50; 22:13; 24:51; 25:30); and the place "prepared for the devil and his angels" (25:41). Pretty strong language, and not just on one occasion (although even that would have been problematic) but repeatedly.

"I'm prepared to agree that Jesus taught about hell," said Graham, "but I can't see why anyone would say it's rational."

What I suggested to Graham was one way that Christian thinkers have figured this one out. The basic thesis is this: The only people who go to hell are those who choose to do so, and they choose to do so because they prefer it to heaven.

What follows is roughly how the conversation progressed from this point on. I'll use Graham's comments and questions as my headings.

"You should tell me first what you mean by heaven and hell."

As I read the Bible, the most important difference between the two is God. In heaven, people live in the full presence of God all the time (Revelation 21:22-23). Hell, on the other hand, means to be excluded from God's presence—"separated from the presence of the Lord and from the glory of his might," as Paul puts it (2 Thessalonians 1:9). Most of Jesus' descriptions of the two, I suspect, are pictures to bring home to us what each means.

The reason anyone might choose hell, then, is because they do not want to be that close to God for that long.

"I still don't see why there has to be a hell if God is love. Is it because God thinks we're so bad?"

Certainly lots of people think that way. So their response to the idea of hell is to say, "I'm not that bad; I haven't done anything to deserve that severe a punishment."

It seems clear from the teaching of Jesus, though, that "going to heaven" has nothing to do with "being good." Think about the thief on the cross who asked Jesus for help, for example. He had no time to begin living well. Yet, Jesus doesn't say to him, "I'm really sorry, but there is no way someone like you can get into heaven. It's far too late now." Rather, he says, "Today you will be with me in Paradise" (Luke 23:43).

"So how come Jesus welcomes him into paradise? What's going on there?"

The answer would appear to be that favorite word of religious people: *faith*. (I'll suggest how we might define faith later.) If that is right—that (good) behavior is not the test for heaven, but faith—then it would hardly make sense to say that (bad) behavior is the criterion for hell. Maybe there, too, the real question is not, "Were you a nice person; were you sincere?" but rather, "Did you have faith?"

In some ways, of course, this does not help us much in coming to terms with the concept of hell. Some people protest that they "cannot" believe, that they have tried to "have faith" and just cannot do it. Others, of course, have never heard of Jesus and never had a chance to consider faith in him. For them, to say heaven and hell are to do with faith, not with being good, really doesn't help. It may even make things worse. After all, I can improve my behavior if I really try, but I'm not sure I can just decide to believe, even if I want to.

"I guess I'm not sure what you mean by faith then. You said you had a definition."

There are lots of people for whom faith is no more than a fancy word for superstition: children "have faith" in Santa Claus, the Easter bunny, and the tooth fairy. This kind of "faith" is associated with the young and naïve, and most people grow out of it as their understanding matures. Although some people think Christian faith is like this, this is not what Jesus means by faith.

A second definition is that faith equals agreeing with certain statements, such as: "I believe that kangaroos live in Australia." This kind of faith isn't wishful thinking. I simply have the fact of kangaroos in Australia in my mind as a piece of information that I believe. I have faith that it is true. Now, again, there are beliefs, about topics such as God and Jesus and the Holy Spirit, which Christians have in their minds, and which other people generally don't. This is a definitely a part of Christian faith, but it's still not the heart of it.

Faith also can mean trust and commitment. You might believe in a particular political candidate, to be prepared to contribute to his or her campaign fund, and to vote for that candidate. You trust her and you're committed to her cause. In this sense you have faith in that person. That's not like having faith in the Easter bunny, and it's not like believing that kangaroos do live in Australia. That kind of faith is much closer to what Jesus means by faith. Jesus generally means trust and commitment when he talks about faith.

"So what's lack of faith, then?"

It depends which definition of faith we're going by. If faith were just superstition, then refusing to have faith would be good. We'd be growing up! If faith were simply a matter of knowing certain facts, and unbelief were not knowing them, then that would be easy to remedy. You'd simply have to find out the facts.

In Christian understanding, however, not believing, not having faith, means something rather more serious. It means not having the third kind of faith, which is trust. Not having faith means not trusting myself to whatever I know about God. God stretches out a hand, and I refuse to take it.

"It still seems really extreme for those who lack faith to be punished with hell."

Well, there is such a thing as cause and effect. God has made the world in such a way that actions have consequences. Actually, one of the great things about being alive is that we have power and influence over many things. In giving us that gift, presumably God hoped that we would enjoy the fact that our good actions have good consequences. Yet the opposite is also possible: our evil or stupid actions also have consequences.

I suppose it comes down to the fact that God has given us free will. God has allowed us to choose how to use our power, but, like a good parent, God doesn't keep us from wrong choices. Most importantly, we are allowed to choose whether we want to relate to God or not, to trust God or not.

"Okay, so help me connect up freewill and faith."

When I use my freewill to trust and follow God (the third definition of faith), that has consequences. On the other hand, if I choose to turn away from what I know about God (that is, I refuse to exercise faith), that will have effects as well. If I have not chosen God in this life, that will have repercussions in the next. In a sense, we judge ourselves by rejecting God; God simply confirms our choice. Author and psychiatrist M. Scott Peck puts it like this:

> God does not punish us, we punish ourselves. Those who are in hell are there by their own choice. They remain in hell because it seems safe and easy to them. The notion that people are in hell by their own choice is not widely familiar, but the fact is that it is both good psychology and good theology.[4]

"Well, then I come back to my first question: How can God judge us on the basis of a single decision?"

If we truly are "judged" on the basis of whether we say yes or no to God in a split second, that would indeed seem unjust. After all, what if I changed my mind tomorrow? Would it be too late? But, in fact, I don't think that "deciding about God" is actually an isolated once-off decision.

Think about it this way. In a sense, every decision we ever make is for or against God. For instance:

• Every time we are thankful (instead of taking things for granted), we prepare ourselves to say the Big Thank You to God for all God has given us.

• Every time we apologize to someone (instead of shouting louder), we are better prepared to make the Big Apology to God for not giving God the rightful place in our lives.

• Every time we acknowledge truth (though it may be painful), we become better equipped to respond to the Jesus, who said, "I am the Truth."

• Every time we stand in awe of beauty, or admit we can't make it by ourselves, or decide to follow our conscience in a small way, we move toward faith in God.

With every decision like that, we become more open to God's influence. We develop habits of heart and mind that make us more vulnerable to God's approaches. Or we do the opposite. This means that a person who says yes to God in that split second decision sense is most likely a person who has been unconsciously responding to God for some time, though possibly without knowing it. On the other hand, a person who consciously says no to God in an ultimate sense is almost certainly a person who has been saying no to God in the small things.

The strange thing, of course, is that you can't always tell from the outside who is going to choose what. In the time of Jesus, it was the religious people, the respectable citizens, who denied his claims and crucified him. And it was the losers, the outsiders, the street people who saw in Jesus exactly what they'd been looking for, and trusted themselves to him.

"But why should these decisions follow me into the next life?"

It's a good question. People say, "I can understand how what you're saying works for this life. I know that my choices have consequences. But how can that apply in eternity?"

Well, I really don't think this is some special, mean, and arbitrary rule that God made up. The question goes back to that dangerous gift of free will, our ability to make decisions that have real consequences. The next step from that statement is to say that we have the ability to exercise our free will, not only to affect the world around us but also (to a certain extent) to make ourselves who we are and who we will be.

So if we choose against God often enough, we get to the point where we become characters who will always say no to God, no matter how often the choice is presented to us. Even if we had another opportunity after death, we would still say no because of the sort of people we have made ourselves into. As C. S. Lewis says, "I believe that if a million chances were likely to do good, they would be given."[5]

Lewis actually wrote a whole book about heaven and hell, *The Great Divorce*.[6] I happen to think it's one of his best. In the story, people on earth are allowed to take a bus trip from earth to heaven to see if they would like to stay. Most of the book describes some of the reasons people use for not staying. These are often very sensible reasons.

There is the self-righteous factory foreman who always stands up for his rights and is not willing to accept anything for free. He refuses even love, which has to be free and can never be a right.

There is the intellectual clergyman who loves playing with ideas, especially ideas about God, but isn't interested in the reality of God.

There is the possessive mother who doesn't want to share her son's love with anyone else, even in heaven. If she can't have him to herself, she won't go in.

There is the artist who is more concerned about his reputation and status than about the beauty he might find in God.

These people have said yes to themselves and no to God's truth and love often enough that they willingly say no to heaven. They have made themselves the kind of people who choose not to be in the presence of God.

"I still don't understand why anyone would not want to be with God in heaven."

Maybe our problem is that we think it would be easy to be in the presence of God. I'm struck by the fact that there are three images for God in the Bible, three places and only three where it says "God is . . ." Each of these three suggests to me that it's not that straightforward.

1. God is light (John 1:15)

I'm sure this is meant to make us think of all the positive qualities we love about light. Light shines and illuminates and clarifies. We could never exclaim, "Oh, I see!" or "Wow! Look at that!" without light. We could never "shed some light" without light. And God is the origin of light. But more than that, God is the one in comparison to whom all created light is merely a shadow. All the good things about light are found infinitely in God.

Yet this light can also be a searchlight, probing the dark places of our conscience and psyche—the thoughts that shame us, the reflex actions we prefer not to talk about, the habits we cannot kick, the prejudices we've held, the fantasies we've never told anyone. Frankly, not everyone wants to be seen in that sort of light. Sometimes the darkness seems kinder.

2. God is fire (Hebrews 12:29)

Fire, like light, has qualities we enjoy. Fire warms and fire glows. But fire also melts off impurities and refines pure metals. The fire that is God not only warms and comforts; it also wants to consume everything that is cheap and destructive, dehumanizing and evil in the world.

We may say, "Well, that's okay. I'm against those things, too." The trouble is, those things that need purging are not just "out there." They are inside us, too. In each of us there is much that is cheap and destructive, dehumanizing and evil. The question is just how much are we against those things? Enough to let the forest fire of God's anger against evil sweep through our innermost being and cleanse us?

If we want to "go to heaven" and live with God, we have to face the fire of God.[7] Quite simply, some prefer not to do that. Yet there is a worse picture; indeed, the worst of all . . .

3. God is love (John 4:8)

God is not just a lover, not just a loving parent, but unadulterated, infinite love. "What's wrong with that?" we ask. "I vote for love. Don't we all want to be loved?"

If we think that, we have never experienced this kind of love. This is a love that yearns for us to be the best we are capable of, and is wounded when we refuse the best. A love that shows us clearly and gently what is best, but doesn't stand in the way if we choose to ignore it. A love that longs to be loved back, but loves too much to impose itself. This love is closely related to light and fire.

There is something infinitely attractive in this kind of love—of course—but also something infinitely terrifying. God is both . . . attractive and terrifying. We want this love, but we also resist it. God gives us the freedom to say no to this love. Lewis's characters do just that. In fact, Lewis says somewhere else: "Some people talk as if meeting the gaze of absolute goodness would be fun. They need to think again. They are still only playing with religion."[8]

Do I then believe in hell? Yes, because Jesus taught about it and I have found him to be a trustworthy teacher on questions where he can be tested. Yes, also because I believe in humankind, in our inherent value and dignity, and in the seriousness of our choices.[9]

If I thought people were less than infinitely valuable, less than the priceless image of God, then the idea of hell would not be necessary; some compromises would be possible.

Or again, if this life were play-acting, if our personalities were just the results of posturing, and if our strengths and weaknesses just props in the play, then once the play was over, we could go back to normality, to reality.

But the play is real and the parts we act are ourselves. We make of our parts what we choose, and increasingly become them, until the play is over. Then we find we are who we have made ourselves, and there is no one else we can be except that character we have become. And on the last day, faced with God, that character finds that it either wants or does not want God-light, God-fire, and God-love. To my mind, no one expresses this more vividly than Dorothy Sayers:

> There is no power in this world or the next that can keep a soul from God if God is what it really desires. But if, seeing God, the soul rejects him in hatred and horror, then there is nothing more that God can do for it. God, who has toiled to win it for himself, and borne for its sake to know death, and suffer the shame of sin, and set his feet in hell, will nevertheless, if it insists, give it what it desires.[10]

That is why C. S. Lewis says that "the gates of hell are locked on the inside."[11] It is not so much that God shuts people out from heaven, as that people want to shut God out of their experience forever.

"I can see the logic of that. But how could a person ever know if they are getting ready to meet God?"

The only way I know to prepare for meeting God is to become a follower of Jesus. Maybe I could put it this way. My mother lives in Wales, and sometimes we have talked about the possibility of her coming to live in Canada. Yet, as she has grown older, the possibility of that happening has become increasingly remote. The acclimatization required would be too harsh for her after a lifetime of living in Britain. She would find the summers far too hot and the winters far too cold. If she were younger, the whole question would be different.

Following Jesus is a way to become acclimatized to the atmosphere of God's new world. What we experience in following Jesus is something of God's light and fire and love here and now, but in manageable quantities. Jesus teaches us the ways of heaven. And Jesus teaches us to let go of those things that would make us unsuited for the culture there. As we live in the company of Jesus, then, we are actually learning to live in the presence of God, so that after death all we want is more of what Jesus has shown us—in other words, we want heaven.

Unfinished business

We both fell silent. By this time, the light was more or less gone, and Graham and I wandered up to the dining hall for the evening snack. We didn't say much as we climbed the hill. I think we were both pretty sobered. We were glad to reach the warmth and the light.

Graham and I lost touch after that summer. He didn't come back to camp as far as I know, and I don't know whether he ever became a Christian. I pray so. But I will always be thankful for his honesty and his insight. I pray that my answer was a seed in his mind that will help him come to Jesus at some point along the way. His questions were certainly a good seed in mine.

13.

Evangelizing Other Religions:

Why Bother?

A pluralistic religious world is not a crisis. It is God's providential challenge and the Church's opportunity. It does not destroy anything but our complacency and smugness.

Lamin O. Sanneh[1]

A S I HAVE TALKED WITH STUDENTS about issues of spirituality, they have asked one question more than any other. "How can you Christians say your way is the only way? That is so arrogant." For Christians, too, I find that one of the most common reasons they shy away from evangelism is that it implies that other people need whatever it is that Christian faith offers. "Surely they're okay as they are? Who are we to say their faith is lacking?" I am asked.

As I reflected on evangelism, this question was always in the background. Should we be evangelizing Muslims? Hindus? New Age believers? Jehovah's Witnesses? After all, the message of our time says, "Believe what you like. Diversity is good. Celebrate difference. Rejoice in people's different understandings of God and learn from them. Don't try and convert anyone, for goodness's sake."

The classical Christian claim, of course, is quite the opposite: that Jesus Christ is the only way to God, and that unless people come to God through Jesus, they are spiritually "lost." The words are harsh, bald and shocking. Can any thinking person hold such a view in today's pluralistic culture?

As I discussed this topic with various groups, often I would hear the Bible quoted—especially Jesus' words in John's Gospel: "I am the Way, the Truth, and the Life. No one comes to the Father except by me" (John 14:6). Groups also would quote Peter: "There is no other name given under heaven by which we may be saved" (Acts 4:12). And Paul: "If you confess with your lips that Jesus is Lord, you will be saved" (Romans 10:9). So that settles the question as far as a Christian is concerned, right? I was not sure. After all, even the devil can use "proof texts" like that (Matthew 4:6).

Since this question was raised so often, I decided to do some research and create a talk that I could present to students on the topic. Here's the way the talk came out.

Do all religions lead to God?

My guess is that you are here today because you are curious or because you have been offended. You have heard the claim from Christians that Jesus is the only way to God, and that all those outside Christianity are bound for hell. And you find it intolerable or at least strange that anyone would make such a claim.

What I hope to do next is to explain as best I know how what this claim really means and what it does not mean. My hunch is that nobody will be satisfied with my answer, but we will have a time for questions at the end when you can say your piece. And hopefully we'll all learn something.

Let me start with some strong statements and then backtrack and do some reflecting. There are three reasons in particular that Christians have for making the claims they do, and they all concern Jesus. Classic Christianity has said things like this:

- Jesus is God in human form, the unique incarnation of God. There is nowhere else, in any religion or culture, where God has been revealed in this kind of way.
- The problems of humankind stem from the fact that we have not allowed God the Creator's rightful place in the world. We have tried to play God and have made a mess of it. But Christianity claims that the death of Jesus is the key to how God puts things right in this world. One early Christian writer put it this way: "in Christ God was reconciling the world to himself" (2 Corinthians 5:19).
- On the third day after Jesus' death, God brought Jesus back from death into a new quality of life that can never be destroyed. Those who follow Jesus share in that quality of life here and now and after death. This "resurrection" of Jesus is God's seal of approval on the work of Jesus, as well as the clearest guide we have to the afterlife.

Before we go further, let me come clean and tell you where I'm at in this whole matter. To be honest, I have struggled with this for years. I find there are two things I hold in tension as I try to follow Jesus.

First, you should know that I hold passionately to those three convictions about Jesus. For me, if I water down those truths, I am betraying what I understand to be the heart of God. If Christianity has anything good to offer to the world, it is bound up in those three truths. You'd be welcome to ask me more about why I believe those things later.

On the other hand, I confess I am horrified by the way some Christians talk. Here, for example are the words of the Council of Florence in 1438:

> No one remaining outside the Catholic Church, not just pagans, but also Jews or heretics or schismatics, can become partakers of eternal life; but they will go to the everlasting fire that was prepared for the devil and his angels, unless before the end of life they are joined to the church.[2]

Although this is a statement of the fifteenth-century church, the attitude is still found in the Christian family today. But this point of view seems out of step with the Jesus described in the earliest biographies of him, and even contrary to the spirit of his teaching. I've come to the conclusion that this kind of statement is not the final word on the subject.

Maybe the best way to come at this is to tell you the most common objections to Christian claims I come across, and how I have tried to come to terms with them. Some of them may be your concerns. If not, you're welcome to add yours to the list later. So, for instance, some people have said to me . . .

Surely all religions say the same thing anyway?

Different religions make claims that often conflict with one another, so I have a problem seeing how they can all be true at the same time. John Hick is a well-known writer on this subject who wants to be as inclusive as possible, but even he admits it's difficult to see how the claims of different religions can all be true.[3] Hick lists some of the questions religions deal with where there are obvious differences, and I have added a few of my own:

- Is the physical world, including its evil, real (as Western religions claim) or is it an illusion (as Buddhism claims)?

- Can God have "a son" in the sense that Christians say Jesus was "the Son of God"? Muslims and Jews would clearly say no.
- Is reincarnation true? Broadly speaking, Western faiths say no and Eastern faiths say yes.
- Is there one book that can appropriately be called "the Word of God"?
- What makes us acceptable to God? Our beliefs? Our moral actions? Our religious actions? Again, religions differ.
- Is it appropriate to think of God as a Trinity, as Christians believe? Or is God strictly One, as Muslims and Orthodox Jews assert?
- Is it appropriate to think of God as (in some sense) a Person? Western religions say yes, Buddhism says no.
- Is the Buddhist concept of nirvana the same as the Christian idea of heaven?

The list could go on. How can all these views be true at the same time? And these are not just secondary beliefs, mind you, somewhere out on the edges of the religions. These topics are all absolutely central.

Perhaps each religion has a piece of the truth.

Sometimes people remind me of the parable of the elephant and the blind men. You may have heard it. It goes like this:

> Several blind men are trying to discover the nature of an elephant. Yet each man offers a different description, according to the part of the elephant he touches. The one who feels the head concludes that an elephant is like a pot; the one with the ear says, "An elephant is like a winnowing basket;" the one feeling the tusk argues that an elephant is like a plowshare; and so on.[4]

The conclusion is obvious: Religious views are different because, like the blind men, each faith grasps only a portion of the truth. Certainly religions are different, but if we could see the whole picture we would understand how in fact they are all part of the truth.

The trouble with illustrations, however, is that we often use them as if they can prove something. In fact, illustrations can do no such thing. All they can do is what the word suggests. Illustrations simply illustrate. Take this particular parable. If it is, in fact, the case that all religions have a piece of the truth, then the elephant story illustrates that beautifully. But how can we know for sure that God is like the elephant? Or how could we know that different religions are like the blind men?

It's significant, of course, that the story is supposed to have been told by the Buddha. In Buddhist tradition, the story works perfectly, because it illustrates a Buddhist understanding of reality—that everything is ultimately one. The story appears to be objective and fair to all religions, yet in fact it speaks out of one particular religious perspective. The real question is: What reason do we have for thinking that that perspective is right? (I'm not assuming it's wrong, you understand. I'm just saying the parable doesn't settle it.)

Maybe different religions are appropriate for different cultures.

Canadian scholar Wilfred Cantwell Smith suggested that comparing religions was as futile as comparing civilizations. Religions are part of civilizations. If you wouldn't think of criticizing a civilization, then don't criticize its religion either. Neither is a subject for value judgments, let alone judgments about truth.[5]

The fact is, of course, we do make value judgments between religions. There are, or have been, religions based on human sacrifice, fear of evil spirits or mass suicide. Should I give those the same degree of respect that I would give to, say, Zen Buddhism? Or what about those cult leaders who claim that God has spoken to them? Should I take that as seriously as the claims that God spoke to Moses or Mohammed or Jesus? I don't think so. In practice, we are only tolerant up to a point, and, I would say, rightly so. We should be discriminating in thinking about religion, especially where such issues as freedom, rights, and human dignity are concerned, which they often are in questions of religion.

The view of religions as just a cultural phenomenon is also difficult to maintain when many of the world's religions are becoming so international. Islam, for example, is found not only in the Middle East but in places as far apart as China and North America. Christianity and Buddhism likewise have adapted to many cultures and languages around the world. Every day it becomes harder to argue that any religion is only appropriate for a certain culture.

Okay, so we may not be able to synthesize religions, but surely we have to admit that ultimate spiritual reality is beyond the grasp of any single religion.

This is a view held by some within the Christian community. For example, in his book *Mansions of the Spirit*, Bishop Michael Ingham takes this approach. He starts with the views of Swiss philosopher Frithjof Schuon. Schuon does not try to synthesize religions. While some people argue that religions are different in superficial ways but the same at a deep level, Schuon will have none of this. Instead, he acknowledges that they are "not only dissimilar in their external but also in their internal character." [6] In other words, the differences go to the very roots of the religions.

At the same time, Schuon believes that God is beyond all religions. To put it another way, "all knowledge radiates from the same transcendent point." [7] Religions are simply "the finite and relative vehicles by which this Truth is known by human beings." [8] Each religion thus has access to Ultimate Reality in its own way. In this sense, the differences between religions really don't matter. What is important is "the Ultimate, or the Real, or the Transcendent . . . that final end towards which religious faith draws us on." [9]

We need to ask, though, if there are so many deep differences, how we can be sure that religions are in touch with the same Ultimate? Ingham finds the connection in that form of religion called mysticism, which occurs in every major religion.

Frankly, I find this point of view very attractive. It would make life easier in many respects. Yet there are significant barriers that hold me back from this answer.

- In this view, we really know nothing about "Ultimate Reality," since he, she, or it is (by definition) beyond anything described in any of the world's great religions. In fact, to judge from the difference between the faiths, it seems that Ultimate Reality manifests itself in ways that are "mutually incoherent." [10]

- Mysticism alone really is not a strong enough foundation for this view. Mysticism, after all, has a different degree of importance and has different meanings in each religion. And if mysticism is the crucial clue, then the vast majority of religious people, who are after all not mystics, have never really "got" what their religion is all about. That seems to me rather presumptuous, even patronizing.

- How could we ever know whether two mystics, on opposite sides of the world and in different centuries, are in fact experiencing the same Ultimate Reality, particularly since they find it impossible to describe? Even Thomas Merton, the Catholic mystic, described himself as agnostic on this point.[11]

- Perhaps most seriously of all, this view forces us to shape a Jesus to suit the argument. This Jesus, we are told, never made claims about his own importance, and so, when the early Christians talked about Jesus' uniqueness, they were actually wrong. Suffice it to say that other scholars disagree with this reading.

Are you saying then that all religions apart from Christianity are wrong?

I don't find that my belief in Jesus leads me to devalue other faiths or their adherents.[12] The way I read the Bible, the truth and light of God are available to people everywhere. They may not always respond to it, any more than Christians do, but it is there. This means I have every reason to respect, value, and learn from people of other faiths and cultures. Clark Pinnock suggests that Christians visiting other cultures "will discover noble insights and actions that are the result of God working among the people."[13]

At the same time, there are significant points at which I disagree with followers of other faiths, and they disagree with me. But I find I can live with the reality of some agreements and some disagreements. My choice is not between having to agree with everything or having to disagree with everything.

This point of view is not unique to Christians. I can imagine someone who is Muslim saying something like this:

Christians respect Abraham and Moses, which is good; and they follow the prophet Jesus, which also is good. Unfortunately, their belief that Jesus is the "Son" of God is blasphemous, and their belief that God would allow one as good as Jesus to die is misguided. And they have certainly missed the best, which is contained in the Koran.

Many Christians today hold this kind of view, on the one hand holding firmly to what they believe, but on the other hand affirming truth and goodness wherever they find it.

Are you saying that people of other religions will go to hell?

I believe that God gives us what we choose. If we choose for God, God honors that choice. If we resist God and push God away, God respects that choice, too. However, we cannot foretell who may say yes and who may say no to God. They may be people of any religion or of none.

Behind the question, I think, is the assumption that religion is the place people go who want to know God and be close to God and follow God.[14] Surely all people who are involved in religion have said yes to God, chosen for God? Well, maybe, but maybe not as well. Bishop John Taylor is typical of religious writers who warn us that no religion necessarily leads to God: "It is impossible to escape the ambiguity of all religions, for in every household of faith it is plain that man [sic] uses religion as a way of escaping from God. This is as true of Christianity as of any other religious system."[15]

Religion as a way of escaping from God? Absolutely. To know this I have to look no further than my own heart. I teach in a religious institution, I engage in religious activities every day of my life, and my mind flows readily to religious language and images. Does that mean I am seeking for God? That I am longing to do what God wants? That I want friendship with God above everything else? Well, on good days, by the grace of God, yes. But I am also quite aware that religious "stuff" can easily become an end in itself. I can be so wrapped up in the everyday life of a "religious professional" that I forget that the purpose of my life is actually to love and serve God.[16] And I suspect I am not alone.

We shouldn't assume, then, that anyone who is involved in religion will be "in heaven." No religious tradition guarantees that a person's heart really desires God. Followers of any religious tradition may want religion (or any one of a hundred benefits of "religion") more than they want God, and the God Jesus taught about is not one who would force them into relationship.

So what about people who have never heard about Jesus? Are they condemned? [17]

I have discovered that there are different answers to this question. Some Christians believe that unless you have heard about Jesus and made an explicit commitment to being his follower, you cannot be "saved." Ignorance of the law (or in this case the gospel) is no excuse. If this seems unfair, the answer is that if God chooses to "save" only those people who hear and respond, that is God's prerogative. After all, nobody deserves God's love anyway, so who are we to argue with any conditions God may choose to lay down for people to enjoy that love?

There is another approach, however. In the Jewish scriptures, there are many people, such as Abraham and Sarah, who apparently had an intimate relationship with God, and who have been regarded as spiritual role models by Christians since the first century. But because they lived before the time of Jesus, they did not hear about or believe in him either.

From a Christian point of view, then, how can people like Abraham be in relationship with God? The New Testament's own answer is that they responded with faith, that is, with trust and commitment, to whatever they knew about God, even if that was only a small amount (Romans 4:20-21).

Does that mean that Jesus was unnecessary for them? Not at all. If Abraham had a relationship with God, it was because God forgave his wrongdoing, and God's forgiveness is inescapably linked to the death of Jesus. The fact that the crucifixion would not happen in history for two thousand years after Abraham's time is a minor detail! The significance of Jesus' death is in this sense "trans-historical"—that is, it works backward in time as well as forward.

Now, maybe people like Abraham offer a clue for thinking about those who have never heard of Jesus in our day. Many Christians would argue that people of any religion or none can find a relationship with God by the same route as Abraham. That is, if they respond with trust to whatever truth God has shown them.

Is Jesus, then, not necessary for them? Again, as with Abraham, Jesus is certainly necessary. But they can experience the benefits of Jesus' death even if they don't know about it, just as I can experience the benefits of driving my car even if I haven't the first idea how it works. (I haven't.)

At the same time, someone who wants to know God will recognize the importance of Jesus when they do hear about him. Jesus anticipated this when he said: "Anyone who resolves to do the will of God will know whether the teaching [I am giving] is from God or whether I am speaking on my own" (John 7:17).

It doesn't surprise me in light of this that pioneer Christian missionaries tell stories of people hearing about Jesus for the first time and saying (in effect), "This is what we have been waiting for." For example, here is the response of an old woman in the Philippines to the message of Christ:

> When being examined for baptism, she was asked: "And when did you believe on the Lord Jesus?" Her poignant and pathetic reply was, "As soon as you told me of him, of course. And wouldn't we have believed sooner had you come sooner?" [18]

Those who have been pursuing the truth about God with humility and faith (resolving "to do the will of God," to use Jesus' words) recognize in the Christian message the fulfillment of their hearts' yearnings.

What of those who never hear of Jesus? My growing conviction is that God seeks to communicate to all people, and gives them the opportunity to respond, whether the light they have is little or much, whether they live in a place where they can hear the Christian message or they are part of another religious faith. John Taylor gives a dramatic illustration:

> The first to be permitted to teach the gospel in northern Nigeria found themselves greeted by a handful of people who professed to being already followers of Jesus Christ. They told the story of Malam Ibrahim, a teacher of the Holy Qur'an whose studies had slowly convinced him that in its pages a unique office is conferred on the figure of Isa Masih, Jesus the Messiah, as the mediator through whom the prayers of the faithful are offered up to the All-Merciful. So he gathered round him a band of devotees who made their regular prayer in the name if Isa Masih. When the religious authorities found out he was charged with heresy, refused to recant, and was crucified in Kao marketplace thirty years before a Christian preacher arrived in the nation. [19]

Do people who sincerely seek God still need to hear about Jesus?

The answer is yes. If you are walking up a steep cliff path with a candle, and someone offers you a floodlight that will illuminate the whole cliff-face including your path, do you respond, "Oh no, it's okay. Can't you see I've got a candle?" I think not.

A more recent objection to exclusive Christian claims is what I suppose should be called a postmodern one: "Your kind of attitude always leads to oppression."

Decades ago, skeptics argued that religious claims to truth were false. Now they argue that there is no such thing as truth. Some skeptics, in fact, contend that people only claim to have "truth" when they want to maintain power and keep other people in subjection. Claims to "truth" are just a club that people use to beat those who do not agree. The story of the nineteenth-century missionary movement and the way it often cooperated with the forces of colonialization provides embarrassing examples of how Christian "truth" has indeed been used to exploit and dehumanize the colonized.

But this is not the whole story. There is good documentation of times when the missionaries worked against the colonial powers, and of the colonizers trying to disrupt missionary work, knowing perfectly well that the missionaries would sow visions of justice and independence that would ultimately overturn their aims. In cases like this, the missionaries' claims to truth actually worked against the powerful and for the oppressed.[20]

It seems clear to me which kind of missionary stands in the authentic tradition of Jesus. He himself was a proclaimer of liberation. Far from believing that truth was oppressive, he promised that "the truth will make you free" (John 8:32), and the marginalized and disempowered of his day discovered that he spoke truly. Nobody can deny that Jesus' followers have sometimes abused truth and power, but that does not invalidate Jesus' intention, nor the fact that others have authentically followed his example.

It is a strange fact that "tolerance" can itself be more oppressive than claims to truth."[21] Take the elephant analogy. It sounds very tolerant, of course. Yet how do we feel toward the blind men in the story? Pity? Perhaps we even smile at their folly. And how do we feel about ourselves as we observe this scene? Superior and even smug. After all, we can see, while those poor blind men can't. Not exactly a pleasant or respectful attitude.

Most significantly of all: how do those watching the scene come to be able see everything? How come they are sighted while everyone else is blind? By what right do they say, "This is how things really are"? The story gives absolutely no reason. So, by a strange reversal, the very story that argues against "objective truth" itself claims to be objective truth. What appears at first sight to be a liberal analogy actually imposes its view just as oppressively as the views it is mocking and relativizing.

The other thing I want to say about truth and oppression is that, in my experience, dialogue and friendship between people of different faiths are not only possible but are, in fact, quite common. Believing that one religion is closer to the truth than another does not necessarily lead to intolerance or persecution, as some fear.

Actually, strong convictions can lead to a greater measure of patience and compassion, rather than less. For instance, I have been present at debates between Christians and Jews, and between Christians and Muslims, which were models of clarity, charity, and respect, in spite of the differences between the speakers. It can work.

More truth, more love

I do hope for my Muslim friends to become followers of Jesus. I would not be faithful to Jesus if I didn't. I know some of them hope for me to become a Muslim. All the same, we enjoy one another's friendship. We enjoy listening to one another and trying to understand one another's faith. We laugh together, tease one another, share pain together. There are issues where we find ourselves closer to one another than to our secular friends. And we have no choice but to leave the outcome of our theological discussions to God.

That, I believe, is pluralism at its best. Not seeking an artificial synthesis, not giving up on our deepest convictions, but committed to searching together for more love and more truth.

I don't think anyone these days can hold to the claims of classical Christianity lightly or thoughtlessly. I for one would say that I hold those views out of deep conviction that they are the most life-changing story the world has ever heard.

If you have been offended by Christians who have talked about Jesus in an angry, loveless kind of way, I want to apologize. But I would encourage you not to dismiss Jesus just because his followers don't always live up to his standards. In particular, I would hate for you to dismiss Christianity's exclusive claims without considering the story that is at the heart of it, the story of Jesus. It is because of loyalty to him that that Christians make the claims they do.

I find myself moved by the words of one convert to Christianity from Islam. He spoke for many of us (but at far greater cost than for most of us), when he said, "I am a Christian for one reason alone—the absolute worship-ability of Jesus Christ. By that word I mean that I have found no other being in the universe who compels my adoration as he has done."[22]

It is this Jesus—intriguing, challenging, infuriating, and delightful—who is the key to this whole question.

Well, that's the way the talk goes. Usually the conversation continues for a long time after the lecture. (During one such conversation, one Muslim student looked me in the eye and told me I was going to hell. That was a new experience.) This is clearly not an issue that is going to go away. Indeed, as the world shrinks, and people of different cultures and faiths inevitably rub shoulders more and more, the questions will become more intense.

What I seek for myself is the ability to be clear about what I believe, and the confidence to commend it to anyone and everyone. In particular, I think Jesus is totally unlike anyone or anything found in other religions of the world. And it is the reality of this Jesus that makes me believe that evangelizing all people, of all backgrounds, whether Buddhist, Muslim, atheist, animist, or indeed Christian, is appropriate—as long as it is done in Jesus' own way.

At the same time, I want to be open to listen to and learn from anyone and everyone. After all, if Jesus is "the truth" there is nothing to be feared and much to be gained. All truth is God's truth.

14.

Beginning and Belonging

The mission of the church is to bear witness, through its life and worship, to the truth of the Gospel, to live as a sign and model of the reign of God, and to work for the reconciliation of the entire world to God through Jesus Christ.

Harold Percy, *Good News People* [1]

I REMEMBER SPEAKING with a woman who had been coming to our church for a few months. I asked her what it had been like as a newcomer, and her response was revealing: "I didn't know where to begin."

Her comment got me thinking. Any church that has been going longer than a week is like a conveyor belt in motion. There are constantly references to things that happened earlier in the church's life. Think of announcements, for example:

- If you haven't yet paid for the tickets for Tuesday's dinner . . .
- It's the first Sunday in October, and you know what that means . . .
- All those whose children are going on the Sunday school outing . . .
- We're all pleased to welcome Bert back from his adventures . . .
- Thank you for praying for my wife last week . . .
- As you all know, our church is deeply in the red . . .

Then I began to notice Bible readings that begin in the middle of a thought, without introduction or explanation:

"After these things . . ." *(What things?)*

"On the third day . . ." *(The third after what?)*

"As they were listening to this . . ." *(To what?)*

"Then Jesus told them a parable . . ." *(When?)*

Or take the proliferation of books so many churches put up with in worship. I think of Ray, a friend of mine who has been "churched" his whole life, who visited our church for the first time a few weeks back. At one point in the service, I looked over and noticed that in one hand Ray was resting an open hymnbook, and on top of that an open prayer book. In his other hand was the weekly bulletin, which directed him to the right pages of the prayer book and the hymnbook. Unfortunately, at various points in the service, he had to turn to another part of the bulletin in order to follow the Bible readings. The point when I noticed his predicament, however, was when we were singing a song not from the regular hymnbook but from the church's new supplementary hymnbook. I decided to share mine with him.

You get the idea. If I am a new person, I am likely to think, "Well, clearly this is a going concern. I'm glad they're having such a good time. But is there a place for me? Will I ever be able to find my way through this service without embarrassment? Is there even one of these events that might welcome a new person? What about the fact that I'm not sure what I believe? I'm not sure I want to be here quite that badly." [2]

Some people might argue, "Well, this is family stuff. This is who we are. Get used to it. If you want to be a part of this family, get with the program. Surely if they're sufficiently strongly motivated, they'll come back and finally they'll get into the stream of things." Well, yes, maybe. But what if their interest is only 10 to 20 percent rather than 90 percent, and not strong enough to make them want to come back? Isn't Jesus interested in the person whose interest in faith is still very timid and tentative?

In any case, this is not how we usually treat guests. After all, if we have visitors in our home, they also come into the middle of a continuous stream of life, just as guests do in church. There are unfinished conversations, in-jokes, references to what happened yesterday, arguments unresolved, and so on. So what do we do? Carry on regardless? Not usually. We will probably take time to explain things, bring guests up to speed, avoid in-jokes, put some conversations on hold till the visitors have gone, and so on. That's just simple courtesy. We want our visitors to feel comfortable and to enjoy their visit. We do not want them to feel embarrassed and to wish they'd never come.

Churches that have visitors on a regular basis have learned how to do this well. (Otherwise they wouldn't have so many visitors!) These churches will, for instance, welcome visitors but not embarrass them by asking them to stand or (even worse) say something. Harold Percy, rector of a growing Anglican church outside Toronto, will sometimes begin a service by saying, "Thank you for coming this morning. You are busy people, and we feel honored that you have made time in your busy schedule, and on a Sunday morning, too, to come to church." Some may feel that visitors should be thanking us for giving them the opportunity to join us in worship, not us thanking them. But it is customary to thank your guests for coming to your home. Sure, you hope they will have a good time, and that they feel grateful to you and say thank you in return. But thanking them for coming is simple courtesy.

If our churches are serious about evangelism, we need to think through our programs in the light of what we have learned so far about how evangelism happens. For example:

1. Evangelism is a slow process. This means we need a place where faith can grow, an incubator, if you like. Church should be a place where faith is not allowed to stagnate but also isn't forced to premature expression.

2. People moving toward faith need to be able to relate to Christians, so that they can "study their faces," [3] see what faith looks like in practice, how it works in the issues of daily life. They need also the opportunity to learn the language "by immersion" and to "try out" the lessons of faith they are learning.

3. Part of the process is having the time to ask questions, to have them heard respectfully, and to reflect on thoughtful answers. Churches serious about helping people find faith need as a priority to provide safe places where that can happen.

In the late twentieth century, many churches in Canada received government money to add ramps and elevators to their church buildings in order to create access for the physically challenged who wanted to come to church but couldn't do so. To my mind, one of the church's tasks now is to create access to church for the spiritually challenged. Like the physically challenged, they find it difficult simply to walk in, the way that others can do. They need the equivalent of ramps and elevators to enable them to access church in a way that is manageable for them. Otherwise, they may give up in despair.

Here are some of the "ramps," the access points, that evangelistically minded churches have found helpful.

Beginners' courses

Sunday mornings services do not generally provide a suitable context for people to ask questions about faith. Many churches now offer just such a safe place for questions and discussion mid-week. Several programs for introducing people to faith are being used across North American and around the world. I think of programs such as Alpha, Emmaus (also known as Seasons of Celebration), Cursillo, Christianity Explored, and Christian Basics.[4]

Some research, however, suggests that home-grown courses are just as effective in helping people find faith as "packaged" programs, not least because they can be tailored to local needs and culture. Because of this, you do not need to feel limited to what is available "out there." Be creative!

Just one warning, however. I have now tried a couple of those books supposedly written for "dummies," and my conclusion is that many of the people who write those books have long since forgotten what it actually is like to be a dummy in their field. As a result, their attempts to help those of us who are truly dummies are inept. They start too far down the road to be of help to people like me. In the same way, we need to be sure that our so-called beginners' programs really do start where people are at.

Dinner with a speaker

Some years ago, when a university put up new buildings on campus, officials were deciding where to put the footpaths. They knew that if they put the footpaths in the wrong places, nobody would walk on them. The university officials did a very smart thing. They put down grass every-where and watched to see where the grass got worn out. That's where they put the footpaths. In evangelism, a similar principle holds. If you put down pathways to faith in areas where nobody goes, however user-friendly they may be, your paths will go untouched. But watch where people walk in their daily and weekly lives, and put down your pathway to faith there, and see what happens.

One such is the dinner with after-dinner speaker. All sorts of groups do it. Fund-raisers frequently take this form. Social clubs do it. It has become a culturally acceptable setting for people to get together and listen to a speaker.

So why not consider holding a dinner party or banquet for your friends and neighbors. Do whatever you can to make it the best party they have ever been to. Choose your setting carefully. For example, the church basement may not be the most friendly place for visitors even if it's fine for in-house events. The question is: Where is the cultural footpath? Where do people in our world feel comfortable meeting their friends? For some, the answer is at a local hotel. After all, that's where special conferences, work-related seminars, wedding receptions, and fund-raising events are held.

Then invite a well-known local Christian (a politician, a doctor, an engineer, or whatever celebrity you can find) to speak. One church in Ottawa invited a woman whose work had been highlighted in the media to speak about the problem of homelessness. During her talk, she described her own experience as a youngster of being on the street and then being "adopted" by a Christian community.

Sometimes an interesting topic can substitute for a well-known speaker. In the days when people used to laugh over the idea that Elvis was alive, I offered a talk called "Elvis Is Alive, Jesus Is Alive: What's the Difference?" I was also invited to speak at gatherings on topics such as "Spirituality Yes, Religion No" or "The Gospel According to Robin Williams."

You might preface the talk with a special musical or dramatic presentation on the theme of the evening. How you plan such an evening is limited only by your creativity. Make it an occasion people will savor for a long time afterward.

Valentine's Day dinner and dance

This is a special variation on the dinner party idea. For some years, Trinity Anglican Church in Streetsville, Ontario, put on a special dinner and dance on the weekend nearest to Valentine's Day. Church members would invite their friends. Both the dinner and the dance would be of high quality. For about three minutes between the dinner and the dance, Harold, the minister, would speak.

What do you say in that kind of context? "My sermon tonight is taken from Leviticus chapter 3"? Probably not. (Don't misunderstand me: there is a place for preaching from Leviticus. I'm just saying that this is not it.) Harold would say something very simple, like this:

> You may be wondering why a church would want to celebrate Valentine's Day. Well, the answer is not hard to find: Valentine's Day is about love, and the church, too, is about love. In fact, we believe that God is the origin of love and that love is one of God's best gifts to the world. What we do at Trinity on a Sunday morning is to gather to thank God for his gift of love, and to try to figure out more of what it means to live a life of love. If you'd like to join us one of these Sunday mornings to check it out, we'd be delighted to see you. Meanwhile, let the party continue!

The event was great. People came and enjoyed themselves, and they went away feeling thoughtful and content. Some of them showed up at church in the following weeks and months.

What about other special occasions in the calendar as an opportunity to welcome guests? I am not thinking just of Christmas and Easter (although we could probably do a better job of making guests feel at home, rather than assuming they'll just fit in). How does your church celebrate Mother's Day, or Father's Day, or Thanksgiving? Those who decided centuries ago to piggyback Christian celebrations of Christmas and Easter onto existing pagan festivals knew a thing or two about evangelism.

A Saturday conference

The Christian message has something distinctive and life giving to say on most issues of concern in our world. A Christian voice in one of these areas can thus give access to Christian faith for someone concerned about the same question. One such topic is the problem of suffering.

A group of Chinese Christian professionals in Ottawa decided to organize a Saturday conference on the question of suffering. They invited three Christians to be on a panel: a doctor who had worked in Africa, speaking from a medical point of view; a local Chinese pastor who was suffering from a painful and chronic disease, speaking from a personal and spiritual point of view; and myself, speaking about the philosophical/theological aspects.

The religion editor of the local newspaper chaired the event. Nearly a hundred people showed up. The morning was brought to a close with a simple lunch, where people could chat over what had been discussed.

The beauty of this event was in the way it drew church folk and non-church folk together over a subject of mutual concern. It was not in one sense a "religious" event, yet it demonstrated that Christians have worthwhile things to say on a universal human experience.

Suffering, of course, is not the only topic that lends itself to this kind of event (though it is a good one). Communication between adolescents and their parents is another pressing one; so are understanding the media (how to think about movies or music videos), marriage enrichment, successful friendship, and financial management.

A reading or movie group

What do you do about books you "know you ought to" be reading but never get round to reading? Or that movie everybody was talking about but you never managed to see while it was in the cinemas? How about starting a reading group or a video group?

Such groups can work well when all the members have roughly the same belief system, but there is an extra level of interest when the group consists of friends who believe differently. Please don't think this means you have to lobby for "Christian books" or "Christian movies" (which, frankly, are not always the best) but to read any worthwhile and thought-provoking book, or to watch any movie that raises important questions. Many secular authors raise issues on which Christian faith has helpful and stimulating things to contribute: questions of personhood and values, of freedom and sexuality, of guilt and meaning.

Here are some questions to get discussion going:
- How did this book/movie make you feel? Why?
- What do you think the book/movie is trying to say?
- What kind of a world is it portraying? How close is this to the world you experience?
- What answers (if any) is it offering to people's problems? For example, love solves everything, violence is the only way, follow your heart, be your own person. What do we think of those answers?
- Does it say anything about big questions such as the existence of God, life after death, or the meaning of life?
- What is the "take-away value" of this book/movie for you? What is the image, character, or theme that will stay with you? Why?

Some books and movies will provide more food for thought than others, of course. But as long as people are asking these sort of questions, and looking for truth and reality, God will be there. What's more, we will all become more thoughtful readers and movie-goers into the bargain.

Visitors' Sunday

I used to be a member of a church where guest services happened once a month. Probably the majority of the people who found faith in that church (and there were a lot of them) made the discovery at a guest service.

Guest services or Visitors' Sundays or "Come Back to Church Month" can be helpful for people who are looking for faith, when they are well done. But we need to do whatever we can to make them "user-friendly" for the person who has not been inside a church for twenty years, if ever.

Here are some practical suggestions:

- Prepare attractively printed invitation cards. Apart from making the occasion seem more concrete, these also make it easier for church members when inviting friends.

- Publicize the event appropriately with posters, information in local papers, on local radio or TV. These are not a substitute for personal invitation, but they can reinforce a personal invitation.

- Decide on your form of service. There are two basic options:

  1. Do everything as you would at a usual service, but to take time to explain what things mean. If you choose this option, you need also to give visitors the choice of not participating in various elements of the service. If I am an agnostic who has come along to check out Christian faith, and I find that I am required to recite the Nicene Creed, believe me, I won't be back.

  2. Offer a simplified form of service, with singing, praying and reading done from the front, but with minimal expectations of congregational involvement. This goes against the grain for people from liturgical traditions. However, this service is not primarily for us: we have guests, and we behave like hosts.

- Everything that the congregation has to know should be on overheads, Power Point displays, or a single service sheet. More than one source of information is confusing. Can you imagine going to the theater and receiving three different programs?

- Include plenty of variety. Things that work well include drama, special kinds of music and instrumentation, or one or two individuals telling the story of their faith journey.

- Make sure the sermon or talk is appropriate for the occasion. Give it a title that outsiders can relate to, such as "Where Is God When It Hurts?" "Finding a Love That Lasts" "Who Needs God?" or "Healing Life's Hurts." Print the title on the invitation card and posters. Consider a question-and-answer period, either during the service, or over coffee afterward. That communicates a posture of openness, which (sadly) people do not expect in the church.

- Provide a nursery (mention it in publicity) and refreshments afterward.

- Advertise opportunities to explore questions further, perhaps in a Christian Basics series or an Agnostics Anonymous group (see below).

Agnostics Anonymous

In an interview with *The Door,* a satirical Christian magazine, psychiatrist M. Scott Peck said that the main thing that brought him to Christian faith was reading the stories of Jesus and being irresistibly drawn to him:

> I was absolutely thunderstruck by the reality of the man I found in the Gospels. . . . I realized that this Jesus was so real that no-one could have made him up. . . . I began to suspect that the Gospel writers, instead of being mythmakers and embellishers, were in fact extremely accurate and conservative reporters.[5]

Whenever someone is interested in studying "the biographies of Jesus" (do we have to call them "the Gospels"?), you know they are going to come face to face with the heart of the Christian message, and the job of evangelism is half done.

If you have ever led a church Bible study, you can probably lead one for unchurched people, where they learn about Jesus. The approach is exactly the same: the group dynamics, the sort of open-ended questions you ask, the atmosphere of acceptance, the hospitality, the sense of being learners together.

You don't have to call your group Agnostics Anonymous, but I still think it's a brilliant name. (I wish I had invented it, but I didn't.) The echo of Alcoholics Anonymous makes people smile because they immediately understand what the group is for, and what it is not for. Just as AA is a mutual support group for those wanting to fight their alcoholism, so Agnostics Anonymous is a mutual support group for those wanting to figure out if there really is a God. Just as AA is non-hierarchical with each person having an equal right to speak, so Agnostics Anonymous promises to be. Both are safe places to be.

I usually begin by saying, "This group exists to be useful to you as you try to figure out what to believe about God and Jesus. There are only two rules around here: one, that we all feel free to say exactly what we think, and, two, that the rest of us respect what is said even when we disagree with it."

Then I invite people to share something of where they are coming from spiritually. I offer them some options as to what they might like to say. Have they ever had exposure to church or Christian faith? What prompted them to come to this group? What do they hope to get out of it? Generally, I share first, so that I model the kind of vulnerability I hope for and how long to speak. Then I listen carefully to what each person contributes and affirm their desire to move forward spiritually.

The main difference between this study group and a regular church study group is obvious: you can't take anything for granted. Language, assumptions, and background knowledge all will be different for every person in the group. I remember one group where a Christian young woman kept quoting Paul ("Paul says this . . . Paul seems to think . . ." —this in spite of the fact we were studying a Gospel). Eventually, one man asked in frustration, "Who is this Paul? Your boyfriend?"

We need to proceed more slowly, check more often that everybody is understanding, explain things more simply. Of course, when it comes to applying the lessons of the study, you cannot assume that everybody will want to believe or behave as a follower of Jesus. A Muslim friend once asked me, "How is it different to live as a Christian from how it is to live as a Muslim?" He wasn't saying he wanted to become a Christian, he just wanted to understand better. So with an "AgAnon" group: what does it look like and feel like to believe in Jesus and follow Jesus? The question of what we may want to do about it will look after itself in due time.

A study like this can be more fun than you ever believed evangelism could be. It will challenge you, keep you awake at night, energize your praying, get you borrowing reference books from your pastor or church library, and make Jesus more real to you (let alone to anyone else).

Individual interests

A university professor I know is a remarkable connoisseur of teas. On my first evening in his home, he asked me what kind of tea I would like. In my naiveté, I shrugged and said, "Oh, orange pekoe would be fine." He looked over his glasses at me and pronounced, "Orange pekoe is not a kind of tea: it is a grade of tea." Well, that was the start of a very interesting visit, during which I learned more than I could ever remember about teas of the world.

By coincidence, while I was there one evening, the professor and his wife held a tea-tasting evening, the third annual such. Ten or so friends came and, during the evening, we sampled a selection of half a dozen kinds of tea (different ones were offered each year), and had some of the little-known wonders of tea explained to us. As the evening wore on, people got into conversation, still nursing cups of various kinds of tea (none of them orange pekoe, I might add). It became clear that some of the visitors (a minority) were Christians, and the rest were of other persuasions, and that some of the conversations were floating in and out of topics of spiritual interest.

I realized that what my friends were doing, apart from creating a very fine and unusual kind of party, was to create a forum where Christians and others could mingle easily. Of course, you do not have to be an expert on tea. But whatever your special interest or hobby, you can use it to create a setting to share something of your home, your interest, and your life.

The ethics of evangelism

In the movie *The Big Kahuna*, three businessmen are trying to win a big contract. Despite their best efforts, only one actually meets the head of the company they are pursuing. Bob is the youngest and least experienced of the three, and just happens to be an evangelical Christian. Instead of talking business to the Big Kahuna, he talks about Jesus.

His two colleagues cannot believe that he would fail them so dismally, and they are not impressed by his argument that it is more important to talk about Jesus than to talk about business. But their other objection is an ethical one, and it is Danny DeVito's character who makes it. He says, "Any time you steer a conversation toward Jesus, you have stopped being a friend." In other words, if you manipulate a person into talking about something they are really not interested in, you are not treating them with respect.

So are the kinds of events I am describing manipulative, trying to make people do something they don't really want to do, like pawns on a chessboard? Are they just a subtle, discreet, respectable form of flashing?

I start with the realization that if I am being manipulative, I am a million miles from the Spirit of Jesus and my evangelism is not going to reflect his beauty. Here are three questions I ask myself, just to keep a check on whether an activity is worthy of Christ or not.

1. Is this activity a legitimate expression of Christian faith?

A dinner and dance is something a church might put on anyway as a celebration of faith; a Saturday conference on suffering is a legitimate activity for Christians to run as a learning event. They would do those things even if everybody was a follower of Jesus and evangelism was not a concern.

Other things, however, are more questionable. Take an extreme and unlikely example: a casino evening. It could be a popular and well attended event for a church to run. People might well be interested in coming, and might even have a good time. Maybe somebody would offer them Bibles or invitations to a Sunday service as they left. But visitors would be deceived if they thought this was somehow a reflection of Christian spirituality and a foretaste of church life. That's manipulation.

2. Is the agenda up front or hidden?

If I say, "Come to this dinner party some friends are putting on. A local Olympic athlete is going to be giving an after-dinner talk"—that's manipulation. I am withholding crucial information in order to get a response my friends might not make if they knew the full facts. They might with justification say afterward, "You never said this was a church thing. You know how I feel about church. I trusted you." It is that last statement—"I trusted you"—that is the real reproach. If we are representatives of Jesus, we have to be trustworthy.

We need to be up front. "My church is putting on a great dinner at the Queen's Hotel a couple of Saturdays from now, and our Member of Parliament is going to be talking about how her faith affects her politics. I think it'll be a really good evening. Do you think you'd like to come?" Now if they come, they know what to expect. If they feel uncomfortable with the idea, they can say no. Either way, our relationship is still intact.

If a person challenges me—"Hey, are you trying to convert me?"— I have to be honest. I will say something like this: "Well, personally, I think it's wonderful to be a Christian, so I'd be crazy to say I wouldn't love for you to experience that, too. But nobody can convert anybody. After all, you haven't converted me to golf after all these years. I think that kind of stuff is between you and God, right? (The faith, that is, not the golf.)"

3. Is there anything being said about this event in private that could not be said in front of guests?

Some preachers would be embarrassed to have an outsider to faith listen in on their sermon about evangelism. The reason is that their emphasis is on how you get people to do what they don't really want to do, so if they knew what you were hoping, they might not do what you hoped after all! This approach to evangelism is also manipulation, and contrary to the spirit of Christ.

It is not a bad principle to say, as we plan this event, would we be comfortable having one of our intended guests listen in on the conversation? Or indeed, to have one of those intended guests actually on the planning committee?

As people taste the reality of spiritual life in the Christian community, they will ask questions. I find it significant that there are no direct exhortations to evangelism in the New Testament epistles, but there are two warnings that we should be ready to answer people's questions (1 Peter 3:15 and Colossians 4:6). So what do we say when our visitors ask, "What exactly is this faith stuff all about?" That's the question we turn to next.

15.

Commitment:

Baby Steps and Giant Strides

I am still not free enough to let myself be held completely in the safe embrace of the Father. In many ways I am still moving toward the center. I am still like the prodigal: traveling, preparing speeches, anticipating how it will be when I finally reach my Father's house. But I am indeed on my way home.

Henri Nouwen, *The Return of the Prodigal Son* [1]

A S A YOUNG UNIVERSITY STUDENT from a respectable Anglican background, the idea of evangelism was new to me. The idea filled me with fear, but also with excitement: the thought that I might be able to make a difference to someone's relationship with God was awesome.

At the beginning of the school year, many of the local churches held guest services to welcome new students; Christian groups on campus likewise made special efforts to welcome newcomers, and if possible to introduce them to the reality of Christian faith.

Alan, like myself, was a new student. Our paths had crossed in the residence dining hall and at some of the orientation sessions for freshmen and, I noticed, at some of the groups for those interested in exploring Christian faith. One night I met Alan on the staircase of the residence, and we got talking.

"Hi, Alan. Didn't I notice you at the Christian fellowship meeting yesterday? Does that mean you're a Christian?" I ventured.

"Actually, no, I'm just checking it out."

"Does that mean you're thinking about becoming a Christian?"

"To be honest, I've been thinking about it for some time, even before coming to university, and I think I've decided I think it's time."

"Is there anything actually holding you back, or do you just need a nudge?"

Alan hesitated and then smiled shyly. "Do you want to come over to my room? I think I'd like to talk about this."

Over instant coffee with powdered milk, we continued the conversation. It soon became obvious that Alan had decided to become a follower of Jesus, and that my main role that evening was to be a catalyst in this crucial stage of his journey to discipleship.

That was fortunate because I didn't really know what to do or say. It was as if I found myself present at the birth of a baby, with absolutely no knowledge of midwifery and only some folk memories of hot water and towels. We knelt on his floor (he seemed to think that was the right thing to do, and I didn't know any differently) and he prayed to Jesus and asked to become his disciple. It was as simple as that.

Alan died a few years later at the age of twenty-eight. He had always had a weak heart, and he was not embarrassed to say that the possibility of death had made him more serious about considering faith. He had finished his degree in chemistry, gone on to study for the Anglican ordained ministry, and had just finished three years as an assistant curate. His last letter to me had said, "I have no idea what happens next, and My Lord (ambivalence intended) is not saying anything just yet."

Whatever his Lord Bishop's plans, the Lord Jesus' plans for Alan were not for this world.

I am grateful to Alan and to God for what I learned from that experience of helping him take his first step in Christian discipleship. A student once told me how he had asked an Anglican bishop, "If I came to you and asked how I could become a Christian, what would you say?" After some humming and hawing, the bishop finally replied, "I'm really not sure. I think I'd have to send you to someone wiser than myself." Sometimes modesty is commendable; in this instance, it seemed to me sad. What I learned from Alan was that the youngest, most untrained, and inarticulate Christian can actually help someone else to find faith in Christ.

Of course, that was a long time ago. Over the years since then, that kind of experience has very seldom come my way again. I have seen many people become Christians, but it has seldom been in such a clear-cut and decisive way. I think now maybe that was a special gift from God.

Since then my understanding of how God works in our lives has also developed and changed. Back then, I had little understanding of faith as a gradual process: it was a black-and-white, once-for-all kind of thing.

Then, I thought evangelism was only what happened with Alan that night: I did not understand that there are many gifts of evangelism and that all of them are needed. Like many from my tradition at that time, I also had little sense of the importance of baptism or of church; I thought of faith primarily as a private matter between you and God.

So what is the lesson of my experience with Alan? How do I incorporate that into my present understanding and practice of evangelism? I suppose I have relativized it. By that I mean there are still many people who come to faith in Christ through that kind of experience. For them the process of God working in their lives leads to a major crisis and turning point. I for one don't want to stop those people from having their crisis! More than that, I believe that every Christian, especially those in leadership, should be able to help someone like Alan take a definitive step if that is how the Holy Spirit seems to be working with them.

But here's where the relativity comes in. I don't want to insist that everyone has to come to faith in Christ that way. Nicky described an experience of being pressured to "pray a prayer of commitment":

> One afternoon I was studying in my room, and heard a knock at the door. It was the leader of the "Who is God?" group I had been attending. I invited him in, and he sat down on my bed, and asked me if I had prayed the prayer accepting Jesus into my life. I was taken aback . . . thinking his question strange. I agreed to try praying in the way that he had described sometime. . . . For my own part, I think that I had prayed the prayer he suggested several times. I began wondering if I wasn't doing it right, or if it hadn't "taken."

Clearly, God was at work in Nicky's life, but not in the way the leader assumed. Nicky's friend Sarah, maybe because she knew Nicky better, was a shrewder judge of what was happening and of what kind of care was needed.

How does a person become a Christian anyway?

Most of this book has assumed the usefulness of the process model of evangelism: evangelism means helping people take steps toward faith in Christ. I have done that partly because it has proved so fruitful for me over the years. But I have also spent time discussing it because it is particularly appropriate in our culture. Christians shy away from what they see as a confrontative approach in evangelism, and in general I think they are right to do so. And because people in our culture generally are nervous about big commitments, especially in relationships (the term *commitment-phobe* was not around much twenty years ago), it is helpful to be reminded that God welcomes our baby steps of commitment just as much as our giant strides.

In this chapter, however, I want to address the following question. Suppose the conversation between you and a friend takes the sort of turn mine with Alan took. How would you respond if someone said to you, "So what would you say it really means to be a Christian?" Or, "I would love to have the sort of faith you have, but I don't really know what it's all about." Or, "So how does a person become a Christian anyway?"

Nicky reached this kind of point with Sarah, and Sarah's response was to encourage the process:

> It was around this time that I realized I wasn't really a Christian. I thought I was, but I wasn't. I remember sitting on my bed one night, saying this to Sarah and asking her what I should do. She wisely suggested that I should continue to learn more about Jesus, and to decide whether I wanted to follow him. She also suggested praying and reading the Bible.

For Nicky, this was right. Yet would it not be nice if we could answer what is (in a way, at least) a simple question with a straightforward answer—even if the end of the conversation is still, "Well, keep learning, keep praying, keep reading"? I have three favorite pictures that I use to answer this kind of direct question about faith:

1. The parable of the prodigal son.   (Luke 15)
2. The image of Jesus knocking at the door.   (Revelation 3:20)
3. The invitation to discipleship.   (Matthew 11:28-30)

I find myself drawn to these passages, because each of the three is found in a single place in Scripture, all three are pictures rather than propositions, all three invite a variety of responses, and all three are the words of Jesus.

So, what does it mean to become a Christian? Here's the sort of thing I might say. In each case, I want to make it clear that I am drawing on the teaching of Jesus, not just my own ideas, and I want to offer my friend various possible responses to the picture, from baby steps to giant strides.

Picture 1: Coming home

Jesus once told a story that, to my mind, explains very clearly what it means to "become a Christian." The story concerns a son who tells his father he wants to leave home. The father agrees to give him his inheritance ahead of time, as it were, so the son has plenty of money to do what he wants or travel as far away as he'd like. In time, however, the money runs out, there is a food shortage in the land, and the son ends up feeding pigs and having only the pig swill to eat.

Then he begins to think about home, and he remembers that even the servants there always had enough to eat. Jesus actually says that "he came to himself" (Luke 15:17)—meaning, I think, that he saw things as they really were. As a result, the son leaves the pig farm and the distant land and makes his way toward home. (I imagine him having to walk the whole way, and feeling very tired and sorry for himself.)

As he heads for home, his father recognizes him off in the distance. (The father was on the lookout, I suspect.) The father runs to meet him. The father isn't interested in the boy's apologies, he's just overjoyed to have him back home. He calls all the neighbors in and throws a great banquet to welcome the son home. Jesus comments that the angels in heaven party over such a homecoming. Churches that follow baptisms with a party seem to me to have the right idea!

Jesus is saying that God is like the Father in this story and that we are like the son who left home. Jesus believed that the heart of what is wrong in our lives is that we haven't followed God as we should. Of course, like the boy in the story, once we get away from God, although we enjoy that kind of freedom in lots of ways, eventually our resources will run out.

In the movie *Patch Adams*, the title character describes all of life as a sort of "coming home." Everyone is restless until they can find their way there. I think that's similar to what Jesus was talking about. We have a sense of being away from home, but we don't know how to get back.

Jesus' story says there's only one thing to do: we need the courage to get up, go back to God, and admit that we have blown it. According to Jesus, God is just overjoyed to have us back. Jesus is telling us that's how God feels when we decide to return!

Of course, I would be surprised if, even after this joyful reconciliation, there are not still days when the relationship between the father and the son is tense. Maybe there are days when the distant land still seems attractive. But little by little the son learns how to live as a true son of the father.[2]

To become a Christian, then, means admitting that we haven't followed God—recognizing that we have strayed from home—and telling God that we want to come back home and live as God's children.

I suppose that, in relation to Christian faith, some people are still having a good time in the far-off land. They're not interested. Others are sitting in the pigpen wondering what went wrong. Some are saying, "You know, I think it's time I started for home." Still others are somewhere on the road, moving toward home, some faster, some slower. Some have caught sight of the father running to meet them with outstretched arms and have broken into a run to meet him. Yet others are beginning to learn the ways of the father's house. If it seems appropriate, I might ask, "Where do you think you are in that sequence?"

Picture 2: Opening the door

There's a wonderful picture at the end of the Bible that for me sums up what it means to become a Christian. Here Jesus says, "Listen! I am standing at the door, knocking; if you hear my voice and open the door, I will come in to you and eat with you, and you with me" (Revelation 3:20).

Nineteenth-century painter Holman Hunt's *The Light of the World* [3] pictures the door as overgrown with weeds. It obviously hasn't been opened for a long time. And there is no handle on the outside, presumably since the door can be opened only from the inside. Jesus stands outside, knocking on the door, holding a lantern in the other hand.

Jesus originally said these words to a church community where at least some of the members had shut Jesus out, and it is possible that the image of eating together may well refer to the Communion service. I asked my wife, Deborah, what she thought about this one morning when we were walking the dog. "Well," she said, "I remember vividly how, when I first began to get involved with Christians, I always had this sense that they knew a reality that I didn't, and, that if I wanted to be fully part of their community, I would have to open the door to Jesus as they had done."[4]

So we can think of the door as the door to our spirituality, our experience, and our personality. The reason Jesus is on the outside is that by nature we find it more comfortable not to let Jesus get too near. We prefer to run our lives our way and not be his followers. Yet Jesus goes on standing outside and knocking. The reason, he says, is that he wants to eat with us. Sharing a meal with someone is often a sign of friendship. (The word *companion* means literally someone we break bread with.) So Jesus says these words as an offer of friendship.

Our friendship with Jesus is not a friendship between equals, of course. Jesus comes into our "house" not just as a friend but also as the landlord who actually owns the property. We are merely the tenants who have been entrusted with our lives. So when Jesus comes in, it is not only to eat with us but also to take possession of what is rightfully his and make whatever changes he sees fit. Jesus brings joy, but he can also bring discomfort. The plans we are drawing for our "home" may be different from the plans Jesus brings.

When Jesus speaks of "knocking," that's symbolic, like everything else in this picture. The ways Jesus gets people's attention, the ways people hear his "knocking," are many. For some people, it's through friends or family whose life is intriguing and attractive because of the faith dimension. (This was Deborah's experience.) Other people may hear Jesus' knocking through a trauma that drives them to serious prayer for the first time, or perhaps a delightful surprise or coincidence that makes them look over their shoulders to see if God is there smiling. Some people experience answers to prayer that they never really dared to expect. Others are over-whelmed by the majesty of nature and come to sense the reality of the Creator. Still others attend a service or a talk or concert and suddenly find themselves drawn and convinced in a way they never expected. The variety is infinite, and God knows what kind of "knocking" will best catch the ear of each of us.

So what do we do? Well, when someone comes to our door, there's a variety of responses we can have. Sometimes we will first check who it is through a "spy hole" or from behind the curtains. There are some people who come to my door I'm not sure whether I should invite in, so I'll open the door and talk to them as they are standing on the doorstep. I trust other people a little more—the pizza deliverer, for example—so I may invite them to stand in the hall while we do our transaction. But then there are people I know and trust, and I immediately ask them in, take their coats, and make them feel welcome.

Getting to know Jesus is similar. Some people are having a conversa-tion with him on the doorstep or in the hallway, just getting to know him, trying to decide how trustworthy he really is. Others are beginning to trust him and have invited him in for a meal. Some people have decided to give Jesus free run of the house and told him to treat it as if it were his own (which, of course, it is anyway).

Picture 3: Joining the school

Christianity is a little like a school, a school for learning about life from the one who created it in the first place. Another way to think about becoming a Christian is joining the school of Jesus. Jesus once said:

> Come to me, all you that are weary and carrying heavy burdens, and I will give you rest. Take my yoke upon you, and learn from me; for I am gentle and humble in heart, and you will find rest for your souls. For my yoke is easy, and my burden is light. (Matthew 11:28-30)

Jesus offers himself as a teacher. He says, "Come . . . learn from me." He speaks to those who are tired of life and its demands, maybe even of the demands of religion[5] and invites them to learn from him a new and better way of living.

How do we learn? We learn by being yoked to him. The picture is of a younger and an older ox, yoked together to pull the plough or the cart. It is as though Jesus is the older, experienced ox and we are the apprentice ox, learning the techniques of pulling the plough and responding to the farmer. In other words, Jesus invites us to become his students, to join his school and to begin a practical apprenticeship in how to live as God's person in God's world in God's way.[6]

Like any program of study, there are days when it will seem tedious and the assignments difficult. But there are also rewards, above all the joy of learning about life from life's Creator, and the sense of becoming the person we were meant to be.

Some people are reading the calendar for the school of Jesus and checking out the course descriptions to see if they sound like what they are looking for. Others are adding up the costs of the program to see if they are willing to spend that much. Still others are actually getting into the introductory courses, doing the readings, getting to know other students, and discussing the assignments.

Taking steps in prayer

I knew Deborah for three years before we got married. Over those three years, there were several stages in the growth of our relationship. One night when we walked back from the library to her residence, we acknowledged that this was a special relationship for both of us. There was the first time we were seen in public as "a couple." I remember other landmarks: the first kiss, the first time we prayed together, the first time we met one another's families. There was the night when I asked Deborah if she would marry me. She said yes, and eight months later we were married.

On one level, the significant stages were: being recognized as a couple, the engagement, and the marriage. Yet those big public things would never have happened if the little daily things had not happened. In a sense, every conversation was a building block in the relationship, every idea shared, every piece of music one of us introduced to the other, every time we met at the library, every argument, every walk, every church service. The bigger could never have existed without the smaller. But at the same time, the bigger, outward and public things were needed, too, in order to validate and nudge forward the smaller.

So with Jesus. The relationship is built of little things: going to a church service, reading the Bible, praying, forgiving a small irritation, asking questions, singing a chorus in the shower, trying out a Bible study group, thinking, "What would Jesus do?" But this relationship, too, is punctuated by public moments. Baptism is the most obvious, but confirmation in some traditions and profession of faith in others serve the same purpose. Those public occasions (in theory, at least) sum up the progress of the relationship to that point and energize it for the next stage.

I believe we can help one another by creating some of those "public occasions," at least on a small scale, by offering to pray with someone. If someone says, "You know, I think I'm like the son on the road. I know I've left, but I'm just as sure I haven't yet met the father," I will offer to pray with them that they may feel the father's arms around them soon. If they say, "Well, I've been chatting with Jesus in the hall for about six months, and I feel now is the time I should let him into the rest of the house," a prayer can help validate that choice. If they say, "You know, I just registered in the school of Jesus a couple of months back, and I'm just starting my first course," a prayer can encourage them to keep going.

"Yes, but . . ."

Often when people are facing the challenge of following Jesus, whether it's the first step or a subsequent one, they realize also that they have questions and doubts that make them hesitate. Here are some of the most common ones I've heard, along with some of the responses I have tried to offer.

"I still have a lot of questions."

They might say, "I have problems with the church, I have questions about the Bible, and I'm not convinced Jesus is the only way to God. Surely I should be further on in my thinking before I get any more deeply involved in this Christian stuff?"

I might say in return, "Questions are great. It's normal to have questions. The Christian life is one where there are new questions all the time. I find it's one of the most stimulating things about following someone who calls himself the Truth!"

This means that real faith is actually compatible with a wide range of questions. I remember clearly, for some years after I began to take my faith seriously, continuing to wrestle with questions ranging all the way from "Isn't it arrogant for me to call myself a Christian?" to "What do people mean when they say the Bible is the Word of God?" In fact, many of those questions I have continued to revisit over the years, and each time I have learned something new in the process.

Of course, some questions do get answered. (There are few questions about Christian faith that have not been chewed over by thoughtful believers at some point over the past two thousand years.) And then, trust me, other brand new questions will come along to take their place.

So if being a Christian doesn't mean the absence of doubts or having answers to all theological questions, what does it mean? I remain convinced that at the heart of Christian faith is allegiance to Jesus Christ. If I bring my questions to him and continue to follow him in the areas where I am fairly sure, I can legitimately call myself a Christian. After all, the person with no doubts or questions, the one with the most clear theology but absolutely no allegiance to Jesus Christ is probably the devil. Of course, some of your questions may be about the devil . . .

"Becoming a Christian can't be that simple."

"You say being a Christian is simply allegiance to Jesus? Saying yes to him? Taking steps toward him and with him? Come on, it has to be more complicated than that."

Many things can be simple if we choose to make them so. I wear a simple gold band on the fourth finger of my left hand. To Deborah and to me that ring symbolizes over thirty years of love, hassle, laughter, sexual pleasure, growing, pain, fun, conversation, working together, child-bearing, and child-rearing. How can a small ring symbolize so much? Simply because we choose to invest it with that significance.

So if our attitude to Jesus is a serious one, if we mean what we say, then to say "yes" to Jesus, to take steps in his direction, is enough to connect us with him. But if we are not serious, then no amount of complexity or ritual will make up for it.

"I was baptized and confirmed—isn't that enough?"

The best answer to this question is: "You tell me!" Some people will say, "God has been real to me as long as I can remember. I try to love and obey Jesus ever day." Personally, I know of no Christianity that is more real than that. If your baptism and confirmation have brought you to that kind of faith, then yes, of course, they are enough. However, baptism (at least in Anglican tradition) is "an outward and visible sign of an inward and spiritual grace," and, in my case and that of many others, while we had the visible sign we had no awareness of spiritual grace.

Your baptism and confirmation may be like that. For me, it was not until a couple of years after my confirmation that I became a deliberate and serious follower of Jesus. I came to see that this was not a denial of my baptism and confirmation but, rather, it was exactly what they had been all about. They had been signposts pointing me in the direction that I had now decided to follow for myself.

"I'm not sure I'm ready for the next step."

The next step in relation to Jesus may be getting involved in a church community, it may be reading the Gospels for the first time, or it may be letting Jesus into more rooms of the house. Whatever it is, we may be right to say, "I'm not ready." It would be irresponsible to encourage people to take a fresh step if they are genuinely not ready. Jesus himself encouraged would-be disciples to count the cost.

On the other hand, "I'm not ready" may be a way of saying, "I'm afraid." For example, my wife and I waited to have children until we thought we were "ready." But when our children were born there was still a deep sense of unreadiness and, frankly, of near panic when they actually came. Still, we coped. Feeling unready was a fear of a totally new experience that nothing had adequately prepared us for.

In facing Christian commitment, sometimes the response "I'm not ready" may similarly mean, "I'm scared." The answer to fear is the supportiveness of the Christian community and the strength of the Spirit within.

Conversions sudden and gradual

The quotation from Henri Nouwen that appears at the beginning of this chapter tells an important truth. When Jesus told the story of the prodigal son, it was in response to the Pharisees' criticism that he spent too much time hanging out with the losers of their world. He told the story to show that these supposed "losers" were the prodigal sons who had returned home, and that his frequent banquets were like the party the father throws at the end of the parable.

The Pharisees, conversely, were like the older brother in the story. In the story, the older brother was still out in the field. In other words, for Jesus, you could say that some people had clearly returned home and others had not.

Nouwen, however, highlights a different reading. Even those followers who have clearly returned home, who know the love of the Father, may discover how little they really know God's love. They may still feel like the prodigal son living in another land, thinking about returning.

Do we have to choose one interpretation over the other? I don't think so. The Bible speaks to us in different ways at different points in our lives. We may say of someone who has just begun to follow Jesus that "the prodigal has returned" and it will be true. We may equally well say after 30 or 40 years of living as Christians that we still have not fully come home yet, and that will be true, too.

I meet Christians who don't want to talk about crisis points in the spiritual life. "Ah," they will say, "but conversion is a daily thing." On the other hand, I meet some Christians who are so concerned for everyone to have a dramatic once-for-all conversion that they seem unconcerned about the need for daily discipleship. I believe there is truth in each, but that each can become an excuse. To talk of daily conversion may be a way of avoiding any conversion at all. To talk of once-for-all conversion may be a way of avoiding the call to conversion in the specifics of daily life.

Once we acknowledge that both understandings are legitimate for followers of Jesus, however, we will be open to either. We will be open to God working suddenly and dramatically in our own lives, and to the daily challenge to live a converted life. As we relate to others on their spiritual journey, we will be sensitive to times when they, too, are at a spiritual crossroads in their lives, as well as to the stresses of daily following Christ.

16.

On Rocks and Mirrors

"Say no more! It is plain enough what you are pointing at." Bilbo the silly hobbit started this affair, and Bilbo had better finish it, or himself. "I am very comfortable here, and getting on with my book. If you want to know, I am just writing an ending for it. I had thought of putting: and he lived happily ever afterward to the end of his days. It is a good ending, and none the worse for having been used before. Now I shall have to alter that: it does not look like coming true; and anyway there will evidently have to be several more chapters, if I live to write them. It is frightful nuisance. When ought I to start?"

Bilbo Baggins in *The Lord of the Rings*, by J. R. R. Tolkien [1]

WE HAVE COME A LONG WAY. In a sense, we have come all the way—from the Garden of Eden to the New Jerusalem. I find that my understanding and my convictions have grown with every step of the journey. Here are four of my main discoveries, the things I treasure most.

1. Evangelism is God's idea, not ours.

In fact, it is one key to understanding what God is about in our world. This I find both challenging and reassuring. Challenging because it means we cannot be serious about following God without beginning to share God's heartbeat for evangelism. Reassuring because it means God is in control of this scary thing called evangelism, and God is, I believe, committed to joy and creativity and wholeness.

2. Jesus embodies God's concern for the world.

His words and his works shape a window through which we see God in action. As I look at Jesus, the New Testament writers encourage me to say, "So that's what God is like!" I love to watch the way he interacts with individuals, with a style that is at once respectful, imaginative, and intriguing. He is, as John's Gospel asserts, "full of grace and truth" (John 1:14), and not one without the other. I want to learn from him.

3. Evangelism is best understood as a process.

This has been an eye-opener. Like any good theory, it makes a lot of sense and explains so much. The gospel of Jesus Christ is something we grow into gradually, both in our understanding and in our practice. Jesus' images of sowing and reaping and his willingness to be thought of as a rabbi with disciples underscore his understanding that kingdom work takes time.

4. Evangelism is the work of the whole Christian community.

If each person does what they are gifted to do, however insignificant any individual piece may seem, a rich tapestry of evangelism will result. There is no single evangelist mold that every Christians has to squeeze into. Indeed, it is because of the diversity of the community and its giftedness that evangelism can take as many forms as there are people to hear the good news. So where does that leave us? What does it mean for us in our churches, our homes, our places of work?

Doing what you know

Sometimes when we read the Bible we don't see what is printed on the page before our eyes. Here's an example. I have often read the following parable to church and student groups, and asked them the simple question: What does the rock stand for in this story?

> Everyone then who hears these words of mine and acts on them will be like a wise man who built his house on rock. The rain fell, the floods came, and the winds blew and beat on that house, but it did not fall, because it had been founded on rock. And everyone who hears these words of mine and does not act on them will be like a foolish man who built his house on sand. The rain fell, and the floods came, and the winds blew and beat against that house, and it fell—and great was its fall! (Matthew 7:24-27)

The answers I receive are varied. They sound very spiritual. The rock stands for faith, Jesus, the church, salvation, God, God's love, being a disciple, the Bible. All those are good answers—in the sense that they are necessary things to have as foundations to one's life. Unfortunately, in this case they are pure speculation and not at all what Jesus actually said! Maybe Jesus' point will be clearer if we isolate these two statements:

Everyone then who hears these words of mine and acts on them will be like a wise man.

Everyone who hears these words of mine and does not act on them will be like a foolish man.

These men are similar in two ways: they hear the words of Jesus, and they set out to build houses. They are dissimilar in every other respect: one is wise, one is foolish, one builds on rock, the other on sand, and . . . one acts on Jesus' words, the other does not. There it is. Not particularly complicated or even theological. The two went to the same Bible study group, sat through the same sermons, maybe went to the same theological college, even read the same book on evangelism. But there the similarity ends. One obeys, one does not. One does something about what he has learned, the other forgets—and the results are far-reaching.

The writer of the book of James understands this principle, too, and uses another analogy to help us see that disobedience is as foolish as building a house with no foundations. He expresses it this way:

Be doers of the word, and not merely hearers who deceive themselves. For if any are hearers of the word and not doers, they are like those who look at themselves in a mirror; for they look at themselves and, on going away, immediately forget what they were like. But those who look into the perfect law, the law of liberty, and persevere, being not hearers who forget but doers who act—they will be blessed in their doing. (James 1:22-25)

It is the evening of the big date, the important meeting, the special party. You are dressed in your best, and as the driver honks from the drive-way, you take one last look in the mirror:

Mirror, mirror, on the wall . . . Whoa! However did your hair get mussed up like that? Look, and at the corner of your mouth, can those be crumbs from that five o'clock snack? Oh no: could that possibly be a dribble of orange juice down your front? And for goodness's sake, you need to wipe your nose.

Two possible scenarios follow:

1. I can't go yet. Tell Pete to stop honking. I need another five minutes. I'll be there as soon as I've cleaned up. I simply cannot go looking like this.
2. Oh well, it can't be helped. Pete's getting frantic out there. Maybe nobody will notice. Let's go.

Does one strike you as more realistic than the other? James says, when we listen to the teaching of Jesus and do nothing about it, we bear a close resemblance to the strange person in Scenario 2. Jesus' teaching, God's truth, is intended to help us clean up our act, identify the junk in our lives that stops us growing, and develop more Christ-like qualities in us. When we ignore what God tells us, the result is not a pretty sight.

That's just a small example, but that is how James recommends that we live all the time—taking the commands and promises of God's truth as seriously as we take the view in the mirror.

So where might God be asking us to be obedient—or more obedient—in evangelism? After all, God is not interested in merely filling our brains with fresh information, but in empowering us to live in a distinctive way as followers of Jesus in the world.

Doing what you're good at

I have said already that I have a strong conviction that evangelism is a ministry of the whole body of Christ, not that of a few outstanding individuals. We do not all need to be Billy Graham. Some members of the body of Christ need his kind of gift, but by no means all. For evangelism to work, it takes each of us doing whatever we are able to do. I know, for instance, that what I am best at is giving talks to try and help people make sense of Christianity's claims. That's my best contribution to the process of evangelism. For me, speaking to someone in the next seat on a train or plane is very, very hard. Yet I know that for many people the opposite is true. They talk to their neighbors very comfortably—and enjoy it—while for them giving a public speech (specially about faith) would be sheer torture. We really do have different gifts. What we need to do is to discover what sort of thing we can contribute to the evangelistic process, and then do it to the best of our ability.

If you are good at inviting people to church, then go ahead, invite them.

If you can lead good Bible studies, try leading an Agnostics Anonymous group for unbelieving friends and neighbors.

If you have a neat group of Christian friends, ask an outsider to come with you next time you go to a ball game or a concert together.

If you find it easy to tell a personal story, tell the story of what your faith means to you when it seems appropriate.

If you love reading, lend a Christian book you have enjoyed. As a result of a chat with my barber, I lent him C. S. Lewis's *Mere Christianity*. Next time I saw him, he told me, to my amazement, that he had not only read it but read it twice—and then he bought six copies to give to friends!

If you love getting to know new people, ask them whether they grew up with church and what that experience meant to them.

If you believe in prayer, tell people you will pray for them. (Of course, then you have to remember to do it!) My friend Maggie told me a story that is typical of her. A friend was describing the problems of a family member, and Maggie asked for his first name. The friend told her, but then added, "But why are you asking?" "So that I can pray for him," Maggie replied.

If you are a party-lover, throw a party for the neighborhood. Make sure the church folk mingle with the non-church folk, and watch what happens.

If you love to serve, look for opportunities to serve your unchurched neighbors with cheerfulness and patience.

If something neat happened at church, mention it when people are talking on Monday morning about how their weekend went.

Each of these may seem trivial by itself, but God the Evangelist can use such acts to pursue a runaway child. Many small experiences go into a person's coming to faith—and many Christians being faithful over such "trivia" contribute more to the process of evangelism than they may realize.

God's evangelism never ends

One more thing. Earlier, I argued that each person we meet is in the process of either moving toward God or trying to get away from God. And God is involved in, indeed initiates, that process—inviting, coaxing, challenging, warning, encouraging people to move in God's direction. Yet the lives of those of us who are attempting to follow Jesus are in process, too. On that scale of 1 to 100 from chapter 6, even if we reckon we are heading in the right direction, the process of spiritual development and growth continues. The difference is that, once we are spiritually awake and choosing to live our life in the company of Jesus, we are aware of the process and more willingly cooperate with it.

In writing to the Christians at Rome, Paul says a strange thing. He expresses his "eagerness to proclaim the gospel to you also who are in Rome" (Romans 1:15). In Greek, "proclaim the gospel" is once again the term from which we get our word evangelize. But how can Paul say that he wants to evangelize those who are already Christians? He clearly says he wants to evangelize "you," those to whom he is writing, whom he has already called "God's beloved in Rome, who are called to be saints" (Romans 1:7), that is, Christians.

If Paul is indeed speaking here of evangelizing Christians, it would be the only time in the whole New Testament that this idea is expressed. This is not an impossible idea. Indeed, one could argue that the whole of the Letter to the Romans is nothing less than Paul "proclaiming good news" (that is, evangelizing) the Christians at Rome. Certainly, by the end of the letter, they have heard much more of the good news than they would ever have understood before. I imagine their reaction might be, "Wow, there is so much more to this Christian faith than we ever knew. This is amazing!"

Maybe the Christian life is simply a life of exploring and experiencing more and more of God's good news. Oh, sure, God breaks bad news to us along the way, too. I well remember a friend high up in government letting slip one day how much he earned, and suddenly realizing that I had a problem with envy that somehow had escaped my notice before!

This is bad news. Yet even something like that can be the prelude to good news: God makes the gift of repentance available, I am forgiven and restored, and God begins to teach me in a new way to be content with what I have. As a result, I actually end up knowing more of the gospel than I did beforehand.

To me, some of the best news in the whole Bible is in two announcements of the apostle Paul about God's long-term plans for the world, one about the human creation, one about what we call the natural world:

> All of us, with unveiled faces, seeing the glory of the Lord as though reflected in a mirror, are being transformed into the same image from one degree of glory to another; for this comes from the Lord, the Spirit. (2 Corinthians 3:18)

> The creation itself will be set free from its bondage to decay and will obtain the freedom of the glory of the children of God. (Romans 8:21)

Both announcements speak of glory, the character of God, clearly visible to all: according to the first, in us who look to Jesus for leadership; in the other, in the natural world, which bears the Artist's signature.

This is the culmination of all the other good news that God has given us, that in the end God will graciously restore us to what we were always meant to be, and that in the end the Creator will restore the creation to what it was always meant to be. And all of the other good news along the way—the possibility of forgiveness, the gift of the Spirit to change us, the breaking down of human barriers, the guidance of Scripture, the sustenance of worship, and a thousand others—will finally reach its climax in a huge, ultimate, literally cosmic celebration of God's goodness, when human creation and natural creation will party together. That would shed some light on why Jesus so often went to parties and used them as illustrations of the kingdom of God: they were rehearsals for the real thing.

Does the good news end when God's restoration of this world is complete? Not necessarily. It would make sense to me that in God's new world, we will simply go on and on learning more and more of God's goodness, and celebrating it more and more. There will always be more things to say, "Thank you, Lord!" about. There will never be an end to what we can know of God's good news. In that sense, God's evangelism never ends.

We cannot say, then, that good news is something that a Christian has, in any final and unalterable way. Certainly we grasp the heart of the good news, that by the death and resurrection of Jesus we are reconciled to God, but there is always more to God and more of God's good news to be discovered. As is so often the case, C. S. Lewis captures this idea with a memorable image. At the end of all the Narnia stories, when the children finally reach Aslan's land, they find to their surprise that there is more to it than they expected. Lucy reflects on it with her old friend, Tumnus the Faun:

> "I see," she said at last, thoughtfully. "I see now. This garden . . . is far bigger inside than it was outside."

> "Of course, Daughter of Eve," said the Faun. "The farther up and the farther in you go, the bigger everything gets. The inside is larger than the outside . . . [It is] like an onion: except that as you go in and in, each circle is larger than the last." [2]

The best evangelists, in my opinion, are those who are constantly seeking to know more of God for themselves. They are those who can say, "Let me tell you the gospel as I understand it; let me share what I know of God's goodness now that I did not know five years ago." Their evangelism is not just what they say (though they are learning to speak clearly and courageously), not just the way they live (though they struggle to follow their Master with integrity), but their evangelism is also a matter of direction: the direction they are looking, the direction they are heading. They are people who can say:

> Come with us. Follow Jesus with us. Yes, it is hard, but there are glimpses of the most marvellous beauty. Yes, there is risk, but there is also glory. Yes, there are questions and doubts, but there is also light and truth that is not to be found anywhere else. Come, take my hand. Let me introduce you to the family. We're making an early start in the morning.

Questions for Study and Reflection

Chapter 1

1. Why did you decide to read a book on evangelism or be part of group discussing a book on evangelism?
2. What, if any, negative images of evangelism do you bring to the reading of this book? What are they and where do they come from? What gives you hope that there is "a better way" of thinking about and doing evangelism?
3. What was your response to the experiences of "evangelism" described by Margaret Atwood and Sandra Tsing Loh? Have you ever had such an experience?
4. If you consider yourself a Christian today, what are the "evangelizing influences" that have brought you to this point? Maybe it was parents, godparents, a pastor or priest, a teacher or friend. Describe what they did that helped you in your spiritual journey.

Chapter 2

1. From your knowledge of the Old Testament, does this description of evangelism in the Old Testament ring true or not? What other themes are you aware of in the Old Testament? Do they relate to this "scarlet thread" of evangelism or not?
2. The author suggests that the Israelites of the Old Testament oscillated between being separate from the culture around them and being assimilated into the culture around them. How do churches or other Christian fellowships you are familiar with handle this tension of being distinctive yet being involved? Do some seem to you to overbalance on one side or the other? Who, in your opinion, has got it about right?
3. What is your reaction to this quote: "For one thing, it was a relief to realize that evangelism is God's project. . . . The desire to reconcile us to God comes in the first place from God's side."
4. How do you respond to the author's suggestion in the final paragraph on page 38?

Chapter 3

1. Do you agree with the author's contention that churches and fellow-ships should consider themselves "centered sets" more than "bounded sets"? If you do, then what becomes of things like baptism and church membership? If not, how can the church encourage "outsiders" to hang around the community and check out the reality of the faith?

2. Think of churches and fellowships you are familiar with. Are they welcoming places for outsiders? What are the things that make them "user-friendly" or intimidating for new people?

3. What do you make of Jennifer's comment: "I'm not a Christian, but, you know, this is a great place to ask my questions"? To you, is evangelism more about asking questions or about providing answers? Why?

Chapter 4

1. How would you explain the church's mission to someone who knew nothing about Christian faith?

2. Share examples from your own experience when words and works have been well blended. Or share times when they have been unhelpfully separated. What happened in these situations?

3. What might this quote mean for you: "In whatever vocation, we are called to bear the image of the Creator."

Chapter 5

1. Think back to those people who first told you about Jesus. In what ways were they like Jesus as he is described in this chapter?

2. Have you ever had the kind of experience Jesus has in this story, when a serendipitous encounter turns into a discussion of faith. Tell the story. How did you feel about this experience? What did you learn from it?

3. How can we become "open" to God working through us? Share your thoughts and experiences.

Chapter 6

1. As you look back on your own spiritual journey, can you see different stages at which God was working through people in your life to clear the stones, plow, sow seed, water, or reap?

2. In the process of evangelism, where do you think you can best play a part? Are you a stone-clearer, a sower, or a reaper? Who do you know in your fellowship who can play some of the roles that you feel you cannot? Is there anything we can do to ensure that every part of the process is nurtured in our churches and fellowships?

3. What does it mean to move in a "Christ-ward" direction? How can you (personally, or together as a congregation) help others move in that direction?

Chapter 7

1. The author describes seven marks of a healthy church. Are there others you think should be added to this list? Are there ways in which they also contribute to "an evangelistic climate"?

2. In which of these areas would you say your church or fellowship is healthiest? What is the area that needs most work?

Chapter 8

1. Where do you see God at work in the so-called "secular" world? How does what you see connect up with the message of Jesus?

2. How is this comment helpful in doing "relational" evangelism: "The good news of the gospel is like a precious button that will fit into the buttonhole in a person's life and understanding. The trick is to link together the button and the buttonhole"?

Chapter 9

1. Can you think of times when your faith in Jesus has caused you to take risks you might not otherwise have taken? Tell what happened and how things worked out. How do you feel about those experiences?

2. Can you think of times when you felt you should have taken a risk but did not? Describe them. What happened and what might have happened. How do you feel about those experiences? Why are we so fearful of taking risks?

3. Can you think of risks God might be calling you to take in evangelism, either as an individual or as a church?

4. Where have you sensed, or where do you sense, the leading of the Holy Spirit in your life of faith?

Chapter 10

1. Do you agree with the author's summary of the gospel as centering on Jesus, human need of Jesus, the promise of benefits from trusting Jesus, and a challenge to respond to Jesus? If someone who asked you what Christianity was all about, how would you answer?
2. What is the gospel according to you? In what ways is Jesus good news in your life?
3. How do the concepts of macro-gospel and micro-gospel shed light on the concept of relational evangelism?

Chapter 11

1. How is translation of the message key to effective evangelism? Who has been the most helpful "translator" of the Christian message for you? Why?
2. What do you think is the most difficult concept or message to "translate" to people who are new to or unfamiliar with Christian faith? Why?
3. What does the phrase "Christ died for our sins" mean to you?
4. Can you think of other analogies, from real life, from novels, or from movies, which might helpfully illuminate some aspect of why Jesus died?

Chapter 12

1. How do you respond to the idea of hell? Does the way the author explains it help you or not? Why?
2. What would you have wanted to say to Graham if you had been there?

Chapter 13

1. What has been your experience of talking about faith with people of religions other than your own? What did you feel? What did you learn? What if anything bothered you?
2. Do you think the author is too exclusive in what he claims for Christianity? Or too open to God's working in people of other faiths?
3. How can one balance the exclusive claims of the gospel with a sense of openness to claims made by other faiths?

Chapter 14

1. Does your church or fellowship think of itself as a place for people to come and explore Christian faith? If so, how did that attitude come about? If not, what would it take for members to begin to think that way?
2. What "access points" does your church or fellowship offer for those who are exploring their spirituality? Do the people come for whom they are designed? Why or why not?
3. Brainstorm some other "access points" that might help your church more effectively reach out to or invite people to move closer to the center—a relationship with Jesus.

Chapter 15

1. Has faith for you involved one main crisis or a series of small crises? Describe how this has been for you.
2. Choose one of the three pictures (the prodigal, the door, the school), and try explaining to someone in the group what that picture says to you about becoming a Christian.
3. What other "pictures" come to mind?

Chapter 16

1. What would it mean for you to be accept Jesus' invitation to become a "fisher of people"? What would need to change in your life?
2. How can you go on learning more about God and having something fresh to say about your faith?

Notes

Introduction

1 Rebecca Manley Pippert, *Out of the Saltshaker and into the World: Evangelism As a Way of Life* (Downers Grove, Ill.: InterVarsity Press, 2nd edition, 1999), p. 16.

2 "In a fallen world such as this, the very ability to change is a golden treasure, a gift from God of such fabulous worth as to call for constant thanksgiving." A. W. Tozer, *The Knowledge of the Holy* (Maharashtra, India: Alliance Publications, 1961), p. 61.

3 Lesslie Newbigin, *Foolishness to the Greeks: The Gospel and Western Culture* (Grand Rapids, Mich.: Eerdmans, 1986), p. 3.

4 N. T. Wright, *The New Testament and the People of God* (Minneapolis: Fortress Press, 1992), pp. 140-141.

Chapter 1

1 T. S. Eliot, "Little Gidding," from *The Four Quartets* (London: Faber and Faber, 1986), p. 48.

2 This wonderful image is from Donald C. Posterski, *True to You: Living Our Faith in Our Multi-Minded World* (Winfield, B.C.: Wood Lake Books, 1995), p. 156.

3 From "Scarlet Ibis," in *Bluebeard's Egg,* by Margaret Atwood (McClelland & Stewart, 1984).

4 The term *strategy* derives from the Greek *strategos* or *general*, "thus suggesting a military campaign, where the 'other' is an enemy who is to be forcibly subdued," from Wilbert R. Shenk, "Mission Strategies," in James M. Phillips and Robert T. Coote, eds., *Towards the 21st Century in Christian Mission* (Grand Rapids, Mich.: Eerdmans, 1993), pp. 218-219. Gary Davis, an American evangelist, highlighted the incongruity of this when he said in a speech recently, "I don't need a strategy for kissing my wife!"

5 "What we need is not more little books about Christianity, but more little books by Christians on other subjects—with their Christianity latent." C. S. Lewis, "Christian Apologetics," in *God in the Dock* (Grand Rapids, Mich.: Eerdmans, 1970), p. 93.

6 From Sandra Tsing Loh, *Depth Takes a Holiday: Essays from Lesser Los Angeles* (Riverhead Books, 1996).

7 Alasdair MacIntyre, *After Virtue: A Study in Moral Theory* (Notre Dame, Ind.: University of Notre Dame Press, 1984), p. 216.

Chapter 2

1 H. H. Rowley, *The Missionary Message of the Old Testament* (London: Carey Press, 1945), p. 32.

2 Richard Middleton and Brian Walsh, *Truth Is Stranger Than It Used to Be: Biblical Faith in a Postmodern Age* (Downers Grove, Ill.: InterVarsity Press, 1995), p. 98.

3   C. S. Lewis, *Reflections on the Psalms* (London: Collins Fontana, 1961 [1958]), pp. 38-40.

4   Martin J. Selman, *2 Chronicles: A Commentary,* Tyndale Old Testament Commentaries (Downers Grove, Ill.: InterVarsity Press, 1994), p. 354.

5   Jacques Ellul comments, "When Nineveh repents, God repents, too." *The Judgment of Jonah* (Grand Rapids, Mich.: Eerdmans, 1971), p. 98.

Chapter 3

1   There is a point, of course, when considering Christian faith becomes deeply unsafe, since it challenges our most basic assumptions about life. As C. S. Lewis says of the Christ figure in the Chronicles of Narnia, Aslan is not a tame lion.

2   "The meanings ascribed to the word *Jew* often come from later Christian and contemporary twentieth-century usage. . . . Judea is simply a place with its environs, air and water. 'Judean' thus designates a person from that segment of a larger ethnic group . . . who comes from the place after which the segment is named." Bruce J. Malina and Richard L. Rohrbaugh, *Social-Science Commentary on the Synoptic Gospels* (Minneapolis: Fortress Press, 1992), p. 32.

3   N. T. Wright, *Jesus and the Victory of God* (Minneapolis: Fortress Press, 1996), pp. 299-300; cf. Gerhard Lohfink, *Jesus and Community: the Social Dimension of Christian Faith* (Philadelphia: Fortress Press; and New York: Paulist Press, 1982), pp. 9-12.

4   Lohfink, p. 42.

5   Luke 8:19-21. "The Christian group acting as a surrogate family is for Luke the locus of the good news. It transcends the normal categories of birth, class, race, gender, education, wealth and power—hence is inclusive in a startling new way." Malina and Rohrbaugh, pp. 335-336.

6   Wright, *Jesus and the Victory of God*, p. 276.

7   Lohfink, p. 44.

8   George G. Hunter III, "The 'Celtic' Way for Evangelizing Today," in *The Journal of the Academy for Evangelism in Theological Education*, vol. 13 (1997-1998), pp. 15-29. Hunter expands on these ideas in *The Celtic Way of Evangelism: How Christianity Can Reach the West . . . Again* (Nashville: Abingdon Press, 2000).

9   This is, of course, scriptural language (such as 1 Peter 2:9). I am only saying that the passing from darkness to light may not happen in exactly the way we have often assumed. For example, one friend pointed out that the chief image of dark turning to light in the ancient world was the sunrise, not the switching on of an electric light.

10   Paul G. Hiebert, "Conversion, Culture and Cognitive Categories," *Gospel in Context*, vol. 1, no. 4, October 1978, pp. 24-29.

11   Ibid., p. 28.

12   "Though meals could include people of varying social ranks, normally that did not occur . . . Roman sources describe meals at which guests of different social ranks are seated in different rooms . . . [Jesus' invitations] to the 'poor, crippled, blind and lame' are evidence of inclusive Christian social practices that are reflected in their meals." Malina and Rohrbaugh, pp. 191-192.

Chapter 4

1   Arthur Conan Doyle, "Silver Blaze," 1892.

2   Walter Brueggemann, *Biblical Perspectives on Evangelism: Living in a Three-Storied Universe* (Nashville: Abingdon Press, 1993), p. 14.

3   John R. W. Stott *Christian Mission in the Modern World* (Downers Grove, Ill.: Inter-Varsity Press, 1975), p. 31.

Chapter 5

1   Rosalind Rinker, *You Can Witness with Confidence* (Grand Rapids, Mich.: Zondervan, 1962), p. 35.

2   The story of where the Samaritans came from, and the reason for the racial prejudice, is told in 2 Kings 17:24–41.

3   The story of Abraham's servant in Genesis 24:11 illustrates just such a custom.

4   Leon Morris, *The Gospel According to John, The New International Commentary on the New Testament* (Grand Rapids, Mich.: Eerdmans, 1971), p. 264.

5   Part of the confusion stems from the question of whether women could divorce men in that culture. Leon Morris explains why it is difficult: "A woman could not divorce her husband in Jewish law. But under certain circumstances she could approach the court that would, if it thought fit, compel the husband to divorce her." Ibid., p. 264.

6   Some have suggested that she is not ducking the issue but moving smoothly to a theological issue that has always worried her. I have tried to read the story that way, but it seems to me the contrast between the vividly personal observation Jesus makes and the theological question she raises is simply too stark for it to be anything but a diversion—even if the question is one she truly wants answered.

7   *The Message: The New Testament in Contemporary English,* by Eugene H. Peterson (Colorado Springs: NavPress Publishing Group, 1993).

8   "Dilige et quod vis fac." *Epist.* Joann. *Tractatus,* vii, 8.

Chapter 6

1   Rebecca Manley Pippert, *Out of the Saltshaker and into the World: Evangelism As a Way of Life* (Downers Grove, Ill.: InterVarsity Press, 2nd edition, 1999), p. 12.

2   Ibid., p. 23. The rest of the conversation is also instructive: "Listen," I responded, "most Christians I know are very hesitant to share their faith precisely because they're afraid they'll offend." "But as long as you let people know that you're aware of where they're coming from, you can say anything you want!" she responded immediately. "And you just tell Christians that I said so."

3   C. S. Lewis, *The Voyage of the Dawn Treader* (London: Collins Fontana Lions, 1980 edition), p. 188.

4   C. S. Lewis, "The Weight of Glory: A Sermon," in *Screwtape Proposes a Toast and Other Pieces* (London: Collins Fontana Books, 1965), p. 109.

5   Eugene Stock, *History of the Church Missionary Society: Its Environment, Its Men and Its Work,* vol. 3 (London: CMS, 1899), p. 125.

6   The woman's statement about the Messiah "is a faithful reflection of the Samaritans' messianic expectation." The Samaritans understood the Messiah or "Taheb" to be "restorer and revealer of the truth." George Beasley-Murray, John, *Word Biblical Commentary* (Dallas: Word Publishing, 1987), pp. 62-63.

7   Anne Lamott, *Traveling Mercies: Some Thoughts on Faith* (New York: Pantheon Books, 1999), p. 3

8   Arnell Motz, ed., *Reclaiming a Nation* (Richmond, B.C.: Church Leadership Library, 1990), p. 145.

9   John Finney, *Finding Faith Today: How Does It Happen?* (Swindon, U.K.: British and Foreign Bible Society, 1992) pp. 24-25.

10 Robert Brow, *"Go Make Learners": A New Model for Discipleship in the Church* (Wheaton, Ill.: Harold Shaw, 1981), p. 81.

11 William J. Abraham, *The Logic of Evangelism* (Grand Rapids, Mich.: Eerdmans, 1989), pp. 95, 104.

12 Brian D. McLaren, *A New Kind of Christian: A Tale of Two Friends on a Spiritual Journey* (San Francisco: Jossey Bass, 2001), p. 62.

Chapter 7

1   Stanley Hauerwas and William Willimon, *Resident Aliens: Life in the Christian Colony* (Nashville: Abingdon Press, 1989), p. 47.

2   Attributed to the fourth-century emperor Julian the Apostate, a persecutor of Christianity. Quoted in Tertullian, *Apologeticus.*

3   Finney, pp. 43-44.

4   Archbishop William Temple gave a fuller definition, which has become something of a classic: "Worship is the submission of all our nature to God. It is the quickening of conscience by his holiness; the nourishment of mind with his truth; the purifying of imagination by his beauty; the opening of the heart to his love; the surrender of will to his purpose—and all of this gathered up in adoration, the most selfless emotion of which our nature is capable." William Temple, *Readings in John's Gospel* (London: MacMillan, 1945), p. 68.

5   John Stott thinks it was Johannes Blauw who first applied the word *centrifugal* to the church's mission, and then J. G. Davies who applied it to the nature of God. Stott (1975), p. 21.

6   David Watson, *One in the Spirit* (London: Hodder and Stoughton, 1973), pp. 89-80.

7   E. M. Forster, *A Passage to India* (Harmondsworth, U.K.: Penguin Books, 1989 [1924]), p. 161.

8   "As partners the two belong to each other and yet are independent of each other. Each stands on its own feet in its own right alongside the other. Neither is a means to the other, or even a manifestation of the other. For each is an end in itself. Both are expressions of unfeigned love." Stott (1975), p. 27.

9   Ray Bakke, *The Urban Christian: Effective Ministry in Today's Urban World* (Downers Grove, Ill.: InterVarsity Press, 1987), p. 134.

Chapter 8

1   I. Howard Marshall, *Acts: An Expositional Commentary,* Tyndale New Testament Commentaries (Grand Rapids, Mich.: Eerdmans, 1980), p. 284.

2   Michael Green, *Jesus Spells Freedom* (London: Inter-Varsity Press, 1972).

3   For example, Pausanius, writing around 175 A.D., refers to "altars of the gods named Unknown" about five miles from Ephesus. Cited in John Stott, *The Spirit, the Church and the World: The Message of Acts* (Downers Grove, Ill.: InterVarsity Press, 1990), p. 284.

4   Diogenes Laertius, *Lives of the Eminent Philosophers,* vol. 1, p. 110. The story is retold in popular form in Don Richardson, *Eternity in their Hearts* (Ventura, Calif.: Regal Books, 1981), pp. 11-18.

5   Theologians Karl Barth and Emil Brunner argued in the 1930s as to whether such bottonholes exist—Barth saying no and Brunner saying yes. It will be clear who I think is right!

6   McLaren, p. 140.

7   John Calvin, *The Acts of the Apostles,* vol. 2, ed. David W. Torrance and Thomas F. Torrance, trans. John W. Fraser (Edinburgh: Oliver and Boyd, 1966; Grand Rapids, Mich.: Eerdmans, 1973), p. 112.

8   F. F. Bruce, *The Acts of the Apostles: The Greek Text with Introduction and Commentary* (London: Tyndale Press, 1970 [1951]), p. 336.

9   Epimenides is quoted again in Titus 1:12, where he is called "a prophet." F. F. Bruce points out that the "God" of these poets is actually Zeus of Greek mythology! Paul seems to think there is enough "overlap" to make the citation valid. See F. F. Bruce, *The Book of the Acts: New International Commentary on the New Testament* (Grand Rapids, Mich.: Eerdmans, 1954), p. 360.

10 Genesis 10:1-32; Exodus 20:11; Leviticus 26:1; Deuteronomy 4:7; 10:14; 32:8-9; 1 Kings 8:27; Job 12:10; 22:2; Psalms 50:12; 74:17; 115:16; 145:18; Isaiah 40:18-20; 46:6; 55:6; Jeremiah 10:16; 23:33-34; Daniel 5:23; Malachi 2:10; and Sirach 28:7.

Chapter 9

1   M. Scott Peck, *The Road Less Traveled* (New York: Simon and Schuster, 1978).

2   McLaren, p. 148.

Chapter 10

1   Charles Williams, *The Place of the Lion* (Grand Rapids, Mich.: Eerdmans, 1978 [1933]), p. 147.

2   James D. G. Dunn, *Unity and Diversity in the New Testament: An Enquiry into the Character of Earliest Christianity* (London: SCM Press, 1990), p. 31. The discussion of this subject in fact began earlier with C. H. Dodd, *The Apostolic Preaching and Its Development* (London: Hodder and Stoughton, 1936).

3   David L. Edwards and John R. W. Stott, *Essentials* (London: Hodder and Stoughton, 1988), p. 330. To be fair, Stott also says firmly that "there is only one apostolic gospel."

4   Dunn, p. 180-183.

5   Lewis, *Mere Christianity* (London: Fontana Books, 1956 [1952]), p. 56.

6   I have suggested that doctrine can be thought of as a summary in point-form of the Christian story in *Growing Convictions: the Story of the IVCF Basis of Faith* (Richmond, B.C.: Digory Designs, 2000).

7   Wright (1992), pp. 140-141. My addition of a sixth act follows Middleton and Walsh, pp. 182, 240. This description of the six acts first appeared in my booklet *Finding a Story to Live By* (Richmond, B.C.: Digory Designs, 2000).

8   C. S. Lewis uses this image in *Mere Christianity*, although other authors may have used it before.

9   "The cross is for Paul the symbol, as it was the means, of the liberating victory of the one true God, creator of the world, over all the enslaving powers that have usurped his authority." N. T. Wright, *What Saint Paul Really Said* (Grand Rapids, Mich.: Eerdmans, 1997), p. 47.

10 McLaren, p. 129.

11 C. S. Lewis, *The Last Battle* (London: Collins, 1980 [1956]), p. 173.

12 "Do you think that God would want a heaven filled with people who cared more about being saved from hell than saved from sin? . . . Who cared more about having their sins forgiven than being good neighbors? Who in fact became worse neighbors precisely because they became so religious in their concern about their own personal souls?" McLaren, pp. 129-130.

13 From *Finding a Story to Live By*, p. 7.

14 I have written at greater length about some of the different reasons people put their faith in Christ in the booklet *Becoming a Christian: A Practical Guide to the Why and the How* (Vancouver: Digory Designs, 1997).

15 Watson (1976), p. 170.

16 C. S. Lewis, *Prince Caspian* (Harmondsworth: Penguin Books, 1962 [1951]), p. 124.

Chapter 11

1   Newbigin (1986), p. 3.

2   Don Richardson, *Peace Child* (Gospel Light/Regal Books, 1976), p. 177.

3   Ibid., p. 177.

4   Ibid., p. 179.

5   Ibid., p. 180.

6   Lamin Sanneh, *Translating the Message: The Missionary Impact on Culture* (Maryknoll, N.Y.: Orbis Books, 1992).

7   Northrop Frye says something similar in *The Great Code: The Bible and Literature* (Toronto: Academic Press, 1982), p. 3.

8   Sanneh, p. 53.

9   Ibid., p. 124.

10 A. S. Byatt, in *The God I Want*, ed. James Mitchell (London: Hodder and Stoughton, 1967), p. 73.

11 Space does not permit discussion of other understandings of the atonement. But I think this one is not only the most central but also the toughest to translate, and maybe principles of translation will surface in this discussion that can be applied to other models.

12 Leon Morris, "Atonement," in *New Dictionary of Theology*, ed. Sinclair B. Ferguson et al (Downers Grove, Ill.: InterVarsity Press, 1988). The book is *The Cross in the New Testament* (Exeter, U.K.: Paternoster Press, 1967).

13 "We must not smuggle in the idea that we can throw the analogy away and, as it were, get in behind it to a purely literal truth. . . . For our abstract thinking is itself a tissue of analogies." C. S. Lewis, *Letters to Malcolm* (London: Collins Fount, 1988 [1963]), p. 54.

14 A survey of teenagers in 1992 asked them, "How much confidence do you have in the people in charge of the lawcourts?" In 1984, 67 percent had replied "a great deal" or "quite a bit." In 1992, however, that number was down to 59 percent. The same survey revealed that, in 1985, only 48 percent of adults trusted the court system, and by 1990 that figure had dropped to 43 percent. Reginald Bibby and Donald Posterski, *Teen Trends: A Nation in Motion* (Toronto: Stoddart, 1992), p. 174.

15 Clark H. Pinnock and Robert C. Brow, *Unbounded Love: A Good News Theology for the 21st Century* (Downers Grove, Ill.: Inter-Varsity Press, 1994), p. 103.

16 Kenneth E. Bailey, *The Cross and the Prodigal* (St. Louis: Concordia, 1971), pp. 56-57.

17 I have also told this story in *Finding a Story to Live By*.

18 Bailey, p. 57.

Chapter 12

1 Charles Williams, *Descent into Hell* (Grand Rapids, Mich.: Eerdmans, 1979 [1939]), p. 115.

2 C. S. Lewis, *The Problem of Pain* (London: Collins Fontana Books, 1965 [1940]), pp. 106, 108.

3 Ibid. 106.

4 M. Scott Peck, *The People of the Lie* (New York: Simon and Schuster, 1983), p. 67.

5 Lewis, *The Problem of Pain*, p. 112.

6 C. S. Lewis, *The Great Divorce* (London: Geoffrey Bles, 1946).

7 Paul speaks of the purifying power of God's fire in 1 Corinthians 3:12-15: "The fire will test what sort of work each has done. . . . If the work is burned up, the builder will suffer loss; the builder will be saved, but only as through fire."

8 Lewis, *Mere Christianity*, p. 37.

9 It is true that this view values human freedom very highly. The alternative is to put more emphasis on God's control of salvation. My observation has been that when people stress God's sovereignty over human choice, they may also argue that all will be "saved" in the end, in order to avoid the unpalatable conclusion that God predestines people to hell. It seems to me that Lewis's view, which I expound here, does more justice to the tensions inherent in the Bible itself.

10 Dorothy L. Sayers, *Introductory Papers on Dante*, quoted in *A Matter of Eternity: Selections from the Writings of Dorothy L. Sayers* (Grand Rapids, Mich.: Eerdmans, 1973), pp. 84-85.

11 Lewis, *The Problem of Pain*, p. 115.

Chapter 13

1   Quoted in Max Warren, *I Believe in the Great Commission* (Grand Rapids, Mich.: Eerdmans, 1976), p. 152.

2   Quoted in Michael Ingham, *Mansions of the Spirit* (Toronto: Anglican Book Centre, 1997), p. 52.

3   John Hick, "The Outcome: Dialogue into Truth," in Hick, ed., *Truth and Dialogue* (London: SCM, 1975), p. 143.

4   The parable is quoted in full in Ingham, pp. 75-76.

5   Hick, p. 142. To compare between them, Smith suggests, is like making value judgments between Tchaikovsky and Bach. One musical friend to whom I told this illustration expostulated, "But there's no comparison! Bach is an infinitely better composer!"

6   Ingham, p. 120.

7   Ibid., p. 120.

8   Ibid., p. 119.

9   Ibid., p. 106.

10   Newbigin (1989), p. 162.

11   Ingham, p. 166.

12   "If you are a Christian you do not have to believe that all other religions are simply wrong all through." Lewis, *Mere Christianity* (1952), p. 39.

13   Clark H. Pinnock, *A Wideness in God's Mercy: The Finality of Jesus Christ in a World of Religions* (Grand Rapids, Mich.: Zondervan, 1992), p. 77.

14   Consider, too, that a religion like Buddhism does not think in terms of "a relationship with God" in the Christian sense.

15   John V. Taylor, *The Go-Between God: The Holy Spirit and the Christian Mission* (London: SCM Press, 1975 [1972]), p. 190

16   I am sobered by the words of George MacDonald to C. S. Lewis in *The Great Divorce*: "There have been some who were so occupied in spreading Christianity that they never gave a thought to Christ. Man! . . . It is the subtlest of all the snares," p. 66.

17   I don't always spend as long on this question as I do here, since it is an "in-house" question generally asked by Christians. Whether and how I address this issue depends on who the audience is.

18   J. Oswald Sanders, *What of the Unevangelized?* (London: Overseas Missionary Fellowship, 1971 [1966]), p. 67.

19   Taylor, p. 193.

20   See, for example, David J. Bosch, *Transforming Mission: Paradigm Shifs in the Theology of Mission* (Maryknoll, N.Y.: Orbis Books, 1991), pp. 281, 287-288, 306-307.

21   Paul Griffiths of the Chicago Divinity School writes: "Pluralists . . . are themselves engaging in precisely the activity they wish to rebuke. . . . [There are] close links between the ideology of pluralism and a voracious, omnivorous modernity, whose surface tolerance of all religions is indistinguishable from a profound hostility to all." "Beyond Pluralism," *First Things*, January 1996, p. 50.

22   Taylor, p. 193.

Chapter 14

1   Harold Percy, *Good News People: An Introduction to Evangelism for Tongue-Tied Christians* (Toronto: Anglican Book Centre, 1996).

2   Statistics suggest that new church plants have a higher number of new Christians than do long established churches. Maybe one reason is that in new churches there isn't such a strong sense of a social machinery already in motion.

3   Hunter (1992), p. 59.

4   Check with colleagues, denominational staff, publishers, and seminaries for resource recommendations. *Christian Basics*, a four-part video (by Harold Percy) and a leader's booklet are available from the Wycliffe College Institute of Evangelism.

5   M. Scott Peck in *The Door Interviews*, ed. Mike Yaconelli (Grand Rapids, Mich.: Zondervan, 1989), p. 248.

Chapter 15

1   Henri Nouwen, *The Return of the Prodigal Son: A Meditation on Fathers, Brothers, and Sons* (New York: Doubleday, 1992), p. 13.

2   I am reminded of C. S. Lewis's description of Eustace in *Voyage of the Dawn Treader*, after he has met Aslan and become "undragoned": "It would be nice, and nearly true, to say that from that time forth Eustace was a different boy. To be strictly true, he began to be a different boy. He had relapses. There were still many days when he could be very tiresome. But most of those I shall not notice. The cure had begun." C. S. Lewis, *The Voyage of the Dawn Treader* (Harmondsworth, U.K.: Puffin Books, 1973 [1952]), p. 99.

3   There are two originals, one in the chapel of Magdalen College in Oxford, the other in St. Paul's Cathedral in London. Apparently, Hunt's model was an agnostic police officer, and, as Hunt painted, they argued about faith.

4   This kind of experience neatly overcomes the dichotomy in which this saying must either refer to a community (which is clearly the original context) or to the individual (which evangelists have traditionally preferred). It can also speak to individuals -in-community.

5   Eugene H. Peterson paraphrases this, "Are you tired? Worn out? Burned out on religion? Come to me." *The Message.*

6   I have explored this image more fully in *The School of Jesus: A Beginner's Guide to Living As a Christian* (Vancouver, B.C.: Digory Designs, 1997).

Chapter 16

1   J. R. R. Tolkien, *The Lord of the Rings* (single-vol. edition; London: Unwin Paperbacks, 1968), p. 287.

2   C. S. Lewis, *The Last Battle*, p. 170.